Arthur Miller and Company

ARTHUR MILLER AND COMPANY

Arthur Miller talks about his work in the company of Actors, Designers, Directors, Reviewers and Writers

Edited by CHRISTOPHER BIGSBY

METHUEN DRAMA *in association with*
THE ARTHUR MILLER CENTRE FOR AMERICAN STUDIES

First published 1990 by Methuen Drama,
Michelin House, 81 Fulham Road, London SW3 6RB

Copyright © 1990 The Arthur Miller Centre for American Studies

A CIP Catalogue Record for this book is available
from the British Library
ISBN 0 413 64220 8

Printed in Great Britain
by Clays Ltd, St Ives plc

This book is dedicated to Arthur Miller,
on the occasion of his 75th birthday,
and to Inge Morath,
with respect and deep affection.

Acknowledgements

The interview contained in this book is an amalgam of separate interviews conducted in the course of ten years between 1979 and 1989. They took place in New York, Roxbury, London and Norwich. Some were for private research, others were conducted for the BBC. A small portion is derived from comments made at the opening of the Arthur Miller Centre for American Studies at the University of East Anglia in May 1989 and on the occasion of the radio production of *The Price*.

I would like to acknowledge the special help of the BBC, Illustra Films, Gerry Cobb, Eleanor Day, Gilbert Debusscher, Ed Thomason, Geoff Wilson and Heide Zeigler. My special thanks go to Butler University at Indianapolis for their assistance.

I would also wish to acknowledge the support of Data General Ltd.

List of Contributors

Actors

Tony Lo Bianco 121
Michael Bryant 208
David Burke 97
David Calder 156
Brian Cox 127
Neil Daglish 208
Richard Dreyfuss 151
Bethan Dudley 100
Michael Gambon 116
Rosemary Harris 50
Pat Hingle 151
Dustin Hoffman 70
Clare Holman 96
Sarah Kestelman 209
Margot Leicester 85
Andrew MacNaughtan 156
John Malkovich 75
Andrew D. Mayor 102
Warren Mitchell 72
Ric Morgan 153
Ruth Nelson 106
Bob Peck 156, 172
Ronald Pickup 36
Gordana Rashovich 107
Vanessa Redgrave 150
David Schofield 212
John Shrapnel 38, 170
Nick Simons 153
Hilary Summers 102
Anny Tobin 153
Zoë Wanamaker 96
Timothy West 152
Tom Wilkinson 95

List of Illustrations

Arthur Miller outside the Royal Exchange Theatre, Manchester. (photograph by Michael Arron)

Jamey Sheridan, Frances McDormand and Christopher Curry in the Long Wharf Theatre production of *All My Sons*, directed by Arvin Brown, New Haven, Connecticut, 1985. (photograph by T. Charles Erickson)

In rehearsal: Arthur Miller with Christopher Bigsby, producer of the gala performance of Miller's work at the Theatre Royal, Norwich, May 15th, 1989. (photograph by Alan Howard)

Tony Lo Bianco and Saundra Santiago in the Long Wharf Theatre production of *A View from the Bridge*, New Haven, Connecticut, 1981. (photograph by Inge Morath)

Arthur Miller talks to Warren Mitchell about his role as Willy Loman in the gala performance of Miller's work at the Theatre Royal, Norwich. (photograph by Alan Howard)

Trevor Peacock and Carmen Rodriguez in the Royal Exchange Theatre production of *Death of a Salesman*, directed by Gregory Hersov, Manchester, 1985. (photograph by Kevin Cummins)

John Cagan, Robert McIntosh and Graham McTavish in the Dundee Rep production of *Death of a Salesman*, 1990. (photograph by Alex Coupar, Spanphoto)

Rosalind Bennett, Natalie Abbot and Kim Benson in the Royal Exchange Theatre production of *The Crucible*, directed by Gregory Hersov, Manchester, 1990. (photograph by Ian T. Tilton)

The cast of the Royal Academy of Music operatic version of *The Crucible*, London, 1990. (photograph by Clive Totman)

Maryann Plunkett and Frank Converse in the Long Wharf Theatre production of *The Crucible*, directed by Arvin Brown, New Haven, Connecticut, 1989. (photograph by T. Charles Erickson)

Zoë Wanamaker and Tom Wilkinson in the National Theatre production of *The Crucible*, directed by Howard Davies, London, 1990. (photograph by Richard Mildenhall)

Pat Hingle and Arthur Kennedy in the original production of *The Price*, New York, 1968. (photograph by Inge Morath)

Nick Simons, Ric Morgan and Arnold Yarrow in the Dukes Theatre production of *The Price*, Lancaster, 1990. (photograph by Arthur Thompson)

Marjorie Yates in the Young Vic production of *The Price*, London, 1990. (photograph by Gordon Rainsford)

Bob Peck, Alan MacNaughtan and David Calder in the Young Vic production of *The Price*. (photograph by Gordon Rainsford)

Introduction

This book marks a birthday. On the day of its publication it will be seventy-five years since Arthur Miller was born and fifty-five years since he began his career as a playwright. There can be few writers whose names are as instantly recognisable around the world, few as respected for their work or their lives. Some years ago at an arts centre in England he read from his autobiography, *Timebends*. On the way out he had to pass through a nearby bar, crowded with people. To his astonishment everyone put down their drinks and applauded him. Just a year earlier he gave a platform reading at Britain's National Theatre. A book signing afterwards had to be curtailed and the bookstore closed as the insistent crowds showed no signs of diminishing.

The British are perhaps too ready at times to claim special relationships of one kind or another but in the case of Arthur Miller the relationship does seem a special one. The British have mounted productions of his early works – either, like *The Golden Years*, never previously performed – or, like *The Man Who Had All the Luck*, seldom performed – and staged highly successful productions of his later plays: *The Price*, *The American Clock*, *The Archbishop's Ceiling* and *Two-Way Mirror*, the last two being published for the first time by a British publisher. In the first six months of his seventy-fifth year, productions were staged the length of Britain, from Bristol to Dundee, and comments by actors and directors from some of those productions are included in the pages which follow.

Such productions were not, of course, unique to Britain. His plays were produced around the world. There were, indeed, two versions of *The Crucible* within an hour's drive of Miller's Connecticut home and further productions in many parts of the United States.

What follows is a birthday gift to Arthur Miller by some of those who over the years have come to know him, in person or through his work. It is not a book of criticism, though several leading theatre reviewers have contributed. It is an acknowledgement, by fellow professionals, of the many and varied ways in which the words he has written on the page in rural Connecticut have lived not only on the world's stages but in the minds and imaginations of all those who have encountered his creations. It is an acknowledgement, too, of a man who has never been cowed by authority or intimidated by consensus. As Linda Loman once insisted: 'Attention, attention should be paid to such a man', a phrase which will echo through this book.

In the late 1970s Arthur Miller sat at a dinner table in Czechoslovakia, with a group of writers. Outside the window, in the street below, was a car filled with plain clothes policemen. The real threat, though, potentially lay within as the possibility of unseen listeners put a pressure on language. Many years before, the previous owner of his first home had stood in a Connecticut field and talked to a friend, of this and that. Later, a transcript of that conversation, faithfully recorded by an agent with a directional microphone, was used in evidence against him. No wonder that a man who had also witnessed that corruption of language in the 1950s which made 'loyalty' a synonym for betrayal, and coined the word 'Un-American' to describe those exercising their civic rights, should see the writer as a key figure. For if it is, as he has suggested, the habit of the state to 'falsify reality', it is the function of the writer to be the 'carrier of the beauty of the language, its development, its poetry,' and, ultimately, its truth.

It is not that he has set himself to challenge political authority, though his version of Ibsen's *An Enemy of the People*, no less than *The Crucible*, could be said to constitute precisely such a challenge. It is that he has always believed that relationships – private and public – turn on contested versions of the real. This most moral of writers has always been acutely aware that the reality which the state can falsify is itself unstable since it is constructed out of memory and desire, composed by the eye which sees and the mind which interprets. What, after all, is *The Crucible* but a debate over the nature of the real and the legitimacy of the language with which we seek to define it?

There is a model of Arthur Miller which suggests that he is a sturdy realist. His plays, it is said, are like the furniture he builds. Each joint is carefully shaped, each product a triumph of the functional. But from the very beginning he has asked himself what happens when we discover that we inhabit different worlds, that my reality is not yours? How can we live a moral life without a knowledge of the parameters of the real? But what is real? Are Willy Loman's desperate dreams not real, or the desires of an Eddie Carbone which can never make their way into language? Who is in touch with reality, the state which sees witches or the man who sees none but has been blind to the dissolution of his marriage and his spirit? In *After the Fall* a man approaching divorce stumbles on the knowledge, no less powerful and disturbing for its banality, that the past which husband and wife imagined themselves to have shared they had not shared at all. The same is true of *The Price*. The past, he insists, is holy, but the past is also a field of contention. And where does that leave the moral logic which ties us to responsibility for our acts and without which we are unable to accuse those who breach that human contract which is the begining and end of art no less than of social life?

Carlos Fuentes has spoken of the risk implied by a 'unitary language' which can kill the novel and society alike, while Salman Rushdie has talked of the danger of privileging one text or one language over others, remarking on the need for fiction to permit a quarrel between languages and narratives. What is true of the novel is, if anything, more true of the theatre in which contending values and languages take social form in a present shared by the audience. And what is true of the theatre is especially true of the work of Arthur Miller. Throughout his career he has staged a debate with his society as characters internalise its values and try to relate them to their own private necessities. Miller's is not a theatre of answers. No redeeming ideology, no self-vindicating faith is available to satisfy the need for a world at moral attention. His plays are full of people baffled by experience which fails to satisfy their need for personal significance. But his is a theatre in which capitulation is never a possibility. These are characters who demand that they be granted their full worth. They shout out their names – sometimes into the wind of history, sometimes at the very moment of betrayal – because they need to convince themselves of their own existence and of the meaning with which they have to believe they have compacted their identities. They are all people who have failed in some significant respect but they are also people who refuse, finally, to allow that failure to be definitional.

From his earliest work Miller has sought to express a tragic sense of life, to see in the losing battle with time a certain dignity and courage. No wonder he was so out of sympathy with the low farce of a Senator McCarthy, who assumed, ultimately, that people crave the redemption of submission, or that he resisted what he saw as the reductivism of the theatre of the absurd, flirting, as it did, with a world resistant to a moral reading of experience. His work bites deep because it insists on the reality of the moral world, on some sense of justice which ties cause to effect, action to consequence, but also because he confesses to the complexity of that world. He has never seen art as detached from the confused social and psychological world which we all inhabit. He acknowledges our capacity for self-deceit and the contingent nature of the values to which he subscribes. But somewhere, beneath the dulling routines of daily life, beyond the seductive simplicities of ideology or a self-justifying materialism, he insists that there are human necessities which cut across class, race or gender. It is out of those necessities, just as it is out of the near impossibility of perceiving or understanding them, that his theatre is born.

Miller's is essentially a democratic art. He writes about salesmen, dockyard workers, second-hand furniture dealers, policemen, farmers, lawyers, surgeons, businessmen. Like Walt Whitman he gives equal weight to their anxieties and illusions, their articulate pleas and their stammering self-doubts. He writes as though there were one society and the lives of every man and woman of equal worth. He writes, moreover, as though there were one audience. They may indeed be fracturing along lines of class, nationality or experience, strangers in a strange world, but he plainly believes that there is a level at which we jointly acknowledge certain truths. For Miller, that is what theatre is about. At university he discovered the drama of ancient Greece and that of Ibsen simultaneously. To him they were both in the same game. What he saw in them was a society arguing with itself and perceiving in the life of the individual the lives of us all. That is why the most American of writers has proved the most international. There is no day without a production of one of his plays somewhere in the world and those plays are not seen simply as pieces of exotic Americana. They have been claimed for their relevance to the life of the individual and the meaning of social action. In whatever languages his characters may speak, from whatever stages the voices of a multitude of actors may sound forth, they never fail to amuse, to challenge, to move. And how could it be otherwise when he has created such characters as Joe Keller, Willy Loman, John Proctor, Eddie Carbone, the sprightly eighty-nine year old Solomon, and a dozen more who will live as long as the theatre is the place to which we turn for images of our mutual failings and mutual possibilities.

Christopher Bigsby

Edward Albee

Arthur Miller understands that serious writing is a social act as well as an aesthetic one, that political involvement comes with the territory. He and I have been at the barricades together often and I am never surprised to see him. A writer's work and his actions should be of the same cloth, after all. His plays and his conscience are a cold burning force. I wish there were more like him.

Ralph Ellison

Congratulating you on your seventy-fifth birthday gives me as much pleasure as that I received years ago upon introducing you to another outstanding writer, Saul Bellow. Over the years we've seldom met but I've followed your career with pleasure and instruction, and would like you to know that for me your example as artist has been important. For despite our differences in artistic form (and often in ideology) your insistence upon bringing the most universal vision and sophisticated dramatic techniques to your material has affirmed and encouraged my own efforts.

   Which is to say that through your art you affirm the democratic vision by redeeming and making visible the marvelous diversity of the human condition. And by giving voice to the voiceless you provide perception to all those who have the heart and courage to see. In other words, you've been an eloquent explorer of America's turbulent and ever-shifting social hierarchy, and by reducing its chaos to artistic form you've given us a crucial gift of national self-consciousness. That I consider a marvelous achievement, and in offering my thanks I wish you long life and continued success.

David Hare

The best thing I ever heard Arthur Miller say was on the radio when a longwinded interviewer, obviously relishing a bit of drama, asked him whether it hadn't needed extraordinary courage to defy the House Un-American Activities Committee. 'Not at all,' said Miller. 'After everything I'd written, if I hadn't defied them, I would have looked a complete idiot.'

Truly, it is as simple as that.

I was lucky enough to miss all his plays when I was young, except for a dreadful film of *A View From the Bridge* with Raf Vallone. The result is I have been able to enjoy each of his great plays, one by one, at an age when they can be stored up, like treats, at two-year intervals. Like Orwell, even when he writes badly, he writes bang on the nose. As with Ibsen, some of the creaky bits turn out to be essential to the power of the glorious bits. He reminds me all the time of a statement of Lord Radcliffe's that 'a sense of gravity is part of the make-up of society.' Miller is grave, not because he is cheerless, but because he thinks needless suffering is grave. The world, to him, seems to be a court-house, which, of course, makes for great drama. But he's too compassionate to hand down a verdict.

Vaclav Havel

We met for the first time at Anna Fárová's in Prague in 1969. My car was in a repair shop and I was to go and fetch it at that time. It was hard to explain what a big event it is in our country to have a car repaired. My problem was therefore great and serious. Was I to enjoy your rare and kind presence and to miss the deadline, or to excuse myself and have my car. I chose the car then because I needed it badly. I was filled with remorse for having made this decision and was suffering for it for a long time. Now I am not suffering so much perhaps because I believe that you will come to Prague soon and that we will meet again. Meeting you will be just as exciting for me as it was years ago.

I wish you all the best for your birthday.
Let me express my respect and friendship.

Joseph Heller

It is with pleasure – and with a smile of pride from ear to ear – that I
sit down to write these paragraphs of praise for Arthur Miller, who
merits all he has received in the forty or so years I've known of him
and is scarcely dependent on any from me. Yet, I insist. This honour is
mine.

Experience teaches us that idealism tends to have a short life span.
And the fervour of morality animating us in youthful years generally
abates considerably with the passage of time, possibly in fatigue and
futility, and in the inescapable realisation that we must attend to our
lives and our work and our families at the same time and do the best
with them we can, no matter what. Not so, I believe, with him. He is
and has remained a figure of majestic stature and great character, and
his virtue has endured.

I have met him no more than three or four times, spoken to him for
no longer than a minute or two, but I am always conscious of him as a
benevolent and reassuring presence. I know him from his accomplish-
ments, and I am therefore never surprised when he reappears in public
as a leader or distinguished advocate in connection with some worthy
person or cause, always benevolent and always with his habitual
dedication to justice, mercy, dignity, and truth.

And I am never surprised when – as seems to occur inevitably in my
vicinity three or four times every season – a work of his for the stage is
produced again and is described and praised once more for the
seriousness and intelligence of its content and intent. His dramas
endure too, because, along with a talent for stage writing that is
unsurpassed in our lifetime, he has put his integrity and uncontrived
ethical sensibility into his plays, with the result that they are always
about something pertinent and always about something of stirring
importance to people who are concerned. His conflicts are disturbing
and charged powerfully, like those we experience inside us as
individuals and those we helplessly observe unfolding around us
constantly in the perilous world in which we live.

But Arthur Miller himself, it seems, remains a comfort, never, to my knowledge, lessening. I find him someone to look up to, as an artist and a good citizen, and I am happy to do so. I feel lucky indeed to have a person to admire.

Harold Pinter

Arthur Miller's socks

Arthur Miller and I landed at Istanbul airport on March 17, 1985. We were visiting Turkey on behalf of International PEN, to investigate allegations of the torture and persecution of Turkish writers. The trip got off to a bad start. I had two suitcases. One hadn't made it. Apart from other things, this left me with no socks. So Arthur lent me his. Bloody good ones they were too. Made to last.

We met dozens of writers. Those who had been tortured in prison were still trembling but they insisted on giving us a drink, pouring the shaking bottle into our glasses. One of the writer's wives was mute. She had fainted and lost her power of speech when she had seen her husband in prison. He was now out. His face was like a permanent tear. (I don't mean tear as in tears but tear as in being torn.)

Turkey at this time was a military dictatorship, fully endorsed by the United States.

The US Ambassador, hearing of our presence and thinking he was playing a clever card, gave a dinner party at the US embassy in Ankara in honour of Arthur. As I was Arthur's running mate they had to invite me too.

I had hardly taken my first bite at the *hors d'oeuvres* when I found myself in the middle of a ferocious row with the US political counsellor about the existence of torture in Turkish prisons.

This rattled on merrily throughout the dinner until, finally, Arthur rose to speak. Since he was the guest of honour the floor was his and he made it his in no uncertain terms. He discussed the term democracy and asked why, as the United States was a democracy, it supported military dictatorships throughout the world, including the country we were now in? 'In Turkey', he said, 'hundreds of people are in prison for their *thoughts*. This persecution is supported and subsidised by the United States. Where', he asked, 'does that leave our

4

understanding of democratic values?' He was as clear as a bell. The Ambassador thanked him for his speech.

After dinner I thought I'd keep out of trouble for a while and went to look at the paintings. Suddenly I saw the Ambassador and his aides bearing down on me. Why they weren't bearing down on Arthur I don't know. Perhaps he was too tall. The Ambassador said to me: 'Mr Pinter, you don't seem to understand the realities of the situation here. Don't forget, the Russians are just over the border. You have to bear in mind the political reality, the diplomatic reality, the military reality.' 'The reality I've been referring to', I said, 'is that of electric current on your genitals.' The Ambassador drew himself, as they say, up to his full height and glared at me. 'Sir,' he said, 'you are a guest in my house.' He turned, as they also say, on his heel and his aides turned too. Arthur suddenly loomed up. 'I think I've been thrown out', I said. 'I'll come with you', Arthur said, without hesitation.

Being thrown out of the US embassy in Ankara with Arthur Miller – a voluntary exile – was one of the proudest moments in my life.

Alan Plater

Hail to the Chief

Early in the 1980s I went on a research trip to Northern Ontario, following the trail of one Archie Belaney from Hastings in England, who went bush, joined an Ojibway tribe, changed his name to Wa-Sha-Quon-Asin and later achieved fame, plus an invitation to Buckingham Palace, as an author writing under the name Grey Owl. I put most of this into a screenplay that remains one of my more interesting abandoned projects.

On Bear Island I met a real, live, Ojibway Indian Chief. His name was Gary and he wore a check shirt, blue jeans and a Chico Marx style hat. He was quiet, gentle and laconic and his main preoccupation was a mineral rights claim.

Later I consulted my designated guide, a sharp-suited Ottawa Indian called Tom, who travelled with a portable hair dryer, about the business of being an Indian Chief.

How, I asked, is a Chief selected?

Tom listed the ground rules.

Rule number one: nobody who wants to be a Chief, and makes that fact widely known, is ever chosen.

Rule number two: the eventual choice is the person who has most clearly demonstrated a willingness to share information.

In conventional Western society, Tom explained, the Chief is the person who has accumulated the most information, and shares it at his or her discretion and then, presumably, only at the highest obtainable market rates. In Indian society, willingness to share and humility transcend all other considerations.

All this is probably a grotesque over-simplification, neatly trimmed to suit my admitted prejudices, but it clearly supports my central proposition: that on any scale of measurement that matters a damn, Arthur Miller is our chosen Chief. It is not an elected position, and its lack of legal and political status has the effect of increasing its moral and intellectual clout. It is a mirror image of conventional power politics where morality and intellect drain away in direct proportion to the altitude of the High Office. The higher the office, the louder the gurgling.

My fairly primitive world view places writers at the centre of the Universe. Along with the painters, clowns and balladeers, they chart the history, geography and psychology of the human condition. Who cares any more whether the Athenian stock exchange was a bull or a bear market? And did anybody keep copies of the opinion polls in Elizabethan Stratford-on-Avon? And, moving smartly to the main item in our agenda, could anybody even begin to understand modern America without reference to *All My Sons*, *Death of a Salesman* and *The Crucible*?

Plays, of course, are things that catch the conscience of all manner of people, including the mean-spirited and disreputable. However congenial the ivory tower, the writer may be called upon, or dragged out, to testify in his own defence, and in defence of what many of us, in our innocence, assumed were self-evident truths. Through the bleak days of Senator McCarthy and his un-merry men and the nightmare of Vietnam, Arthur Miller was a bright light in a wicked world: the writer as citizen. It is a difficult and demanding role, especially at times when people are easily fragmented into the familiar categories: the Good, the Bad and the Shifty.

Those of us who drew winning tickets and found ourselves at the 1989 celebrations in Norwich remember, no doubt with advantages, the gala performance at the theatre, introduced by the author. At the

6

end, there was a standing ovation for Arthur Miller, and those with the sharpest memories may recall that the writers in the audience were the first on their feet. It was an instinctive response but, at the risk of analysing the moment into the ground, let me try to explain the tribal sub-text.

We were saying thank you for the plays and books; for the civic example; for not compromising; and for restoring integrity to the phrase Man of Letters. We were also saying, in a mood of total admiration and affection, Hail to the Chief who shares his knowledge and wisdom, and who understands that the proper way to deal with power is to hand it back immediately to those who gave it to you. And, perhaps above all, we were saying: attention must be paid to this man.

William Styron

Americans, including writers and artists, are supposed to be compulsively sociable but I lived for six years as a close neighbor of Arthur's in Roxbury – a rural village then populated with but 600 souls – before we ever laid eyes on each other. Even then we met in, of all places, the lobby of the Hotel Vier Jahreszeiten in Munich, where we had converged on separate literary missions. Arthur was as aware as I was of the oddness of our not having met, for in Munich his first words to me were those which Stanley might have wished he had actually used upon encountering Livingstone, i.e., 'At Last'. This was in 1961, a short while after his marriage to Inge Morath, who was accompanying him and who helped make our brief sojourn in Bavaria such a pleasure. Like Eckermann on his first visit to Goethe, I think I was prepared to find something about Arthur that was fairly Olympian. I am regrettably susceptible to unsubstantiated opinion, and in New York several years before this an academic gentleman of forlorn mien told me, after I said I was an unfulfilled neighbour of Arthur's, that when I finally met him I would be encountering a man of 'sadness and incredible dignity, like Abraham Lincoln.'

This asinine impression derived more, of course, from the general gravity of the Miller oeuvre than from the man. Arthur, I discovered, has as much dignity as the next person but the primary characteristic he shares with Lincoln is that of great height; as for sadness, Arthur

7

manages to conceal his with deftness. The salient feature of Arthur's personality is, as a matter of fact, humour, and his comedic gift is the quality that makes him such buoyant company.

It is a sense of humour born out of the memory of neediness and hard times, and is one that haunts his otherwise intense and rather somber view of life. In the past thirty years I've spent many hours listening to Arthur, at each other's house in Connecticut or on certain peculiarly conceived trips that have taken us to the globe's far corners – Chile, for example, or Egypt. When I remember Arthur settling back in a deck chair on a luxurious boat cruising the Nile, exclaiming expansively, 'What is it that the working class is complaining about?', I realise that the laughter induced in me by the mock-plutocratic tone has an ambiguous quality owing to my knowledge of his working-class experience and allegiances. Likewise, an exquisitely American perception of the dynamics of class and power overlaid his response to the colossal Pharonic effigies sculpted into the cliffs of the Valley of the Kings. They were created, Arthur observed, in precisely the same spirit as that which caused to be erected the various façades of the First National City Bank and bore the identical intimidating message for their beholders: 'We're in charge here. Keep the hell out.' Travelling with Arthur as I have over so many thousands of terrestrial miles has not been like travelling with your run-of-the-mill CEO, say, or a politician. His curiosity is unquenchable, his ability to make associative connections is formidable, and it is all held in equipoise by a marvelous sense of the absurd. However, his pleasure in travel seems provisional. One feels his longing to get back to the Connecticut countryside and his fine but sensibly proportioned house, where he can look at the woods and fields which he has been looking at serenely for over forty years.

Critics have adduced many subtle reasons (and will continue their analyses for generations) to explain Arthur's mastery as a dramatist, but few are likely to come up with the crucially simple truth that he is a consummate storyteller. Having watched him on numerous occasions, clad in his gentleman farmer's rumpledness, sidling into my crowded living room, I have etched on my mind his expression of richly amused dejection, that of a man experiencing both pleasure and anguish, one deathly afraid of bores and of being bored yet warily hopeful for that blessed moment of communion that sometimes happens. And after a while it usually does happen. Arthur has found an audience – or, more significantly, they have found him, which is the rarest tribute of all since only a great storyteller can exert such magnetism without a trace of self-devotion. As the yarn unwinds Arthur's eyes sparkle and his voice becomes sly, conspiritorial, reflective, studded with small abrupt astonishments, the denouement craftily dangled and delayed: he is also an actor of intuitive panache. Is it a performance? Perhaps. But whatever it is it unfolds with eloquence and his listeners are lost in it, and it is then that I am able to perceive, simultaneously, the inspired vision of the playwright and the energising charm of the man.

Peter Ustinov

The first impression of Arthur Miller is that of a man who has left his mark on Mount Rushmore, so chiselled is his face, so deep the furrows of determination bracketing his mouth. The eyes are inquisitive and quite ready to be puzzled by the incongruities of life, even if the traces of time on his face allow no room for doubt; he is a man of opinion, with a mental architecture of his own which leaves no areas of intelligence vague or ill-digested. He is a strategist rather than a tactician, with a scientific application of his acquired values to the matters at hand: an unhurried judge as well as a passionate, yet reasoned, advocate.

The second impression of Arthur Miller is more surprising. It is that of a charming friend, with a delightful felicity of mind, who can elegantly make light of most things, including himself. He is not one for parties where no voice can be comfortably heard. He prefers a background of silence, and is well aware of the importance of stamina, and an ideal climate for either work or conversation. Very little of either is wasted.

He is a man who commands respect by according it to others, even if he is redoubtable in debate, and will not concede vital points for the sake of convenience, or even mere politeness. He has elements of the best of both worlds. While better qualified to Mount Rushmore than most, he is also, quite simply, fun. But all in good time.

Kurt Vonnegut

My old friend Arthur Miller and I met most recently, as I write, at the mansion of the Mayor of New York City, David Dinkins, for breakfast on February 23rd, 1990 with the President of Czechoslovakia, the playwright Vaclav Havel. Someone raised the question of which American playwright would make the best President, and the matter was quickly settled. No dramatist in this country's history, and no President, for that matter, has ever looked more like a President than Arthur Miller.

His appearance is, of course, testimony to nothing but genetic good luck. His great gifts as a writer, however, have allowed him to justify his magisterial persona with admirable acts of statesmanship. I mean those plays of his which speak movingly about America to almost all Americans, while telling the truth about America. Most of the rest of us who write here can't find any way to do that while being truthful. It is as though Arthur Miller had squared the circle.

Or saved the Union.

Bigsby: You were born and brought up in New York but a rather different New York from the one we know now. Can you tell me something about that world?

Miller: Well, I was born in Harlem (in the southern limits of Harlem) and it was a very pleasant place to be for the most part. Harlem is actually, in my opinion, one of the most beautiful neighbourhoods in New York. It's higher than the rest of the island. In those days there were still trees, large trees, on 7th Avenue, Lennox Avenue and 5th Avenue, and the place was, for a young kid, an idyllic place to be, within limits, and the limits were that anything you had would probably get stolen, but that was part of life. Incidentally, the place was occupied by about twenty to twenty-five per cent (this is a rough estimate) of blacks. The rest were every other kind of people you can imagine – Jews, Italians, Irish, Germans and it wasn't, incidentally, the blacks that were stealing. They were country people in those days. They came up from the South only recently around World War I – I am speaking now of the 20s of course – and it was the whites stealing from the whites – but it was a major preoccupation always in New York.

Bigsby: Do you mean that New York then was in a sense like a small town – the part that you lived in?

Miller: Yes, well it tends to do that anyway you know. It doesn't seem to from the naked eye, but New York does congregate in neighbourhoods and people do know each other in those neighbourhoods. It seems terribly anonymous when you drive through and you see all the populated hurly-burly but in my neighbourhood you knew just about everybody; you knew a lot of peopole and the school was behind my house on the next block so I could look out of the window and see when the flag was pulled up and then I knew I was late. My mother had gone to the same school. The same lady, Miss Fisher, was in charge of the school as when my brother and I went there and she used to lament to my mother that I was not the student that my mother had been. My grandmother lived in the neighbourhood, and my grandfather. I had an extended family, as they say today. There were cousins, aunts and uncles all over the place. Not only there but in Brooklyn as well. We were a very large family and I lived opposite Central Park, where you had a front yard of one the most beautiful parks in the country. In the winter you went ice skating. If you looked out of our window you could see when the red ball went up and everybody would come pouring out of these apartment houses with ice skates. In the summertime we played ball out there and rode bikes.

Bigsby: You then moved, later on, to Brooklyn?

Miller: When I was about twelve or so we moved to Brooklyn where it was even better. Brooklyn was then far less crowded than it later became and we called it the country. It wasn't really, but there were some empty lots and we could play football on a empty lot and go fishing in the Atlantic Ocean. It was quite wonderful.

Bigsby: I suppose the central image of *Death of a Salesman* is of an almost countryfied world which then slowly closes in on them as the apartment buildings go up.

Miller: Well, that was the way it was, yes. In Brooklyn through the first World War and up until, I would say, the late twenties/early thirties, there were few apartment houses. There were a lot of one family small houses. You could stand on the back porch and watch your kid going to school a mile away. There were still tomatoes being raised all over the place, grapes – the Italians raised grapes and made wine, picked dandelions – it was a great place, I thought, but it rapidly got crowded in like everything else. It was in microcosm, I think, what happened to most of the urban world that we know about now.

Bigsby: So many of your plays are about father/son relationships. How would you characterise your own relationship with your father?

Miller: Well, the actual relationship was quite good. My father was a very ordinary kind of a businessman really and his attitude was very tolerant. Whatever you wanted to do, you did. If not he was uninterested, basically. He just assumed you would come out all right.

Bigsby: That reminds me of a line in *Death of a Salesman* where Charlie says his great virtue was . . .

Miller: Yes, that he never had any interest in anything. Well, it's like that.

Bigsby: But I never understood that line because, in a sense, why would that be a virtue?

Miller: It's that he never leaned on his son. He never insisted that he become something that he might not want to be. He never forced him to do what the son might not have chosen to do. He was not living through his son as much as Willy was living through his children. That's what that means, really.

Bigsby: Was yours a noticeably Jewish household?

Miller: My mother was born in the United States. My father came from Austro-Hungary when he was about four or five years old so that fundamentally it was as American a group of people as there was at the time in this country, I suppose. They certainly were Jews but they were trying to become, and in some ways did become, indistinguishable from anybody else.

Bigsby: Does that mean that there was a price paid for that?

Miller: Oh sure. There always is, yes. In any ethnic group you lose roots and you gain something else, perhaps, but it's a trade off, it's a question of what you do lose. I think in their class of people in their time, in the development of this country, it was probably as common a development as there was. Now some people came out of a different kind of emigration, like the Russians from Odessa or from Kiev or one of the places in Europe where there had been heavy Socialist agitation due to the pogroms of the Tsar. But my grandparents came out of a much less painful environment. It was bad enough but it wasn't anything like that because they were under Franz Joseph, who was a far more liberal tyrant than the Tsars ever were. It was a German/Austrian domination which in those days, comparatively, was less onerous. So consequently they didn't react with the fever of an Israel or a Palestine, the way the Jews in Russia did. Israel really was set up by Russian immigrants for a good reason – they were reacting against this dreadful anti-Semitism in Russia. There was anti-Semitism in the Austrian-Hungarian empire to be sure but for their moment in history, apparently, it led to a different development. They thought that they could become like the Germans. My mother was the bridge. She was born, raised and educated in New York. My father was the immigrant but my mother's education was pretty good. She read everything. She was quick and had a phenomenal memory. She was a very good student. It was the curse of the era that a woman rarely went on from high school, from lower schools. They married her off and that was the end of her but she could have been any kind of an intellectual worker, I would imagine.

Bigsby: So if she was the bridge was there a space between you and your father for cultural reasons?

Miller: Well, he had no European memories, that was the odd thing. He was only four or five years of age when he left. He was astonished when I became old enough to go back to Europe to visit on the usual American tour after World War II. He wondered why I bothered. What was there? And I had to explain to him that there were some beautiful great cities and a civilisation. All he remembered was some lousy little village in Poland someplace near Krakow, where they drank out of the same water they washed their clothes in and the place was full of mangy idiots and there was no asylum for the crippled. Those were his memories and why anybody would voluntarily go back to that continent was simply beyond him.

Bigsby: Am I right in sensing a gulf between your parents: your mother, on the one hand, committed to culture, actually hiring a student to read novels to her; and your father, much more committed to the material world, and, indeed, barely literate.

Miller: That's right, there was a cultural space between them, and as I went on I made much of it because a kid growing up needs to learn to read, he needs to learn to absorb the culture that is given him, and my father could be of no help there. He was barely able to read and write and so I naturally gravitated towards my mother for that. But, as time went on, I found he had a certain taste which was basically mine, much more than hers. She was very sentimental about books, about people, about everything; he was far more realistic, in a peasant-like way. Some idea had to operate; he had no intellectual pretensions whatsoever, so just having an idea was no great thing for him. He wanted to know what happened as a result of it, where did it lead, how did it change anything. Fundamentally he was on the right track. So I was caught between the two of them and I think it was fruitful.

Bigsby: On the other hand when you became a writer, wasn't that a way of taking sides, almost a betrayal?

Miller: Well, it was a way of pleasing her, fundamentally, because in fact when I started to write I had to create some career for myself that would make sense to him and if I told him I was going to be a writer he would give me one of his long, blank looks and I would then have to invent something. So I invented the idea that I was going to be a journalist, because he knew that journalists work for companies and they had payrolls. But, of course, I wasn't a good journalist because I had no real interest in it.

Bigsby: The very first play you wrote when you were a student at the University of Michigan was in some ways about your family, and your father emerges from that a rather bewildered man, certainly not in tune with what then would have been called progressive forces. He was a decent man but in a way a failure. I notice that in your autobiography you list a number of American writers whose fathers were failures or whose sons regarded them as failures. Would you place yourself in that category?

Miller: I certainly would. That was the ethos that I grew up with in fact; it was the standard operating procedure. I think it may still be. One rarely hears of an American writer, I don't know about England or Europe, whose father was to be regarded as, in any way, adequate or successful. The writer in America is surplanting somebody, correcting him, making up for his errors or failures, and in the process he is creating a new world. He is the power that the father had lost.

Bigsby: But isn't that another way of denying history, which is what you often accuse American society of doing?

Miller: Yes, sure. It is. We want to create a new cosmos and each man in America is going to create that cosmos all by his little self and he is not going to need a society. That is the reason why America has no great socialist tradition.

Bigsby: But do you mean by this that the writer, instead of opposing society, actually becomes an archetype of American society, inventing it anew?

Miller: I think that is a good way of putting it. He does invent it all by himself, all new, until he has to come to terms with it sometime later which is a different procedure. Take Hemingway, for example: his father shot himself just as he was fated to do and though I don't know enough about his psyche to say, I bet that he arrived at some kind of an inner confrontation with that fact very late in his life. He was struggling with that damn father of his until he died. And Faulkner was that way too.

Bigsby: You were still writing about your father in *The American Clock*.

Miller: Right. It is an incubus and an impulse to go on. It's something you need in order to create whatever you are creating, apparently. Maybe it's a universal thing. Oddly enough I've noticed that in a number of Chinese stories and novels there are an enormous number of stories about fathers who are gradually losing their marbles and their authority. And then the Crash, of course, had a tremendous impact because I was so convinced of the authority of the system that I lived in and in which my father was a great success. That success had flowed over on to him, so that when the actual physical crash

15

came what it took with it was the authority of anybody who claimed authority.

Bigsby: Was there a moment in which you became aware of the fact that you were Jewish? Was that always there from the very beginning?

Miller: Of course, I always knew it but I knew that I was in a semi-beleaguered position. Very early on, its hard to know when exactly, I just knew that my parents were on the defensive. I caught this in the air. They were not hiding the fact that they were Jews; it was just that if you wanted to move up in the society, you'd better take on a colouration like the society. My father, for example, happened to look like your average Irish policeman, which was quite weird. He was as tall as I but he had blue eyes and reddish hair and a square head like the police on the street in those days. Many policemen used to think, as he went by, that he was a member of the department in plain clothes or something. He could always get a taxi, for example. He had tremendous personal authority. Now that made his friction with the surrounding world minimal. He had moved into that very easily.

Bigsby: Can you remember the first moment when you personally came up against anti-Semitism in the United States?

Miller: Yes. It was rather late in my case. I was already about eighteen, because fundamentally we lived among our own clan. I was protected in a sense, even though I went to a school where there were all kinds of people. Then again, in New York City the Jews were always numerous. My first job was in a auto parts warehouse, which was a Jewish company, and I had to be let go because business was so bad they didn't need a truck driver any more. So I was out of work for a while and then I saw this ad in the newspaper and I recognised the firm immediately because for a year I had been picking up auto parts from that firm to deliver to my firm in Long Island City, which is an industrial area outside New York City, over the river. I knew all the guys up there so I hurried there because it was a hell of a good place to work. They interviewed me and I told the boss whom I'd worked for before that I was applying, and if they asked him about me, that he should tell a lot of lies and say I was just great. And nothing happened. So he waited about three or four days and he called me up. He said, 'Did anything come of that interview?' I said 'No, it didn't.' I was just a kid then. This was a clerk's job, unskilled work, really. He said, 'Well, that's because you're Jewish!' and I was shocked. I said, 'Really?' He said, 'Yes, there's no other reason. They wouldn't find a kid your age who knows what you know about auto parts.' And I did know the business. By this time I'd spent a year in it with him. So he picked up the phone, he called them and he said, 'You know, most of your customers are Jewish and if you don't give this kid the job that he applied for, I'll know why.' Next day I got the job. I worked there for almost three years. While I was there, I was the only Jew they had ever hired and probably the only one they ever would hire. In those days it was pretty tough once you got a company like that. It was just rough.

Bigsby: You not only worked there but you worked also for a while, briefly, for your father's company.

Miller: Oh yes, well that was different. That was in the garment centre and that was practically all Jewish.

Bigsby: What was your response to the business world. Did it shape you in any way?

Miller: Well, through these experiences I learned a lot about it from the underbelly. These were small businesses that were highly competitive and in a Depression period which made it even worse. I had, I guess, a torn attitude about it. On the one hand, I shared the mores of business, that is that you had to work hard and keep your nose clean and if you succeeded it was good and if you failed it wasn't. On the other hand, the scale of values always bothered me a lot. I usually got involved with the failures in the place, of which I concede myself to be one, the people who didn't fit in this scheme of things, including a lot of salesmen who passed through, and they always moved me very much. Some of them were very sensitive, intelligent men who were simply scrapped. It was by nobody's will. It was really a dog eat dog situation, much more so than today, probably, excepting maybe on the highest levels of industry where they cut each other's throats on principle; but down below, there, it was a rough place for anybody to work and I found myself thrown in with a lot of these men from time to time.

Bigsby: You were what, fourteen, when the Crash came?

Miller: Yes.

Bigsby: What sort of impact did that have on your life and your family's life?

Miller: It was revolutionary. I remember I was playing handball on the street one day against a wall of the building and some fellow was playing with us. He was older than I was. He was already at University somewhere. And he started to tell me that the reason the Depression had occurred was because the workers hadn't been paid as much as they should have been and they couldn't buy back what had been produced. It was a Marxist argument. I remember standing there and thinking, everything is upside down. Of course I'd been brought up to think that workers belonged where they were. The reason they were workers was that they couldn't get to be bosses. Therefore it was always better to be the boss than the worker because the boss represented the end of your striving, your perfection, and the worker was a state of imperfection. So that day I recall very clearly thinking, 'My God, the whole thing is upside down. I should be wanting to be a worker.' You see. Anyway, it was revolutionary in all different ways. You suddenly realised that the great leaders of society were full of hot air. The thing was built on smoke. There were really no underpinnings. The head of the Stock Exchange had landed in prison for seven years for some crookedness. Certainly you had to believe in the banks, but they were closing up all over the place.

Bigsby: What happened to your own family?

Miller: Oh, they were ruined by it, just destroyed by it and very quickly. It was a story that was repeated millions of times in the United States on a larger scale than ours but it was big enough. My father had a business that probably employed eight hundred to a thousand people. It was one of the largest coat companies in the United States and in a period of, I don't know, probably a year or so, there was absolutely nothing left of it. The bottom dropped out of the whole thing. People forget, you know, that the American Banking Association went to Franklin Roosevelt and asked him to nationalise the banks. That came from the bankers. It was simply out of control. They didn't think they could bring back any kind of a usable banking system. So if they were talking about nationalising banks, you can imagine what we were talking about. When it first happened, people imagined that this would pass in a few weeks. After all the Stock Market had gone up and down a few times. But it kept going down and when they said it was all over, it kept going down again. Pretty soon nothing was worth anything and the effect on us, my family, was tremendous because, like a lot of other people, my father had realised, some time in the early or middle 20s, that while he had a perfectly lucrative business manufacturing women's coats, he could make immeasurably more money on the Stock Market than anybody could ever make in a business. So, like a lot of other businessmen, he put more and more capital into the Stock Market. And things were great for about four years until 1929–30 when the bottom fell out of it. So, in short order, like a lot of other people, he lost his capital and he lost a perfectly viable business which, had he not gambled with capital, would probably have survived. And the country went into hock. That is, everybody was in debt, whether it be for their home or their business or whatever, and the banks found it impossible to collect on the loans that they had made because people had lost what they had borrowed and the banks began to fail. I remember very clearly the time when I was on my bicycle passing a bank that I passed a thousand times on my way to school and there was a crowd of people out front and a policeman standing in front of the closed gates of that bank. It was about eleven o'clock in the morning. The policeman was explaining what had happened to their money. You can imagine the desperation involved in asking a policeman to describe what had happened to their money. And he, of course, was as bewildered as anybody. There was simply no Governmental regulation to catch the falling bodies. These people could go nowhere. Suddenly, of one morning, they had no assets. They couldn't buy food. They had what was in their pockets or what was in a drawer in the house. So the structure of the world shook. This big heavy looking bank turned out to be a fraud. What could you believe in, then? One banker after another on Monday would make a statement that everything was going to be all right and on Thursday he had jumped out of a window. So, within about six months of the Crash, I would say, possibly a little longer, you were naked on the beach. There was nothing to lean on. There was no security anywhere. The country was a fraud. It stunned my parents at first and then my father went back and tried to start a new business. He borrowed money from some place or another. He was now going into business in a period of Depression when the unemployment was something like twenty per cent after a while, that was the countable unemployed. There was no purchasing power so no business could survive then and he never recovered in his whole lifetime. Everybody was scrabbling around for any kind of a job. I went to work delivering bread and rolls at four thirty in the morning before I went to high school. I got four dollars a week for about twenty five hours. I was fortunate, I thought, to get this job. Four dollars sounds like a ridiculous sum, and it was, but you could buy a quart of milk for eight cents and, later on, I could buy some smoking tobacco for nine cents or something.

Bigsby: It occurs to me that it must have been almost a double blow to your father, because surely, in a sense, it was a blow to his manhood. That's to say, his status was being attacked. When you were a teenager and presumably of an age to challenge his status anyway, did it make relationships between the two of you difficult?

Miller: It didn't make them overtly difficult. I had great pity for him. Somewhere in my head I knew that it was not his responsibility that this had happened. However, he thought it was his responsibility. That was a distinctive thing about the American Depression of the 30s. The people blamed themselves, not the system, by and large, which is why the country never got radicalised in any way. They didn't blame the system. On the whole there was more self-blame than anything else. And it therefore became my job in effect to teach him that he should stop blaming himself so much. I did that because I slowly became more and more Marxist as the thing went on, as did my whole generation to one degree or another, because it was the only viable explanation, as you could imagine, for this whole thing having happened. We were not accustomed, in those days, to think of the thing as a system anyway. I never heard the word used, frankly – the word 'system'. You weren't in the system. You were in some sort of a free arena where each person went out to test himself. And that didn't change, of course. We are still in that arena, many of us. I went into my life not expecting any help from anywhere. I was amazed when the Government started to create programmes where you helped the people somehow. You expected people to get knocked off, destroyed, by bad luck. Then you either had to become entirely cynical about the whole world, which I was not set up to do, or you had to get busy creating a new one so that that creation of the new one and the rejection of absolute cynicism has really been the theme of much of my work. I'm not a fatalist. I don't believe there is no hope for man, but I do believe we stand on a very thin edge and that it is liable to go down at any moment. It was interesting in the late 80s, with the Stock Market on the slide again, to listen to a replay of the same speeches that were being made in 1929. Ronald Reagan announced that it was just an adjustment. That's like saying that the collision of two major planets is an adjustment of the universe. And it was some of what the hated Roosvelt put in place in the great hundred days after he got into office which prevented the unravelling of the whole sweater, though of course no one was going to admit that. Had we had the free economy, that we are all of course in favour of, we would all have been in the drink by now. But we don't have a free economy. We haven't had one at least since 1934, thank

God, and the result was that you could stop these haemorrhages by certain measures that were put in then.

Bigsby: Presumably, this was the period in which your own personal political views were beginning to crystalise? How would you characterise your politics in the late 30s?

Miller: I was totally confused but what I knew was that you couldn't simply wait. You see, after the first shock of the Crash, there was a period when everybody said, 'Well, you wait a few months and the whole thing will heal itself,' and the few months went by and your life was changing. In my case, for example, normally when a kid my class and age graduated from high school, he went on to college. Well you arrived at that June and then you came home and there was no college. So what do you do with yourself? You're untrained, in a market where nobody needs you, and you wait for the great change and the great change doesn't happen and slowly you are sinking into some kind of morass. I remember young fellows on our street playing ball all day long – some of them had Masters degrees in various disciplines. There was a hopelessness around that was devastating. It simply transformed the world from one in which there was an authority of some kind to one in which you were on the verge of thinking there was absolutely nothing upstairs whatsoever, good, bad or indifferent, that nobody was running the store.

Bigsby: So you were drawn to Marxism.

Miller: Oh yes, I was drawn to Marxism and also there was one other element. Hitler came into power in Germany at about the same time. Of course the early Fascism people didn't recognise for what it was. It was just sort of a crazy German movement of some sort which was going to be thrown out as soon as the sensible Germans caught on to what a ruffian this guy was. But within a year or two it was quite clear that he wasn't going to be thrown out at all and the anti-Semitism became more and more open. So that clouded the situation here because it aroused anti-Semitism in the United States for the simple reason that refugees started to want to get into this country and there was competition for jobs. Not only was there competition between Gentile and Jewish workers but the Jews were here and Jews were coming over and they didn't like that either. This is an untold story but it's true. For a time in the 1930s the Germans were milking the Jews by taking away all their property and in return were letting them get out. It was before the concentration camp system had reached its apogee – before it had really been developed – and they arrived here and then were turned away. They were turned away because Roosevelt feared that it would generate a terrific reaction against both him and the Jews. They tried to land in Cuba and the Cubans turned them away and they went back to Germany and were killed.

Bigsby: Presumably Marxism is the very antithesis of everything that your father believed in.

Miller: Oh yes. This was a challenge to him. I overthrew all his values. I now identified myself with the workers and indeed I had to be a worker for a number of years. He never took this kind of thing seriously. He was all but illiterate and he left all that to the people who had heavy thoughts. He didn't think his opinion amounted to anything. Actually he was wiser than a lot of people. He went purely by existential instincts. He knew what he had seen and you couldn't budge that and he knew what he hadn't seen and you couldn't budge that either but he'd listen and nod and figure, well that's not his line of work, this kind of thinking. So our conflicts were minimised because he never assumed he had a right to an opinion about all this stuff. He knew the coat business; he knew all about that. He knew about the market; he knew all about that. Beyond these small areas he had no competence, he thought.

Bigsby: Presumably as it was a family business he must have wanted you to go into that business and now it no longer existed.

Miller: Yes. Well that hurt him some. Of course, you see, he was of that generation of immigrants who thought that the best thing one could do was to find some way of life that was less cut-throat, less competitive, because they were scrabbling at the bottom of this pit every day, trying to come up with the golden egg. Their ideal was a profession of some kind where people could be ladies and gentlemen and didn't have to go into this dreadful battle for survival. That's what he thought he was in. Dog eat dog. He knew that much. So, he wasn't against my turning my back on that, although my brother became a businessman and they were closer together than I was, because my brother shared a lot of his viewpoints with at least half his head. The other half didn't. But none of this lapped over onto me. I just discarded the whole business ethic from day one. It just seemed to me to be an absurdity.

Bigsby: What's the most acute memory you have of that period that in some way sums up the 30s and the Depression to you.

Miller: Endless, boundless waiting. The 30s have been characterised as a time of great struggle, which they were in the sense that our trade unions were formed then, or reformed, and the country became conscious of the Government's obligation to extend help in various ways, but any neighbourhood you went into was full of grown people with nothing to do. That's where I grew up. Grown men were playing football in the streets in the middle of the work-day, living with in-laws, and the conversations were about how somebody had hit it rich somehow or somebody had sung a song and gotten on the radio and made twenty-five dollars. Everything was about money, you see. This was obsessional. Where was the next dollar going to come from. It's almost impossible to imagine any more a country with no public assistance. You see, people were living on each other. There were six-roomed houses with eighteen people living in them, tripping over each other to go to the one bathroom, all related and all calling themselves middle-class people. They might even have a car. The absurdities of it all were what hit you. It was a dusty time and the summers were the most dreadful time of all for a young guy because you had gone through school and thought that in the fall you would go back to school and the point arrived where school was coming up and you weren't going back. What do you do all those October/November/December days? That was what was dreadful. Everything was put off. Whatever you thought of was greeted with a sigh that maybe someday one could do that again, but not soon. It was agony, especially in a country where in all our memories, even mine, you thought you could pretty much do what you thought you wanted to do.

Bigsby: With money so tight, then, how was it that you managed to go to University?

Miller: Well, I had to work about three years. The University cost about sixty-five dollars a semester, for the first term, and sixty-five afterward. However, the University required, in my case, that I show them a bank book with five hundred dollars in it for fear that the state of Michigan would have to support me. It's a state institution. So I earned the money. I saved up five hundred dollars in about two and a half years, working in various jobs. The longest job I had was in that automobile parts warehouse I mentioned. That's the only reason I could go.

Bigsby: When did you first start thinking of yourself as being a writer?

Miller: I had this illusion, I think, by the time I was fifteen or sixteen. My mother loved to read; she did a lot of reading and she would direct me toward books. They were mostly popular novels but the idea of being literate in some way was something that we lived with in the house. The earliest memory I have of such a thing was called *The Book of Knowledge*, which was a ten to fifteen volume set sold to parents of schoolchildren. It was in effect a primitive kind of encyclopedia for young people. And in that was an etching of Charles Dickens with a sort of halo around his head made up of about fifteen of the major characters of his novels. I saw that when I was about eight or nine and I was struck with amazement that somebody could imagine people and then you could draw pictures of them, because it seemed to me that they had to be accurate pictures if they were in a heavy book like this with a leather binding. That idea of creating something out of your head and making it visible was very strong with me. I went around for days wondering how that could be possible. But the actual idea of writing something didn't come until I was about sixteen or seventeen. I used to clown around a lot. There were some corny radio programmes, allegedly newscasts but in true American fashion these were very theatricalised since the newscasters were people who over-dramatised everything. If somebody fell on the subway it sounded as though Christ had just arisen. So I did a take-off of this man and I wrote it out because there was an amateur radio hour. Amateurs would be put on the radio for a few minutes to sing or amuse people, and you could win a prize if you were voted the best. So I wrote a take-off on this newscaster and I went down there and I read it for the producers and they promptly stole the thing and I heard it on the radio about three weeks later. A comedian, Phil Baker, who was then a household name, was reading my stuff and when I wrote to them I never got an answer. They stole the thing right then. So literature was already larcenous; it was tainted, and I learned then and there that the first law of literary life is never trust anybody.

Bigsby: What did you know of the theatre?

Miller: I had by this time seen a couple of plays in New York. One was an Ibsen play, in Brooklyn, of all places. Nazimova, who was a great star, played in Brooklyn, at Brighton Beach. It cost me thirty-five cents and the fare. I went down there to see her in *Ghosts*. That was a big shock, that a play could be that way. I had heard about Ibsen; I'd read one or two small things about him but I'd never read his plays, so I started reading them then. And, let's see, what else could I have seen? I can't remember now what else I'd seen on the stage. I think I saw *Waiting for Lefty*. Anyway, all that kind of social rebellion was in the air anyhow. There were all kinds of articles and novels written from much the same point of view, practically a religious repetition of the notion that the middle class was doomed. It stood between the workers and the bosses and was therefore in a position that made it morally confused. It didn't know what to give its allegiance to. It was the job of the middle-class person to recognise that his interests lay with the workers. This was the fix, and indeed, when I looked at it, later on, that was really the firm pattern of all the left-wing writing, in one way or another. It amounted to the fact that the middle class had lost its way. And they were the ones to be saved; they were the lost sheep. Workers, theoretically, knew where they were going. Of course, this was all total nonsense, but this was the way. You see, it was all new, this whole idea of looking at people as members of a class; it was totally un-American. One never did that. One never thought of it.

Bigsby: Did you take any drama courses at university?

Miller: Not at that point. I had been writing stories in the Freshman English class, and one or two teachers who read these stories got interested in me as a writer.

Bigsby: But why drama, if you began by writing short stories?

Miller: You know, the theatre suddenly became an arena. There were eight million short stories. Everybody was writing short stories, and there were magazines devoted to the short story. But, somehow, the theatrical instinct in me took over. The other thing seemed remote. You wrote a story and even if it got published, which never happened to me – I hadn't published anything – it was sort of lost in the general mill. But already I sensed that there was an isolation around any good play. It stood out, and one felt that one was really talking to people. Whereas a short story was talking to nobody.

Bigsby: And then you wrote your first play, *They Too Arise*, originally called *No Villain*. Didn't that win a competition?

Miller: Well, yes. One of the reasons I went to Michigan in the first place was the Hopwood Awards. A friend of mine in Brooklyn had been there and flunked out, but he told me about the Hopwood Awards. I had already started writing in Brooklyn, or wished I could write; I was, in any case, fooling around with it, and this guy told me about the awards. So I got interested in that because it indicated that at Michigan I could get some help, some cash. There was money involved. It was impossible to imagine in those days that anybody would give students $250. To give you an idea of what that meant, I worked two years to save $500, and they were running a prize of $250, for writing a few pages of something. It was incredible. Also Michigan gave cheap tuition, so I went there. Anyhow, *They Too Arise* was written in the hope that it would win the Hopwood Award.

Bigsby: And you wrote it very fast?

Miller: I wrote it in a vacation. The kids went away, I think, on Friday, and then they came back the following Sunday night. In other words, I had a week plus the weekends. I had started it on, I think, a Saturday, after the classes had finished, and the hall was empty because everyone had gone home. I worked all week, and I remember finishing it on Thursday evening and giving it to my friend across the hall, who was a costumer for the University theatre. They did mostly Shakespeare, and he manufactured these beautiful costumes out of nothing, with no money. Anyhow, he read it and was surprised that it was good; he thought that it was a play. He was my first audience, and I could hear him chuckling in the other room. Anyway, from there I gave it to my English teacher who, later on, many years later, became the Dean of the University. Anyway, he got excited about it. And I submitted it and it won the prize.

Bigsby: And it was produced?

Miller: It was then produced by the Hillel Foundation, which was the Jewish group on campus, in a very amateurish way, but the WPA (Works Progress Administration) theatre picked it up.

Bigsby: How did that happen?

Miller: I think that they had somebody in Ann Arbor, because it got reviewed. In those days student work was never produced by anybody. Of course plays had been written in Ann Arbor for ever; there had always been plays, but nobody had ever dreamed of putting on an unproven play. They always put on Broadway plays, and the play production department was a very active place. They were doing plays all the time, but it was beyond anyone's imagination to put on student plays. Anyway, it became quite a success on the campus. People kept coming in, and they were going to keep it on for another night, so it was a bit of a stir. And I became known in that little pond as a playwright, and some of the faculty came, and they got interested in it. And then I won the prize, and later on, the following Fall, I think it was, I won another prize with it, which was a national playwriting contest. One of the other four or five winners was Tennessee Williams. He was in Missouri then, I guess, the University of Missouri. And, then I began thinking of myself as a playwright,

26

and I wrote another play, and that won another prize, the following year.

Bigsby: Can you remember what those early plays were liike?

Miller: They were interesting plays. Take *The Great Disobedience*, for example. I had spent time visiting with a friend of mine who got a job as a psychologist at the Jackson State Prison. That was then, maybe still is, the largest prison in the United States. It had something like eight thousand inmates. They had a lot of hard-timers, they had a lot of murderers, and I used to spend the weekends there. Jackson was – I don't know – forty miles from Ann Arbor and the place, it seemed to me, was fifty per cent insane, and the job this guy had was to keep the sane from going crazy. He had very little training; he had a degree and a couple of courses in psychology, and he was the psychiatric department of this hospital, if you can believe it. He later became the head of the parole board in the state of Michigan. Anyway, as a result of those visits, I wrote this play about a doctor trying to keep people from going crazy in this prison. It was full of class consciousness, and not wrongly so because the prison population in those days had a large proportion of economic crimes. I remember even now there was one farmer, a sheep farmer from up the peninsula, which was a very frontier-like place, a finger of Michigan into Canada, and he shot a sheriff of that area, who came to collect his sheep, because he hadn't paid some mortgage or whatever on his land. And he was a very simple fellow, and he still didn't understand why anybody took objection to this because they were his sheep, and the man had come to steal his sheep. There was a lot of that, and it was by no means a black prison. I would say the majority were white men in that prison. A lot of auto workers, unemployed, and it was clearly, as prisons usually are, a reflection of that society, and what was wrong with it. These guys were people who were out of work, a large number of them.

Bigsby: *The Great Disobedience* was never produced?

Miller: No, nobody ever did that.

Bigsby: Did *They Too Arise* get any other productions?

Miller: They did it in Detroit. They did one or two performances of it, maybe a week.

Bigsby: Were you tempted, once your career was successfully launched, to go back to that play?

Miller: You know, I've never been able successfully to go back over anything. I seem to lose it. The work that I've done a year ago is like somebody else's work, in a way. Of course, I recognise everything, and I remember more or less what I felt when I was working on it, but the past is the past. I can never go back. Now, I have tried to do it from time to time, but I've never succeeded. You can tell where one mood leaves off and another one begins. I muck around with them, maybe, but it never succeeds. Now it can take a year or more of work, like *All My Sons* did, but I'm continuously working at something, and that's one strain of the motion, which is continued. If I drop it, it closes the book, that's it.

Bigsby: *They Too Arise* was very close to your family circumstances.

Miller: Oh yes, it was the most biographical play I ever wrote. I think most young writers start that way. At least here they do.

Bigsby: Did you feel intimidated in writing that play as very often writers do when they address their own circumstances and their family life. Did you feel your father as a presence who might one day read it or see it?

Miller: I always got along with my father very well, but I did that by staying away from any conflict, that's all. But I enjoyed him, and he certainly thought that I was OK, well not always, but he wanted me to succeed. That was a basic immigrant's idea anyway. And once you did that, anything else was gravy. So it was a kind of metaphysical idea of a father I was using. I never felt that it was really him. I never had that problem of having him see it or not see it. Ever.

Bigsby: The various versions of the play are quite different. One is described on the title page as a comedy, and it ends up with the two sons marrying the people they want to marry. It's almost a comedy of manners with a social play hidden somewhere. And in another one, it's the social play which is in the immediate foreground. Can you recall that sense of moving between those versions?

Miller: I think I wrote the comic version when I came back from university. I didn't work on that at Michigan. I would think that I worked on that much later, because I thought that it could be made into a play that could be done on a stage in New York.

Bigsby: So you were thinking Broadway?

Miller: Well there was only one theatre then. There was no such thing as Off-Broadway theatre. You either went on Broadway or you didn't exist. But, of course, Broadway meant all sorts of things, then. That play, for example, could problably have been done for six or seven thousand dollars on Broadway. And in those days, there were still productions that would have cost twenty, so that would have been an inexpensive production. And I vaguely recall that there were people who were interested in it, they were taken by the idea, but they felt it wasn't finished, so I was trying to finish it. And my instincts were all wrong for that, because I wasn't into that kind of writing anyway. Of course the Theatre Guild saw that play and gave me a prize for it.

Bigsby: And that didn't involve production?

Miller: Not necessarily. You see, Tennessee won the same prize and they didn't produce his play either. They didn't produce any of those plays. They were just trying to collect some new writers by virtue of this contest, and we were among six or seven. I don't believe that I've heard of any of the others since, but none of them got produced.

Bigsby: What led to *The Golden Years*, your play about Montezuma and Cortez?

Miller: Well, first of all, there is a context. *The Golden Years* requires around twenty-five characters and I would never have dreamed of writing a play of that size excepting that there was a Federal Theatre at the time. The Federal Theatre was roughly speaking like a National Theatre. It was a government-supported theatre set up to absorb unemployed actors and keep them going. When I got out of college, in 1938, I managed to get taken on to the Federal Theatre in the playwriting department. Now a playwright, then, if he wrote a play that was somehow acceptable, could call upon endless numbers of actors; nobody cared, they were all being paid by the government anyway. Otherwise I probably would never have written so vast a play. I would go through spasms of wanting to be an historian and I think in one of those I read the story of the conquest of Mexico and it is a great, great story, just as a story. So when I got home from college and got on the project I thought it would be a hell of a tale. I also wanted to stretch the realistic theatre anyway; I was very impatient with it. I didn't know how to do that except by the use of language which always seemed to me to be terribly important in theatre. The fact is that we weren't using it, with the exception possibly of Clifford Odets who invented a kind of New York English which never existed in the streets. Apart from him, playwrights were using very crabbed and naturalistic language and this was a chance to get up off your feet and use the language a little bit and that was attractive. To make a long story short, by the time I had finished the play the Federal Theatre was dissolved by Congress so nobody would touch a play of that size any more than they would now. That was the end of it. *The Golden Years* really came out of Fascism. Since the early thirties we had lived under the threat, not just of Nazism, but American racism. It was terrifying, and anti-Semitism was very strong in the United States. The more it surfaced in Germany, the worse it got here. It became OK to be anti-Semitic, and we had some terrible incidents, and I thought that it was getting worse all the time. I thought personally that we would be destroyed by it one day, if a reaction against it didn't really materialise. So I lived a life of defensiveness against Fascism. That may seem putting it too simply, but that's what it was. And *The Golden Years* was what I saw as a kind of metaphor for the paralysis of the West, in the face of this cobra, which was forming itself in the heart of Europe, and quite clearly intended to destroy the whole civilisation. Hitler was talked about as if he were simply another politician who was a bit crude now and then.

Bigsby: How did you make the leap from the situation in Europe to the relationship of Cortez and Montezuma?

Miller: There's a fantastic book by one of the conquistadors, Bernard del Castello, who was one of those who served with Cortez when they conquered the country. Then he was made a chief or mayor of some town. And once he had that job he had nothing to do, of course, so he wrote this absolutely marvellous account of the conquest, which is basically the fundamental document upon which everything else stands. And, just as a piece of literature, it is a remarkable piece of work. I can't remember now at what point I got hold of that, but I read that and knew that I had to do something about it. It's such a beautiful story. And he suggests, from the Spanish viewpoint, but a totally honest viewpoint I thought, that in effect, from a long distance of hundreds of miles from the coast of Mexico to Mexico City, over those dreadful mountains, they hypnotised Montezuma. It's a marvellous idea. They'd never met. They'd never laid eyes upon each other, but Cortez, every step he took, was mesmerising this king, and one felt that in relation to Hitler. Well, look at the English especially, although Roosevelt was no better for a long time. Everything was falling into his hands. He couldn't do anything wrong. His mistakes were good mistakes, and wherever he stepped, it turned out to be the right step to make. And that was what was going on between 1932 about and 1939. That's a long time. That's damn near a decade.

Bigsby: What was the history of this play? What happened to it after you completed it?

Miller: Nothing. By the time I'd finished writing it it was 1939 or 1940, and, in the meantime, I was writing a lot of radio plays, and making my living that way. I realised that it was an impossible play to be produced on Broadway, because it would cost too much. I was totally unknown. I sent it to the Group Theatre but I never heard from them one way or another. They were so fixated by this time on just doing basically realistic social drama, and this thing was a big, classical tragedy, and it was something that nobody could touch, I suppose. They wouldn't know what to make of it, and I can't imagine their actors playing in it anyway, excepting one or two of them. Luther Adler could have been fantastic as Montezuma. He could have played Cortez, too. He was a wonderful actor. He was one of their great actors. If they had had any brains, they would have tried it. In later years I asked Harold Clurman, who directed a couple of my things, 'Whatever happened? Why didn't you guys answer me?' He didn't even remember ever having seen it. His wife, Stella Adler, said, 'Well the reason was that they were always so desperate, but they never made a dime'. They had all this publicity. Everybody said what an important theatre it was, but they were broke all the time, and failing. They were staggering from one financial failure to another, except that one of Odets's plays made money, so they were simply sitting on Odets's doorstep to give them another play. They never got organised as far as plays were concerned. It was one of their greatest failures. It wasn't just me. They never could branch out to another writer. It was rather their tragedy.

Bigsby: You mentioned the language of the piece. It does have the odd bit of over-heated prose. On the other hand these are characters, both Montezuma and Cortez, who are in a way the victims of their own rhetoric.

Miller: Yes, this play really is the story of two illusions. I am sure that Cortez really had rationalised himself into a position where he thought he was spreading the Christian religion and incidentally picking up as much wealth as he could for his King and himself. As he says in the play, there is Empire in it but there is also Jesus Christ in what he is doing. Therefore he could not approach life on a purely realistic level. I don't think anybody knows how sixteenth-century Spaniards spoke in real life, but when people are impelled by large 'ideas' they tend to use large rhetoric. Certainly they did in their letters, their reports and so on, which, incidentally, were very elaborate. Now Montezuma had a different illusion. His illusion was that he was already the richest, most powerful individual on the face of the earth and that what he needed more than anything was not what Cortez needed, which was Empire, he had the Empire; what he needed was God. He needed to believe that he had been ordained by the heavens to be, in effect, transubstantiated, lifted off from the human level into something that was eternal because he had conquered, as far as he knew, the entire world and here was somebody coming in from the coast, white, bearded, a being who had a strange metal costume and was riding on a beast that nobody had ever seen before. And the Aztecs had an ideology that told them that one of the great gods, Quetzalcoatl, had left Mexico, walked on the water, spoken of peace, and eschewed all violence. Now these people were coming back, bearing a cross which was the sign of Quetzalcoatl. So Montezuma wanted desperately to trust Cortez and Cortez wanted him desperately to trust him and they grappled to the death. The rhetoric, therefore, is on, I hoped, the level of those illusions which are of course world-shaking illusions, in which power is ultimate, infinite. The play goes over the edge occasionally but I think, after not reading it for almost half a century, I was quite surprised it had a certain power.

Bigsby: That play was written nearly half a century ago and now it's been produced on the radio. What's your response to that?

Miller: Well, I love it. Because I love radio. I worked in radio for many years, that's how I made my living, but I was never really allowed to write anything too good because it was commercial radio and I worked on historical subjects for the Cavalcade of America, which was the Dupont's Corporation's voice to the public. But the language is appropriate to radio, that is, it is self-descriptive. A lot of the time the character tells you where he is and what he is doing and what he is thinking, quite overtly. That makes good radio, I think.

Martin Jenkins

Director of the BBC World Premiere of The Golden
Years, *November, 1987*

In many respects radio is an ideal medium for concentrating upon
Miller's richness of language and imagery. Working as a director for
the BBC Radio Drama Department, I have in recent years recorded a
number of the plays including *All My Sons*, *The Crucible*, and *The Price*,
the last two with members of the Los Angeles based LA Classic
Theatre Works. *The Crucible* was recorded in a tiny makeshift studio
created in a corner of a huge Hollywood sound stage at Culver City,
formerly home to such legendary movies as *Gone With the Wind* and
Citizen Kane. The cast consisted of American film and TV stars, many
with little experience of radio technique. It was fascinating to watch
them adapt to a new challenge and succeed in recording the whole play
within the alloted time of four and a half days. I was naturally pleased
when I learnt that Miller had approved of the production; however, I
was even more delighted when in 1986 I was asked to direct the world
premiere of his previously unperformed play, *The Golden Years*. Written
in 1939/40, when he was twenty-four, the play was Miller's response
to events then sweeping Europe. As with *The Crucible* he had chosen an
historical setting to highlight a contemporary political situation. He
equated Hitler's expansionist policies with the invasion and destruction
of the Aztec Empire by the Spanish conquistador, Hernando Cortez.
Intended for performance by the American equivalent of the National
Theatre, the play proved to be both epic in conception and
presentation, requiring, as Miller wryly observed, 'the whole Aztec
army'. With a cast of around thirty, the play was shelved and had
virtually 'disappeared,' the only copy being deposited amongst various
Miller papers at the University of Austin in Texas. It was re-located by
Chris Bigsby who brought it to the BBC with Miller's agreement.

Having secured Miller's approval to adapt the play, to undertake
certain re-writes, and to make textual additions to explain the key
visual moments, I made certain other decisions before embarking upon
the actual work. The first concerned the crucial question of
presentation. Miller had introduced a Narrator who read the stage

instructions before each scene, thereby providing the listeners with vital information. I believed this a somewhat outdated device which could break the natural impetus of the writing but I also knew the audience required specific indications of time and place. My solution was to incorporate as much information as possible into the opening credits and then to devise a series of sound montages which would create a sense of period and atmosphere. These were enhanced by a highly original score by Christos Pittas. A chanting priest swiftly signalled a temple, drums represented the Spaniards, flutes the Aztecs. For the very opening, I created a sequence of sound images to convey location and distance. The noise of the sea symbolised the exploration of the Spaniards and the isolation of the Aztecs. Cannon shots and tramping horses denoted the first battle between the two sides as well as introducing sounds which would have been alien to the Aztecs. Finally, I ended the sequence with two echoing cries of 'Montezuma'. Here the aim was to suggest the mountains and the space between Cortez and Montezuma. The cries were also brought from a distance towards the listener thereby taking them from the coast to the heart of the Aztec kingdom. However, having heard the edited play *before* transmission, I was acutely aware that the listener might still find the first scene confusing. Miller offered to record a thirty second introduction which highlighted the main themes and offered the audience the equivalent of 'the programme notes'. He stated: 'the story basically involves the conflict of two illusions – Cortez, the illusion that he was bringing Christianity to a heathen people, and Montezuma, the illusion that he would be deified by the strange white creatures from the coast'. This provided vital information too often missing from major radio productions.

My second concern was the large number of characters, many with unpronounceable and in some cases instantly forgettable names. From bitter experience with large cast plays on radio I knew that identification for the audience could be a major difficulty, especially when up to ten characters appear simultaneously, each with a particular impact on the development of the drama. I had to steer away from dialogue such as 'Ah, my lord Guatemotzin here are Cuitlahua and Cagama and as you are Montezuma's nephew what is the latest news on the Sun Emperor and his daughter, Tecuichpo.' But I still had a duty to ensure the listeners knew at least the main contenders.

Thirdly, the clarification of purely visual moments involved writing new lines which had to conform with Miller's own style and also obtain

34

his seal of approval. In the past, I had written lengthy chunks of blank verse for *Vivat Rex*, a 26 part serialisation of Elizabethan history plays, imitating as closely as possible the changing styles of Marlowe and Shakespeare; but they at least were dead! Here I was striving to match a living writer whose work I had, in the past, believed virtually uncuttable never mind alterable. However, Miller understood the problem and approved all the amendments. Interestingly, some months later, I directed the first ever Neil Simon play for radio. His agents insisted that not a single word should be altered. It took several lengthy letters to educate them into the techniques of radio production before they appreciated that however brilliant a visual moment might be on stage, on radio it passes for absolutely nothing unless illuminated for the listener. When I finally spoke to Simon, he, like Miller, instantly recognised the problem.

The two most complicated visual moments in *The Golden Years* proved to be Montezuma's death and the helmet revered by the Sun Emperor. In the original text Montezuma never once refers to the helmet as a helmet. In the theatre the audience would know from his reactions his feelings towards the helmet. All this had to be conveyed with new dialogue. The death presented real problems. In attempting to persuade his people that he has acted in their best interests, the captive Montezuma appeals to them from a balcony. Half way through he is mortally wounded by an arrow fired by his brother. On stage both events would be clearly visible and dialogue unnecessary. For radio, I believed it was essential the listeners should know he had been killed by his brother and with an arrow. The first was overcome by Montezuma reacting to the impact of the arrow and recognising his assassin. The arrow was referred to later.

My fourth and final concern was the vexed question of accents. Although written for American actors I could see no justification for using American accents for a British production of a play about Aztec Indians and Spanish conquistadores. Also I wished to avoid comparison with Hollywood epics. Equally, I did not want pseudo-Shakespearian styles of speaking. In the end, the Aztecs used straight accents but devoid of poetic overtones, whilst the Spaniards aimed at a roughness and coarseness of delivery without falling back on varieties of 'mummerset'. Having decided to use English actors I then excised a number of Americanisms such as 'gotten' from the original and tightened and strengthened some of the speeches to achieve a more natural flow for British audiences.

The broadcast enjoyed considerable advance publicity and provoked at least a dozen reviews, all favourable. Several critics spent time analysing the suitability of the play for the stage. Miller himself had wanted to use the radio production to assess the impact of the play and gauge the possibility of a stage presentation. He seemed genuinely pleased by the power and impact of his dialogue and characterisation.

Ronald Pickup

The challenge of *The Golden Years* is that it presents the actor with a thrilling mixture – full-blown language bursting at the seams with richness and power (doing justice to an epic story of the kind that Hollywood has always drooled over), and the exploration of two wary men both at crisis points in their lives, one an innocent the other a pragmatic bully.

Encountering the play for the first time the sheer pace and excitement of the story make it compulsive reading. Then you wonder why it has never been done. You think of the cast of thousands and the sets and you know why! But we, in the radio production, had only to worry about the language of the play, its outer and its inner language; and there is no better medium than radio for enabling actors to follow their instincts about the language of a play. On the debit side, there is occasionally not enough time to explore, or merely to try a different *tone* because the need to commit to tape is urgent. But I think in our production, thanks to Martin Jenkins and a marvellous cast, which included Hannah Gordon and John Shrapnel (as Cortez), I think I found Montezuma one of the most tantalising experiences of my radio work. In simplistic terms I settled (because of time!) for seeing him as an Indian Richard II and Cortez a Spanish Bolingbroke – a parallel which had its uses when you look at the broad contrasts of character. But where Arthur Miller's characters become treacherous and wonderfully difficult is that there are areas of overlap. Montezuma is a poet, an innocent (more innocent, spiritually, I think than Richard II), but he is not completely so. Cortez is a brute, but a brute who somehow commands the respect of hard-nosed men, a beautiful princess of the land, and, most strange of all, Montezuma. Power is fascinated by power. Fading power, as evidenced in Montezuma, is fascinated by *new* power, as evidenced in Cortez. I think this wary, shifting admiration and suspicion, pride and humility, was the area we concentrated on most in the radio production, because it so well suited that medium – the stillness, the pauses, the moments of unbearable tension, as when Cortez mistakenly attempts to touch Montezuma, who recoils with an animal shriek.

This brief preamble about the radio production, and the few generalisation I have made about the play, merely set the scene for a year or so later, in May, 1989, when John Shrapnel and I presented a brief scene from *The Golden Years* in a programme distinguished by many fine actors who performed extracts from Arthur Miller's other plays.

The occasion was the opening of the Arthur Miller Centre for American Studies at Norwich. We actors were to perform an extract; Chris Bigsby and Arthur, sitting on stage right, were to talk about the plays and their relationship to that particular part of his life.

We rehearsed some 'bits' in the afternoon under Arthur's benign and yet formidable presence. To say we weren't nervous would have been a lie, but to someone like myself, who had never met him before, it became clear in a moment that, as he confirmed later in a moving and public statement about actors, I think he is at his happiest and most relaxed with this tribe of people who, as he modestly says, 'give life to his plays'.

He is so matter of fact and practical. One of my extracts was a marvellous soliloquy of Montezuma's, full of doubt about the implications of Cortez's presence in Mexico. The speech ends with a plea to the 'Great God Quetzalcoatl' to give him a sign. So I did it, all a bit careful and well enunciated, and that was about all. When I finished Arthur just said 'the guy's hooked on spirits isn't he'. Which meant everything about the part. So he then made a simple, superbly simple, theatrical suggestion. He said that when I call out to the God at the end of the speech I should throw my head back in such a way that I am facing absolutely, directly, upwards, not slightly or diagonally, but straight upwards. The difference, when you let an idea like that filter through into other aspects of the part, is the difference between playing safe and playing dangerous – going for broke. It reveals, if one ever doubted it, that theatrical *size* of presentation is as crucial to the Arthur Miller approach to the human condition, as are the minute details which go to form the whole. But the size must always be welded

37

to the truth. The Gods were truth for Montezuma, so the head would be thrown back, vulnerable and awesome.

Hence my remark earlier about the radio performance of the part being so tantalising. Montezuma is boy-man, man-girl, innocent-demonic, vulnerable-awesome. In the final analysis the sheer theatrical space is necessary to achieve all that, plus a few weeks of rehearsal! But it strikes me as a play which could be done in a very simple space and without a huge cast. The size of the language and the ideas fill the stage, and, although John and I had the advantage of doing a hitherto unknown play on the stage at Norwich, the stark simplicity of the setting for the extracts we did seemed to enhance an impact which only a very special play could command. Miller's presence, though, contributed so much to that, because, true to the sentiments he later expressed about actors, the pleasure which watching his own work 'being brought to life' gave him suffused the whole evening with generosity of spirit and optimism.

John Shrapnel

Obviously, the big thrill of doing *The Golden Years* was speaking lines which no one had ever spoken before (except maybe a youthful Arthur Miller trying them out over a Smith-Corona in some rooming-house).

And what lines. When you read: '. . . We will tear this people from the claws of anti-Christ and Jesus will reign in Mexico and blood and stone will not stop us!' you just want to get in the car and put your foot down.

It's a completely fearless play, and what I love is the vastness of the theme (Montezuma, Cortez, elemental rivalry) and the fact that the dialogue veers from the clouds to the streets: from Montezuma's teeming description of his city, and the electric moment of physical contact with Cortez: 'I . . . . I AM NEVER TOUCHED . . . .' right down to '. . . . Hernando, there's going to be trouble!'

I think it's this anachronistic quality which gives the play its life; the fact that it can accommodate Shakespearean weight ('. . . . Do I not bleed?') and quick-cut cinematic drama (and dialogue), as when the Spaniards fake a huge army by the ruse of sending the same few horsemen thundering past the door many times. This always felt to me like a Western moment.

Radio seemed a natural home for all this, because you just had to trust the dialogue to do the work and create the images.

As Cortez, my final line was my favourite: '. . . Then? We break for the open streets! (Draws sword). Come! . . .'

I mean, if you don't jump on that like a spare-rib, take a job in a bank . . .

Bigsby: When you did hit Broadway, it was with a play that turned out to be something of a disaster at the time, *The Man Who Had All The Luck*.

Miller: Yes, it lasted four or five days.

Bigsby: What went wrong?

Miller: Well, I didn't know anything about how to do a play. I had no connection with a theatre – it's typical. And this was done on Broadway by a very nice man, who smelt something there that he loved, but he didn't know how to do the play, and I'm not sure you could do the play. I was after the story of a man who can't seem to fail, and it should have ended tragically, I think; maybe that would have really made it make sense, although I hadn't written it tragically, I hadn't set out to write a tragedy. I'd set out to write a kind of myth, and the myth was simply mythic in the sense that a myth pays most attention to the process of fate, as it works itself out, rather than to realistic character. A character in myth is a persona; he's not an ordinary person. Well, I was trying to make this guy both mythic and ordinary at the same time, and succeeded in making him more ordinary than mythical. But I still thought – and I'm not sure that I'm wrong yet – that, treated properly, with sufficient theatrical cues as to what we're about, that we're not in a folk comedy (because that's the way it was produced – it was produced as a realistic folk comedy), it makes some sense. If it had been produced as a kind of semi-whimsical and yet terribly sad story, it might work.

Bigsby: Now you've redone it.

Miller: Well, I did do the last few pages again and they are the best I can manage now. You see, the play ended too completely. The issue is, if you put it in the crudest sense, how much of our fate do we make and how much is accident, or what the ancients would call fate or fortune? And I thought that the central character was sick, because he couldn't believe in his own identity, his own contribution to what was happening to him.

Paul Unwin

Bristol Old Vic, May 1990

An actor, I can't remember who, said that the art is 'knowing what kind of play you're in'. Good preparation is as much about finding out what kind of play you're directing as it is about solving the practical issues any production throws up. Writing before I start rehearsals for *The Man Who Had All The Luck* I'm deep in the what kind of play debate.

The Man Who Had All The Luck has a chequered history and is, whoever had written it, the product of a very different time and, to my experience, a very distant world. I first read the play, barely aware that it was by Arthur Miller, as part of a half dozen texts I'd taken away for a weekend. What struck me immediately was how direct, passionate and bold it was. While the other writers in the pile seemed to struggle to avoid collisions, *The Man Who Had All The Luck* burst with them.

The Man Who Had All The Luck is a perverse play. I can't think of another drama based on the astonishing notion of things in life going right and yet for David Beeves, the play's hero, this is exactly what happens. As drama's first model is life, perverse may be an understatement. Miller was struggling with a particular element of life in writing *The Man Who Had All The Luck* and created David to test it. At a time when Europe seemed to be abandoning itself to tyranny and America abandoning Europe, Miller was testing the notion of individual responsibility. Do we affect events or are we simply their victims? For America, where fantastic prosperity was haunted by potential catastrophe, Miller was writing a fable in which good fortune, rather than disaster, tested a young man.

The Man Who Had All The Luck tells an 'unrealistic' story. We can all imagine how life can go terribly wrong but find it harder to imagine it going right, at least consistently so, and we know, from experience, it is unrealistic to imagine that it will. In the play, events – such as Gus's arrival or Falk's timely death – are problems because, to our pessimistic imaginations, they are unlikely.

It is tempting to bypass one's own doubts about the play. Something that is 'unrealistic' could be simply bad writing. We all recognise artifact as distinct from bad construction. Was Miller able to achieve what he aspired to in writing the first drafts of *The Man Who Had All The Luck* or was he uncertain of style and unable to complete the matrix that, in the end, makes up a 'realistic' plot? I don't know and won't know until I've seen the play on stage. However, we do know from Miller's autobiography that he was sufficiently obsessed with fate, good fortune and luck, to want to throw the unlikely together.

When I talked to Miller in Connecticut about the play he was clear that the piece cannot be constrained by a 'naturalistic' production. Clearly the play's original and disastrous production, albeit of a different version, was set entirely naturalistically and directed by one of Broadway's foremost comedy directors. What went wrong, and Miller's willing to take his share of blame, was the signals the production gave about the play. Nowadays Miller wants the play's heightened qualities to extend to the setting and as we talked he described options as radical as the one-dimensional designs used in the traditional Japanese theatre. I, and the designer Sally Crabb, have found there is a relatively complex contradiction here as the play demands, for example, that a car is on the stage, that it starts and so on.

I'm attempting to solve some of this by working on the production with the jazz saxophonist and composer Andy Sheppard. Rather than use music to cover a scene change or set the location, Andy is creating a score for the piece that will, I hope, underscore the action, heightening it, perhaps even teasing its implicit melodrama.

The externals of production – set, music, lights – are frequently given too much attention. Whatever the stylistic problems of a play, a production stands on the quality of its acting. Without acting the theatre is nothing and the rehearsal, for me, is an attempt to get good clear acting out of everyone involved. This may be a statement of the obvious but as I don't have a theory about the play I want to express, the obvious is happily all I'm left with. I've been very lucky with *The Man Who Had All The Luck* because it has been possible to attract a perfect cast, by which I mean a group of actors who fit their roles, can act, and have the balance of skill, sanity, and ego to ensure that rehearsals don't become neurotic battleground.

How will we begin? Or rather what have we got to achieve? First, everyone has to know who they are and to do this we'll trawl the text for clues. We may go beyond the published text; I've got three other versions of *The Man Who Had All The Luck* and in the earlier ones some key elements are different. Miller has a special feeling about *The Man Who Had All The Luck* because it gave him one of the main ingredients to his work: families and, more specifically, the relationship between brothers, fathers and sons. In the first version of the play David and Amos aren't even related. To explore how this handicaps the play may well give us an insight into how the play now works.

The rehearsal process isn't scientific. Building from the facts the text offers, we'll start to establish each character's subjective reality. I might ask the actors to write their character's diary, in other words, express, as their character would, the events that occur to them. At the same time, I have asked the actors to bring to rehearsal some information about the play's environment and I've been faxing Miller with questions. For example, what would the attitude be to Gus coming from Europe? Answer: 'The Midwest couldn't have noticed it less . . . Europe I mean. It was Lunar'. Constantly in rehearsal one is trying to find a character's action. What do they want, and what are they trying to do?

Finally – and I do always want to delay this moment – the talking is done and the standing up acting begins. The fact that the sofa, we discover, is in an impossible position instantly removes questions of naturalism or realism. However, there are things to hang onto. Miller's characters are direct. While they may be neurotic they speak their mind and confront issues directly. We must keep the lines of communication open and not clutter them with excessive detail. The play is a 'fable' and as such focuses on clear dilemmas and their consequence for one person, David. While, of course, the other characters are important, they all exist in a David-centred world, in a David-centred drama.

The Man Who Had All The Luck is dramatic and deals with the big issues. We mustn't let British understatement soften its guts or lessen its melodrama. Like Steinbeck, or Woody Guthrie, or Edward Hopper, Miller was trying to find a form to express the scale of the American experience when he wrote *The Man Who Had All The Luck*. As such it should punch hard.

Bigsby: So, your first stage play to be produced in New York, was a flop. What impact did that have on you?

Miller: Well, it sent me into novel writing. That's a pretty big effect. I thought I was finished with the theatre. I thought it was a lunatic asylum, which of course it is, but you've got to become one of the inmates and not observe the whole thing. I simply decided I would never write another play. I couldn't recognise my play on the stage, you see, but this is a common thing among neophyte playwrights. They are thinking of some idealised or perfect characters that they have written and then some mortal actor comes up and he's got the wrong face and he has the wrong body and the wrong voice and you can't put him together with what you wrote. So it ended up like scrambled egg, as far as I was concerned. It had no relation to anything I'd done and I couldn't imagine trying to do it again, even though, by that time, I'd written I don't know how many plays that I hadn't gotten produced.

Bigsby: It was about this time that you got married, and you got married to a Catholic.

Miller: Right. Of course, she was a lapsed Catholic. She wouldn't have that much to do with Catholicism by that time and hadn't for years.

Bigsby: How did you survive in those years?

Miller: Well I began writing radio plays, which was a viable means of support. That of course was before television when the large corporations were still subsidising radio programmes. Some of them were historical programmes and you could just barely eke out a living. The only good part about it was you could do them quickly. I could write one in a morning and if I did six or eight of them I got two hundred and fifty dollars a piece. I could live pretty good. Life was cheap then and my wife was working.

Bigsby: One response to the anti-Semitism of the times was to produce a novel, *Focus*, which is still the only novel you have written.

Miller: Yes, well I did that because I had been so burned by my first Broadway disaster, very simply. It was also a better subject for a novel than it was a play. It came out of my years in the Navy Yard. During World War II I was rejected by the army for an injury to my leg and I wanted to do something. I was writing radio plays and whilst I was writing the radio plays (they were very patriotic radio plays) I got bored with that whole thing and so I went to the Navy Yard and got taken on as a shipfitter's helper and I worked there for about two years. And in the yard I became additionally concerned not just about anti-Semitism but about racism which was sometimes ferocious. I used to think sometimes that when the war would be over, we would begin eating each other alive. It was a crazy place. There were sixty thousand men in there where formerly, in peacetime, there would be six thousand. They were crawling over each other, preparing ships mainly, and I had some very good friends and some ferocious enemies. I worked the night shift, fourteen hours a night, from four in the afternoon to six in the morning, thirteen days out of fourteen. Most of them were wonderful guys but there was a kind of semi-organised pro-Fascist group in there. They used to attack British sailors, incidentally. We had a lot of British ships in there and we repaired them and the Italians would gang up on them. The Navy Yard was at the edge of the city, naturally, and it was pretty dark there at night and they would gang up on those guys.

Bigsby: *Focus* is concerned with anti-Semitism and yet that issue, and in particular the question of the concentration camps, doesn't come into your plays until the mid-1960s, with *After the Fall*, and *Incident at Vichy*.

Miller: I couldn't find a way to deal with it. The first chance I got to go to Europe was in '47. I went over purely as a tourist with a friend of mine who was an Italian-American and we toured France and Italy, southern Italy, Sicily, which was in ruins at that time, and I simply was aghast at the whole thing. It was beyond me to deal with it. I simply couldn't grasp it. The enormity of the whole thing was too great.

Bigsby: What was it that it made it possible to deal with it in the 60s?

Miller: I went back and it became possible to look at it with some perspective. I had remarried. I was now married to my present wife and she had been in Germany during the whole war. She'd been, part of that time, in forced labour at Templehoff Aerodrome where they were bombing the hell out of it all the time. Suddenly I got a human view of the whole thing. It was not simply a Jewish view of it. It was human in the sense that the wholeness of that tragedy began to seep in on me. I could begin to deal with it.

Wally Daly

I was asked if I would like to adapt Arthur Miller's book *Focus* as a radio play, and a 75th birthday tribute to him, totally out of the blue.

I've never adapted anything before, and hadn't told anybody that adaptation was something that appealed as a challenge – which, at this stage in my career it does.

I said fine, love to – but (an appropriate comment for an ex-Chairman of the British Writers Guild to make) how about asking Miller himself if he'd like to adapt it?

I thought the idea of writing a radio play for the English audience might appeal to him as fun not knowing he'd actually cut his teeth on writing radio plays back in the forties.

Three months passed then I was approached again. I presumed he'd been asked and turned the job down, but didn't push my luck by asking.

Reading the book the two major problems it was going to present in adaptation leapt off the page. Firstly the book walks a purposeful and dangerous anti-Semitic tight rope. Virtually every page is full of hatred for the Jew forcefully expressed by all major gentile characters and only ameliorated toward the end when Newman finally comes to see how stupid and wrong he has been in his anti-Semitic view all these years. Plus of course the wonderful last line pay-off when he admits to being a Jew – even though he isn't – makes the whole point of the book very forcefully, and the whole journey worthwhile.

Secondly, nobody in the book (apart from Finklestein who doesn't speak until two thirds of the way through it) is likeable, never mind loveable.

Add to that various other little problem areas, an example of which would be the Itzik story. Highly important to show Finkelstein's view, in the book it's a thirty-five minute internal monologue spoken by Finkelstein's dead father in his brain. Getting that down to size and palatable for the radio listener's span was going to be a great challenge.

Not knowing how you go about adapting somebody else's work, and not going along with the commonly held view that the way to do it is to read the work twice, then forget about it and write your own version, I went at it blindly. A good point to start seemed to me to get the book's dialogue into the computer. (Great procrastination as well.) It turned out that there was two hours of it. The arithmetic wasn't looking good. If I had a 90 minute radio slot in to which to compress two hours of (depressingly) brilliant dialogue, plus four hours of story telling, then I was on to a loser.

Luckily it was at this point a brief meeting was arranged with the author in the middle of his busy London schedules. He first of all confessed that, having written the piece fifty years previously, he wasn't exactly as up to date with the story as he might be. And then as I started to talk through problems of necessary compressing and cutting, he interrupted to say quite an amazing and incredibly trusting thing, which I doubt whether many writers, including myself, would have the courage to say. He said 'Do it. Whatever has to be done – do it. I've written radio plays – I know the problems – just do what has to be done.'

So – I did just that.

Bigsby: After *Focus* you did turn back to the theatre and produced a play which was enormously successful, *All My Sons*. It was a wartime play, but it was produced after the war.

Miller: Well, I didn't know it was going to be produced after the war. I wrote it during the war. It took about two years to do it because, as I've said, we were in the midst of a commercial theatre and there was no place to go excepting to the commercial managers. And I had realised by this time – I was, I guess, turning thirty – that I had to make a choice. I loved the theatre. I wanted to be a playwright. I had written by this time, I don't know what, six or seven plays, and probably thirty or more radio plays, and if I wanted to be a playwright I had to settle for the fact that I couldn't any longer submit a script that I wasn't sure of on every page. So I took about two and a half years on this one. I was writing radio plays, and I submitted it and it was wanted by two producers immediately; one was Elia Kazan, the other Harold Clurman, who had gone into business together. Needless to say, the crime in *All My Sons* now seems quite minimal. Joe Keller was manufacturing faulty parts for aircraft engines. We've got big crimes now. Just recently a company that supplies stabilising machinery for missiles admitted in court that they had falsified the documents of inspection, and that had resulted in some deaths. Nowadays, we do it on a much bigger scale involving hundreds of millions of dollars; in those days it was just a few cylinder heads that the man was charged with having passed when they were faulty. Everything got bigger since 1947.

Bigsby: But there was also another theme in that play which doesn't seem entirely worked out and which has to do with the guilt of the idealist who presents an impossible ideal.

Miller: Yes.

Bigsby: Why is that not completely worked out?

Miller: I didn't know how to do it. I could only carry the impulse to a certain end. In fact every play leaves something. You can only raise the questions, as the old cliché goes, you can't give all the answers.

Bigsby: Was it in some sense the pressure of the moment, the immediacy of the principal theme, that left no space for anything else?

Miller: There was no space for it, yes, that's true.

Bigsby: It's a play that owes something to Ibsen, and Ibsen was a figure who mattered to you, wasn't he?

Miller: The first time I really felt I could become a playwright was at the University when I was reading, quite by chance I think, a Greek tragedy and Ibsen at the same time. And I assumed then that everyone was aware that he was carrying the Greeks into nineteenth-century Europe, principally because they were both obsessed with the birds coming home to roost: the effect of the past, of which Oedipus is probably the clearest example. That is, something happens x years ago, unbeknown to the hero, and he's got to grapple with its consequences. This is Ibsen, and there's something in me that understood that very well, partly, incidentally, because of my attitude towards the Crash. You see, America had been on some kind of an obscene trip, looking to get rich at any cost, right through the 20s, any cost to the spirit, and had elevated into power the men who could most easily and comfortably lead that kind of a quest. That aggrandisement is what led finally to the disaster of '29 and to the Crash. And what we all discovered was that there was nothing to them. All they were was aggression. They were a lot of aggressive sharks who were leading, not only the economy, but the spiritual side of the country. There's a bit of that today, not only here but all over the world. There's never been a more materialistic moment in history since I've been around.

Bigsby: Indeed, didn't *All My Sons* have a very successful run recently in Israel?

Miller: It ran longer than any play they'd ever done there. Incidentally, it's being produced more and more in the United States now, for some reason.

Rosemary Harris

All My Sons ran for nine months at Wyndham's. It was an incredibly bonded company; in fact I think we all feel the ties still. I know I do in a way that is quite unique. Colin Blakeley had turned down the Number One dressing room (which opens almost directly onto the stage), so we decided to make it into the Company Green Room, and a wonderful time was had by all. However, an entrance or two came perilously close to being missed, one of which was mine and once I had to shout my lines from back stage to avoid a hold-up. All such blips were duly recorded in the Log Book. A few days before the end of the run we were in Act Two, and I, Kate, had just come out of the house to welcome George, with a 'broken speech' ending with the word 'Larry . . .', which is interrupted by someone else coming out of the house. No someone else appeared. I could sense it, because George was facing upstage with a look of horror on his face. A few seconds passed while I considered what to do. Then I had a brainwave. In the first act Kate has a speech in which she describes her dream of her son Larry's plane, crashing through the apple tree. Suddenly I realised that George hadn't *heard* it. I knew I was good for at least two minutes. So off I launched into it. It was a wonderful feeling. Someone on stage started to interrupt me and say 'Oh, for God's sake not again!' then wisely thought better of it. George was enthralled (and relieved) and so were the unsuspecting audience, even though they had heard the dream before. People listening in the Green Room thought I'd gone mad until they realised what had happened. The missing person was found (in the telephone booth telephoning their son to make sure he'd done his homework) and the day, or rather the night, was saved. In the Log Book an entry was recorded, 'Rosemary was heroic!' of which I was very proud, not least because it helped to exonerate me from my previous lapses.

As to the play itself, one of the fascinating aspects of playing Kate, is the question of how much she really knows or suspects. It is a very thin line. The hope of Larry's return has to be kept alive at all costs and some of the profoundest feelings I've felt on a stage I felt during Anne's reading of Larry's suicide letter. It's hard to describe: a complete and utter emptiness engulfed by grief. I was always awfully jolly after the curtain came down but I used to wake up in the morning with a curious sense of heaviness and sorrow. After all 'my husband' and 'my son' had killed themselves the night before.

Playing Kate has been one of the joys of my theatrical life. I realise it doesn't make much sense talking of joy and sorrow in the same breath but those were the feelings. I am grateful to Arthur for that character and for all the people of his imagination. And I retain more than memories. All these years later I still have the costumes from that play.

Gregory Hersov

Royal Exchange Theatre, Manchester

'To me the theatre is not a disconnected entertainment, which it usually is to most people here. It's the sound and the ring of the spirit of the people at any one time. It is where a collective mass of people through the genius of some author is able to project its terrors and its hopes and to symbolise them. Now, how that's done – there are thousands of ways to do it of course . . . . I personally feel that theatre has to confront the basic themes always.'

Miller, of course, is talking about other dramatists but I feel these words sum up the essence and achievement of his plays in the theatre. In directing his three great early works, certain basic themes have presented themselves strongly.

Miller always strives to create a fully rounded character. He has no problem with seeing individuals in their most private and their most public capacities. Many writers can only manage one or the other, if that. As he says 'the fish is in the water and the water is in the fish. Man is in society but the society is in man and every individual.' However large or small a part, everyone who appears in a Miller play has this wholeness. Actors respond to that; so do audiences.

Miller always brings his characters to a crisis point where their basic identity is tested. They cannot walk away from this process. It is how they find out who they truly are. Their past, present and future existence is summoned up with no compromise or flinching from the frequently tragic results. In Miller plays the characters' destinies are fully written; there are no holes or evasions. The crisis that lies at the heart of the plays is never melodramatic or self-indulgently willed. It has an inevitability and rightness that comes from a deeply felt and thought-out response to the world. Part of the enduring power of these plays is that these crisis points contain basic themes that still bear strongly on our modern world.

Joe Keller's crime in *All My Sons* is the modern riddle of our free market world. In the interests of our own well-being, self-esteem, love for our family, business decisions are taken that destroy those very possibilities in other human beings, whom we may never meet. One sunny day, in his own garden, Joe Keller finds out the awful truth of his actions. His whole family and neighbourhood are also brought face to face with this trouble. Their previously held ideas of themselves and their world are destroyed, their 'connection' with everything discovered. The setting of the play, with all its reassuring images coupled with its basic issues, connect directly with our modern existence.

Willy Loman is a salesman. We live in a world where buying and selling, competition, and work-rate are fundamental to our identity. *Death of a Salesman* shows the consequences this system has for our humanity. Again, the most intimate unit, the family, is torn apart by the protagonists' inability to find feeling, sustenance, love and meaning in that system. If Willy was dismissed as a neurotic loser in the 1940s (wrongly!) by 1990 he has become an Everyman. We all know how much we live by buying and selling. The play shows how we can die by it too.

In *The Crucible* a whole state cracks up. Persecution, scapegoating, hysteria and killing reign. A society devours itself in front of our eyes. However, this process is not irrational; it is done in the name of belief. Everyone has coherent reasons and can articulate them. We don't need witches now to know how societies conspire in millions of different ways to repeat this cycle. Whether through bigotry, racism or the systematic exploitation of other human beings, the spell of Salem still holds us in thrawl. *The Crucible* is Miller's most complete tapestry of the private and the public. From a child's bedroom to the marriage home, developing to the open court and state prison, the basic theme is explored. 'This projection of one's own vileness onto others in order to wipe it out with their blood,' as Miller says in *Timebends*, reaches from the youngest to the oldest. We haven't lost our need for witches; they just have different names.

In Manchester we work in the round. Philosophically and

aesthetically we believe that environment can provide the freshest and most genuine of dramatic experiences. The audience is placed to share the play, to connect; they breathe the same air as the actors. The actors have to confront each other directly; they have nowhere to turn away and are inextricably bound together with each other. Only plays that contain individual characters that come from a rigorous observation of human behaviour, combined with a deeply felt and authentic moral design, can achieve the three-dimensionality the round demands. Over the last few years, whatever the merits of the individual productions, thousands of people have seen Miller at the Royal Exchange and felt that deep connection with the basic issues of their lives that only theatre can provide.

Miller has said his characters are trying to find a proper home in the world. To my mind his achievement has been to provide a home for audiences and theatre workers alike, where we can all find a deep and proper meaning in Theatre.

Michael Holt

On designing All My Sons *and* The Crucible
at the Royal Exchange Theatre, Manchester

We decided on the design and stage management teams that this was probably one mark of a good play. The prop lists for both *All My Sons* and *The Crucible* are so short. Not much for us to search for or make; in the first play the odd newspaper, a saw, two coffee cups, grape juice, and of course the letter. *The Crucible* was similarly unproblematic.

These plays clearly rise above the ordinary household settings in which they occur. Suddenly an everyday problem of life management is the catalyst for the exploration of much more fundamental Why's and Wherefores, issues that more often find expression in religions and churches than in theatres.

'Of course,' said my director on discussing *All My Sons*, 'What we see at the end of the play is the fall of the house of Atreus with Clytemnestra sobbing before the temple'. In this context the Royal Exchange Theatre's shape, with its in-the-round stage and tiers of audience, provides a natural 'orchestra' in which to recreate the temple/theatre of the Greeks. The wooden facade of the American dream house automatically provides the imitation classical features of the scene.

Similarly, in the other play, the theatre shape itself is a crucible in which to create an image of a 'wooden' society melting down to separate the base metal from the valuable.

But our mundane prop lists remind us that the plays are rooted in the everyday. Our lightning conductor, like Arthur Miller's, is naturalism. We used real grass and trees to draw our audience, which sits so very close in this theatre, into an extension of their world. The *Crucible* costumes are fashioned for a hardworking farming community as much as for a fanatical religious sect. These are very real worlds but ones in which the confronting of truth, honour and human responsibility have fundamental 'religious' significance.

'What colour grape juice do you want for the scene where the mother tries to draw the families together?' asks the stage manager. There could be only one answer; 'Red, – like the wine of the eucharist'.

Bigsby: *Death of a Salesman* is a contrast in a number of ways. It seems to me the most lyrical of your plays.

Miller: That's true, yes. Well, I had always done that. Most of the plays I had written before had been reaching toward it. I was trying to find a poetic voice in the theatre while at the same time making the scenes and the characters believable. Then I was also interested in time. We don't stop when we remember something; we go right on talking or doing whatever we're doing. Meanwhile, in another compartment of the brain the past is working. That was what I was trying for with that play. That was the form.

Bigsby: Do you ever feel, in looking back, that there is a kind of rift in *Death of a Salesman*, in that our dramatic attention is on Willy Loman but the play's moral resolution really turns on Biff's self-realisation? Is that why some people thought of the play as pessimistic, because they were looking in the wrong place?

Miller: Well, I'm sure that's why. There is a rift in it in that sense. You know, Thomas Mann saw that play, and he said, 'You know, the thing about the play is that it is a lyric play, but you never tell them what to think. It is simply an experience that they can't escape.' Now of course this is part of the reason that there's all this debate about the play. You see, I never allowed them to go beyond their intellectual and emotional capacity. There is no line in there that goes beyond what they could possibly have realised. The consequence is that, unlike standard tragedy, where you have the right, so to speak, formally speaking, to make self-aware statements where the character is aware of the play he is in, I never let them become aware of the play they are in. All that was driven out, ruthlessly, because at that time I resolved that I was going to make that audience never escape, even at the risk of losing objectivity, if I could do it. Because, I believed in squeezing out all the self-consciousness in the play. Every scene in that play begins late. There are no transitions in the play. It starts with a man who is tired. He doesn't get tired. He's tired in the first second of the play. You can tell from the way he enters the play. On the first line, she says, 'What happened?' Nothing happened but he's exhausted. You know you're somewhere. The same is true of every scene in that play. I completely drove out the usual transitional material from the play. That's the form of the play, that I never

55

allowed into it the self-conscious statements, which Mann wisely recognised. Now, he thought of it as a pessimistic play, but he loved the fact that the younger generation did not. You know, when I was writing that, there wasn't a younger generation. I was the age of Biff. I wasn't Willy's age. You don't regard yourself as the younger generation. But the key is in the requiem at the end, which everybody wanted me to cut out. They said the audience were never going to stay there because Willy Loman is dead; there's nothing more to say. Of course, they did want to stay there, just as you do want to go to a funeral. And what is the point of a funeral? You want to think over the life of the departed and it's in there, really, that it's nailed down: he won't accept this life.

Bigsby: He had all the wrong dreams. But, that's the dilemma isn't it? Most of our attention has been focused on the man who has now gone and the moral resolution naturally comes from the character, Biff, who's been less central.

Miller: I think what is missing, if you want to look at it that way, is what is missing in *Lear*, which a lot of nineteenth-century commentators didn't like for the same reason. It's unalleviated, setting aside the beauty of the poetry which relieves us of the gloom. Lear is unredeemed; he really goes down in a sack, in a coal chute. *Hamlet* has relief, moral relief so to speak; there is a structure remaining.

Bigsby: But you did say that there is a force that is in a race for Willy's soul, which is love. I am not quite sure what you mean by that, Linda's or Biff's, but do you in any way regret not giving Linda more resources to make the battle a bit more equal?

Miller: I regretted it at the time but I couldn't honestly give her what I didn't think she would ever have. You see, if that woman were more articulate in terms of her ability to handle it, probably they would have broken apart earlier on; she couldn't have stood it. You know, he's a cruel son of a bitch that guy; everybody is charmed by him but if you objectively face some of those scenes in the bedroom, he just wipes the floor with her from time to time. You see a woman who was thinking of herself more would simply not have been there one morning, or else she would have put up such a fight as to crush him because he would never be able to accept any independence around him. This is part of the disease.

Bigsby: Is there something of a risk that in emphasising the state of Willy's mind – and he is getting into a kind of deranged state, in which past and present are indistinguishable – the play might become a pathological case study?

Miller: It depends how you do it. You see, they made a movie of it which did just that. I hated that movie. Let's talk about it for a minute, because it applies to some of the things we have been talking about. I wrote that play in 1948 and it was produced in 1949. It ran for years. They bought the film rights, let's say in 1950. The right wing had not yet taken over in the culture so they would buy a play of mine. They made the film but as they were making it the country was swinging far over to the right. What did they do? They made Willy crazier and crazier. Interesting. Now I happen to have been a very good friend of Freddy March, who played Willy. We nearly cast him in the original play. He was a marvellous actor. Freddy was a real actor in the best sense; he was an animal and he knew that there was something wrong with making him so crazy. He knew that. I certainly didn't tell him. Of course these people making the film had to make him crazy or they couldn't make the film. The social and moral dimensions of the picture had to be resolved in this pathological side. By this time I was being attacked left and right as a red and here they were stuck with this x million dollars that they had sunk into the film. They were threatened with boycotts from the American Legion, the Catholic war veterans and all those yahoos. They came to me and said, 'would you make a statement to these people to placate them?' I said, 'I'll placate nobody. You bought the picture, fellas, you're stuck with it.'

You know what they did? Columbia Pictures had another film made which they filmed at City College, New York City, the Business School of City College, about the life of a salesman. It was a short, like fifteen minutes, in which they interviewed professors of business administration and heads of corporations and other such people who were experts in this field who said that Willy Loman was absolutely an atypical American. Really! Well, they were using my title in and out of the film and they got nervous about a law suit, so they called me in. Now my picture had not been released yet and they said, 'we'd like you to see this.' So I saw it and I said, 'why did you do this? You've just destroyed the film you've made, because if this is true then my film must be some aberration of an idiot'. 'Well, we didn't think it would be bad.' And I said, 'well, look, I'll sue you'. They wanted to play it with my picture and I had a financial interest in my picture, I suppose, although I doubted if I could make it stick in court. But as far as I was concerned they were injuring my property rights and apparently they were worried about this too or they wouldn't have even consulted me. I convinced them that they would be laughed out of existence, which I doubt would have happened at that moment since nobody was laughing about anything. Anyway, productions of *Salesman* shouldn't be about pathology but it can happen if you play Willy like a real mad fellow, yes. But it would be bad acting and it would be a stupid way to do the show. However, I think that this is a real danger whenever you get into a highly charged personality like Lear. You can make *Lear* an absolutely meaningless play. In fact you can do it easier than you can with Willy, because what kind of an idiot is it who cannot glimpse what we all see, the fact that he has a good daughter who he thinks is the bad daughter. Well, he's for the looney bin. The audience knew what *Salesman* was about. They knew he wasn't crazy. They were right up with him. See, let me not underestimate it, I was ironically stating all the things that they always state seriously. A man can get anywhere in this country on the basis of being liked. Now this is serious advice, and that audience is sitting there almost about to smile but the tears are coming out of their eyes because they know that that is what they believe. This man is obviously going down the chute and he's telling them exactly what they believe. So I don't have to make a speech that this is wrong. The irony of the whole situation is what is making it work.

Bigsby: But it's not a play which only works in an American context.

Miller: No. Let me put it this way. That play was a great success in Western Europe, Eastern Europe, Japan, it hardly mattered where it was done. You see all countries have people with reveries of how they're going to conquer life. It's just that in this particular situation he is a salesman.

Bigsby: Incidentally how far is Willy's brother, Ben, intended to be simply a product of Willy's mind and how far an independent character?

Miller: He's a real brother but Willy has invested him already with the whole mythos of that vast brutal success which is larger than life. Nobody can be that successful. Ben is an expressionist figure; every time he opens his mouth he is talking about diamonds, or wealth, or the land, or exploitation of some kind, and that's the way it would be for Willy. Willy wouldn't think of him excepting as the one who won, the victor. *The Crucible* is built on what I would call autonomous

58

characters, who bring on their personalities encased in their social roles as we do in real life: one is poor, one is rich or whatever. *Death of a Salesman* was conceived literally on two dimensions at the same time. On one level there are autonomous characters while on another there are characters who exist as symbols for Willy Loman.

Bigsby: You mean that Happy and Biff together are aspects of Willy's mind.

Miller: Exactly. It was done up in Minneapolis by Guthrie and I sat with him and he said, 'you know I was never aware before but this is a lyric; this is a long poem by Willy.' It is, you know. John Proctor's voice is not all the voices but in a certain sense Willy is all the voices.

Bigsby: Is that why the play was originally to be called *The Inside of His Head*?

Miller: Yes, I conceived it as taking place inside his head and that's why it is different from any other play.

Bigsby: So, the gulf that I was suggesting existed between the physical attention on Willy and the moral resolution through Biff would not have occurred in the original because they would all have been aspects of Willy's mind.

Miller: Yes, that's right. But at that point when he dies his consciousness vanishes and there is a space between the requiem and the play. It takes place on the earth, so to speak. We've left Willy's head now; we're on the earth.

Bigsby: You've seen, obviously, a lot of Willy Lomans over the years? What have the principal actors brought to that part that was different?

Miller: Well, there have been three chief players, as far as I am concerned. One was Warren Mitchell, who played it marvellously in London. I didn't know Warren and I just saw him in the play and we chatted for a while but his Willy and Dustin Hoffman's are related. They are both small men, feisty fellows. They've got a large world that's trying to kill them and a small man reacts with a kind of nervosity. That is in the part. It is obvious that Willy is leaping from one contradictory attitude to another very rapidly, sometimes with hardly a line in between, and to me that also was the characteristic of a little man, a physically small man. And I wrote it for a small man, if I wrote it for anybody. Lee Cobb, who did the original, was a giant, he was six feet whatever and he weighed a lot and he looked like he was in mourning for his life. He had always been a sad sack and he had what we conventionally think of as a tragic air because he was so damn sad. When he laughed, you wept. He had a dark air about him.

Dustin is of another order. First of all, because he is so diminutive he has to create people, literally create them. I don't know how he gets into the skin of Tootsie or of Kramer or of any of the other parts he's done but he has a true actor's imagination. You see Warren was playing closer to Lee Cobb. Dustin had to make Willy Loman happen as far as he was concerned and what I get from Dustin's Willy is tragic in a completely different sense. It isn't the tragedy of the portrait but of the idea. Probably Dustin's is the most lucid of all the Willys that I am aware of. I have been so closely involved with the production, maybe it seems so because I know what he is doing and how he arrived there but he is a fantastically intelligent actor. That's a rare thing in anybody. Actors being feeling people, first of all, we don't normally think of them as being very intellectual. He's by no means intellectual and he doesn't want to be, thank God, but he's very bright and he can analyse his own feelings and know what part of himself he needs to use in order to become Willy.

Bigsby: Have audiences changed, the audiences to *Death of a Salesman*? Do they respond to the same things?

Miller: I tell you, I was just talking about that the other day. I don't see any change whatsoever, in thirty-five years. Everybody, including me, has been saying that that kind of a play isn't possible any more, purely and simply because nobody's going to sit there that long with that degree of attention. The television has destroyed them. They can only listen for ten minutes and then they start shifting around. Well, it's nonsense. They are doing exactly what they did, in my memory, in the beginning, and what they do in China and what they'd done in Germany and anywhere else I've seen the thing. I think their potential hasn't been used in some years.

Bigsby: Willy Loman is a person who comes out of a differnt kind of time. He has a different sensibility. He wants to work with his hands. He looks back to the time before the city when things were simpler, relationships were simpler. I wonder if his nostalgia and Biff's nostalgia isn't also partly yours in that play?

Miller: I am very sceptical about that, quite frankly, and I am one of the ones who does not think that in the Depression time people were better. You know there's a whole romance going on about the Depression that because everybody was broke they were kinder to one another, because they understood that everybody was broke. Well, all I can remember was that I wanted to go to school outside New York because I thought that we were cutting each other's throats and that it would be nicer in a small town where I could breathe easier. I think the Depression time was a ferociously competitive period. There was idealism. There was radicalism, which gave a loftiness to some of the sentiments, but underneath it was murder.

Bigsby: I don't think I was meaning quite so much the 30s as a period for which he was nostalgic, as the nineteenth century.

Miller: That, of course, I share. But I have to say that one of our best writers was Thoreau and he trembled at the sound of the railroad. He thought that this was going to be the end of everything. Maybe it was. But intellectuals are always afraid of change. They are really the most conservative psychological types. They don't want it to change and they want to look back at some better era and what they're doing, of course, what I do, what I think everybody does, is look back to when you were young and you were so dumb and ignorant that you thought the world was full of hope.

Bigsby: Doesn't the logic of that play almost confirm that nostalgia in that, at the end, we are left with Biff Loman who's come to an understanding of who he is and is presumably about to return to a farm in Texas, to light out for territory like Huck Finn. But the territory isn't, for the most part, there any more, is it?

Miller: No, it isn't. But it would be wrong to say that it isn't. You see there is a different life in certain parts of the United States still, as compared to the New York, Chicago, Los Angeles life. Life can be much more pleasant in a smaller place and Biff wants not to be an integer, a simple little factor, in this gigantic business and industrial operation that the United States is and like most other countries are. And there is an escape in that, of course, a desire to assert different values. He is a precursor of the hippy movement in a way. Vermont, the most remote northern part of the United States, is full of people, young people, very competent, professional people sometimes, who have simply given it all up and have gone to these places to live a human life. That's really what he's doing. But I had no cultural tools at the time. Biff was not part of any movement.

Bigsby: I wonder, though, if there isn't a sense of doubt on your part when you move on to *The Misfits* in which you have a person who is working with horses . . .

Miller: And you see what it comes to.

Bigsby: And you see what's happened.

Miller: Oh yes, no doubt, it's directly connected with *Salesman*. Sure it is.

Bigsby: Were you aware of that when you were . . .

Miller: No. One of my failings is that I have a very short vision. When I am writing I think that I am inventing it for the first time. I guess if I didn't, I wouldn't write it. But that's true, though. *The Misfits* is what happens when you are in the great outdoors. You are killing horses for dog food.

Bigsby: I wonder also if there isn't a sense in which you yourself at this stage were feeling a misfit?

Miller: Yes. Well, I've always felt a misfit. I've always identified with those fellows, even down in the middle of New York. I didn't have to go out to Reno, Nevada to feel that way. Yes. Sure. And not only identification with them but identification with the problem, which is to assert value apart from the society, to assert some kind of a human life apart from the society. That's pretty tough because it's got its own contradictions and its own paradoxes. I don't know whether you really can do it.

Robertson Davies

I may describe myself as a convert to Arthur Miller. When his *Death of a Salesman* first appeared it was rapturously hailed as a tragedy, and my critical colleagues could not find praise high enough to serve for it. I resisted, because I stuck with Sir Philip Sidney's judgement that 'tragedy concerneth a high fellow', and nothing could make a high fellow of Willy Loman; he did not so much fall, as slump. But time and better judgement changed my mind. The play is indeed a tragedy. In my days as a newspaper editor I had met scores of Willys and their existence was a tragic indictment of society. Since that time I have become convinced that Arthur Miller is the true successor to Eugene O'Neill, and in my judgement superior to O'Neill in his perception of the tragic downfall of people who, through the malignity of society or their own weakness, or a combination of the two, have become psychological cripples. They are not great people, but suffering is relative; their pain is as much as they can bear, and does tragedy demand more? Arthur Miller's concept of tragedy has enlarged my understanding, and of how many men can anyone truly say as much?

Doris Lessing

Nothing is more interesting than the way plays, books, authors, are different at different times. *Death of a Salesman* is now an American classic and taken for granted, as classics are. It is a bit of a monument and we are all respectful of it. But I remember it when it first appeared and how it struck us then. I read it, for I was not likely to see it acted in Southern Africa, where the local amateur groups were not going to put on untried new plays from America. But people who read at all read everything we could get hold of from the United States. It was not only Arthur Miller, for he was part of a wave or movement of exhilarating work that could never have come out of Britain. Arthur Miller and Dreiser and Steinbeck, Dos Passos and Hellman wrote with

63

uninhibited energy, in a new idiom. About *Death of a Salesman* we thought, 'This is a very good play: it is the real thing, and yet it is about people we recognise, and written by an author who is still alive.' And, too, it was about The Slump, and we had all known people hurt by The Slump.

Much later, in London, I saw *Death of a Salesman* on the stage. It had changed, seemed more of an exotic than it had in Africa. People living outside the metropolitan heartlands find it easier to identify with American people, American situations. But it still shocked and electrified, as it had done on the page.

The play will always seem relevant to people in hard times, just as *The Crucible* comes alive in any oppressive political situation. But it is interesting to speculate what new air, or place will set *Death of a Salesman* before us as it seemed then, when it first came out.

David Mamet

I saw the *Salesman* Dustin Hoffman did on Broadway; and, later that week, had the pleasure of spending part of an afternoon with Mr Miller. I needed a telephone and he led me to a joint in the theatre district which had recently sold him a telephone he found particularly useful. It took me a while to muster courage sufficient to address Mr Miller on the subject of his work, and, finally, said, 'you know, Arthur, watching *Salesman*, I felt I was watching my own story – that you had written the story of my father and me – don't you think that's strange?' I saw a small courteous smile on his face that said that he did not find my remark strange at all – that, on the contrary, he had heard it from the vast majority of men who had seen the play and offered him a comment on it – that our response to a work of genius on stage is: that is *my* story – not only did you write it about me, but *I could go up on stage right now and act it*.

He told me that he had been told the same thing about the play by audiences in China, 'that is the story of my father and me.' We all stole the fountain pen – none of us won the football game – it was our story that we did not know until we heard it.

Arnold Wesker

You're 75. Stop writing for Chrissake and give the rest of us a break. I mean it's bad enough for those of us who live in England under the shadow of Shakespeare, but to have to live under the shadow of a Yank, too?

When my first work appeared the critics did the usual thing of saying he's like this one and that one, and the name that kept coming up was Odets. They were wrong – when are they not? Even when they're right! The name they should have referred to was Miller. A perceptive observer would have noted: the last line of the first play in The Wesker Trilogy, *Chicken Soup with Barley* – 'If you don't care you'll die' – obviously has its lineage in the last line in the Miller classic, *Death of a Salesman* – 'Attention must be paid' . . .

I don't know where you got your line from, mine came from my mother, but I'd never have identified it as dramatically resonant without the precedent you set, even though I'd only ever seen a Miller play as a film. We could afford movies not theatre. The plays I saw were those I acted in as an amateur!

Of course I owe you more than a line! But what? Perhaps now is the time to think about it and repay debts.

I had a fortunate beginning as a writer. From the start I'd been alerted to the dangers of 'prescription literature': literature contrived to prove theories about the way life is lived or should be lived. I'd also recognised early on the need to distinguish between metaphor and anecdote. How often we become excited by an event in our lives which suggests itself as material for drama and then, as we contemplate it, toss it around in our minds, fit dramatic structures to it, discover that nothing really hangs properly, realise it is significant of nothing more than itself.

Where did I learn this important lesson, that the power of any work lies in its resonance? From many quarters, naturally, but some stand out in memory. The characters in *Death of a Salesman* and *All My Sons* were reflections of my own family. If such characters and their preoccupations could reach beyond the specific settings of an American/Jewish milieu then so could the personalities who inhabited my world.

But it's not as simple as that. It never is. We all know that the great universal works of literature are very specifically something: Chekhov is very Russian, O'Casey is very Irish, Singer is very Yiddish, Ibsen is very Norwegian. None of them sat down to be 'universal'. They wrote about what was to hand. But more is required, isn't it. What?

I've often thought about this question and I keep returning to a simple answer. What makes Chekhov's plays universal, resonant, rippling with relevance beyond their very Russian life is the quality of his perceptions about his experience of that very Russian life. Instinctively he perceived what was essentially human in the Russianness of his characters.

I discovered you before I discovered Chekhov, and from you learnt that fundamental lesson: characters must first and foremost be human rather than ciphers. Your characters existed in their own right before they became symbols for something else. All art, as we know, is selection. I learned from you what to select. A debt. I acknowledge it. I hope my plays repay that debt.

Now *The Price* is on in town, the first preview of which we shared together. What an experience! Didn't it thrill you to see your work bringing whoops of joy and recognition from such a young audience? I remember the first time I saw it in London, many, many years ago, and I remember my reaction. 'Thank God!' I thought, 'for an intelligent play at last!' And here it is again, intelligent, passionate, about four people whose very human complexities and contradictions resonate with that reassuring familiarity which immediately gives them universality.

I was weaned on your work. My children studied you at school. You've formed and continue to form generations of thoughtful and enquiring minds. And every tear, every laugh, each emotion and each thought is hard-earned there. You're rare, dear friend, you're not only an audience's playwright you are a playwright's playwright, a source for us all.

Many happy returns. And on second thoughts, don't stop writing. With affection and admiration.

Benedict Nightingale

The Times

There were two major productions of *Death of a Salesman* in the early eighties, both interestingly similar, both interestingly different. One was at the National Theatre in London, with Warren Mitchell as Willy Loman, and the other at the Broadhurst in New York, with Dustin Hoffman in the role. Both were, as it happened, staged by the same director, an American long resident in Britain, Michael Rudman. Both reportedly received a good deal of input from Arthur Miller himself, and hence presumably reflected, at least to some extent, his own views of the play.

In each case, one at first felt the terrible exhaustion of the salesman himself. Mitchell, naturally a rather spiky, aggressive actor, traipsed onstage with his shoulders slumped, jowls creased, face colored pumice-grey. In his voice, too, were the disappointments and frustrations of wasted days, weeks, months, as they were in Hoffman's deeper tones, too.

Both men are smallish, but Hoffman the shorter of the two. The image he presented was of a dumpy penguin waddling home after a long, long battle with the fish he had hoped to have for supper. His shoulders sagged too, but not only because of those feelings of defeat. He was carrying as vast a sample case as it is easy to imagine. What *could* he have been selling? Surely not stockings or any other article mentioned in the play. Tree-trunks, more likely. Or perhaps what Miller once said he was selling: himself. The case was just about large enough to contain the crumpled Hoffman.

Yet in neither actor did exhaustion turn out to be the dominant note, even at those times in the play which are inexorably set in the dismal present. Miller reportedly admired Mitchell for what he called his 'feistiness', the same quality he had brought to the combative Cockney Alf Garnett in *Till Death Us Do Part*, the TV role that was eventually converted to Archie Bunker in America. As he launched into conversation with Doreen Mantle's Linda, one could see the Loman he once had been: winking at the shopgirls, swapping dirty jokes with the buyers, living off his wits, making decent commissions and, not incidentally, irritating some of his supposed friends with his self-conscious pep and drive. One of the marks of the major actor is to show us what *was* as well as what is: Mitchell, a more considerable talent than is usually recognised, implied an ambiguous past as well as presenting the here and now.

Hoffman followed suit. He laughed, he cackled, if not very humorously, at least loudly and often. He persistently clapped his hands for emphasis. On the line, 'you're my foundation and support', he jokily tweaked his wife's literal foundation and support, her behind. He did a little dance with her, and then exuberantly brandished his own rump before making an exit. Once again, you could see the not-unsuccessful hustler behind the chalky facade. This Willy too would have enjoyed flirting with the secretaries and occasionally even seducing them. You could see, as you often cannot in productions of *Salesman*, the emotional logic of the bedroom encounter with the unnamed girl in Boston. Again, you could imagine this Loman talking, talking, talking, and getting something of a reputation as a loudmouth in the process.

Both actors, however, went on pretty vividly to show the character in crisis. Hoffman's smiles became more forced, his laughter more empty, the slaps of the hands testier, more irritable. Even the slick silver hair above the trim suit – this Loman, more than Mitchell's, was a natty dresser – seemed to lose some of its shine. Suddenly he was wildly blustering at a pained Howard and banging on his desk, or tearfully clutching and pushing at his old friend Charley, or down on all fours and thumping the carpet in impotent resentment.

Mitchell had his physical moments too; but they were less flamboyant, more restrained, less audacious if you like. When Hoffman's Willy made his last, fatal exit, it was not with the 'gasp of fear' that Miller's stage directions require and Mitchell came rather nearer to providing. It was with a big grin, a skip and a bounce, and yet another peppy clap of the hands. All he was thinking about was the prospect of Biff achieving belated success with the help of the insurance money he expects to be paid him after he has pulverised his car and killed himself. Hence his glee as he scuttles out, salesman to the very end, off to clinch his last and largest deal.

The performance went daringly far, presenting (as it did) suicide as a creative con-trick, the ultimate manifestation of despair as an expression of American optimism. Mitchell was less busy, yet more successful in suggesting that some compensating, balancing dread existed even in a mind so adept at avoiding reality, so superficially sure that black is white – or, rather, gold. The American 'method' actor was, oddly, sometimes more external, more interested in bravura body-language. The English actor, whose studiously philistine interviews would suggest he had never heard of affective memory, had the more human heart.

Yet there was one moment, one central moment, when that was not at all the case. Indeed, it showed a basic difference between the American and English productions and perhaps even between the American and English theatres. Mitchell's final rapprochement with Biff, played at the National by Stephen Greif as a big, lumbering sort, too awkward for any Manhattan office, had no particular power. It was touching, but no more so than his scenes with Miss Mantle, who herself gave a strong, grieving performance. Compare that with Hoffman's reconciliation with John Malkovich's Biff, a slighter man physically, and until then a rather wan, flimsy presence, but actually someone with feelings of a suppressed intensity beyond either grief or Greif.

The result was one of the most astonishing moments I can remember in any theatre. Hoffman cradled Malkovich for longer than one would have thought possible. Had I been professionally checking my watch, instead of joining the sniffs and gulps of the audience around me, the time-span would probably have turned out to be no more than a minute or so. But it seemed to stretch on and on; and on Hoffman's face was the kind of disbelieving tenderness you might expect to see on a father who has picked up his newborn child for the first time. His whey-coloured cheeks visibly reddened, and he inarticulately gurgled in total surrender to what always had been the primary bond of his life. One realised that when he babbled ludicrously on about Biff's 'greatness', he meant something very simple. He loved him.

Yet that moment's very success may paradoxically have explained a limitation in the American production as opposed to the English one. At the Broadhurst, even more than at the National, we were made aware of Willy's defining context. A huge, looming fretwork of windows and fire escapes showed what he was up against: a society with the power to oppress, overwhelm, even destroy the individual. Yet it remained a decorative image. Its significance was not so obviously embodied in the production, as it was in London. The text of course makes it clear that Willy is a victim of his place and time. The idea is unavoidable. But Mitchell's Loman, more the little fellow failing to

69

survive in a hostile world, less the adoring parent, ended by projecting the point more eloquently.

That, probably, is the way Miller would have preferred it. On the sole occasion I have met him, on a visit to his alma mater, the University of Michigan, he imprecated against the American theatre's current imperviousness to social and political realities. He regretted its failure to recognise, as his plays recognise, that character and relationships must at least partly be determined by environment. With the English theatre the opposite tends to be true. Depth of relationship is often sacrificed to an emphasis on its context, its social meaning.

It would be too much to argue that the American *Salesman*'s greatest strength was also its greatest weakness. Nothing would have been lost if Mitchell's cocky vulgarian had managed just such an emotional encounter with his Biff. Indeed, what the two productions may have shown is that you can tilt the play one way or the other, towards the personal or towards the social; and still it is satisfying, still it is alive. That kind of elasticity may leave one feeling one is missing something; but it is an infallible sign of a large-minded play.

Dustin Hoffman

The first time I met Arthur, when I stage-managed *A View from the Bridge*, I thought I was going to faint when he came in to see the cast. He was my hero. So articulate. He's this great storyteller. He sounds like this New York cab driver; he's so unpretentious and earthy. You're laughing one minute, then you're thinking the next, and touched the next. He is a storyteller, just in the way he frames his stories. He's hitting the colours on the canvas.

My brother gave me a collection of plays when I was sixteen years old, before I even thought about being an actor. I don't know why he gave me a book of plays because I'd never thought about acting. It was the Gassner edition of *The Best American Plays* and the first play in it was *Death of a Salesman*. I'd never read a play, so I read that play and I had a kind of small breakdown for about two weeks after that. I would walk around just suddenly bursting into tears every once in a while.

Arthur said, 'Well, what are you going to do now?' and I said, 'I'd like to do a play'. He said, 'Why don't you do *Salesman*', and I said, 'I can't play that part' and he said 'Sure you can'. So we began a series of informal meetings just sitting on the grass there for about two months. He knows this play. I mean he knows *Salesman* like no one knows *Salesman*. It would be like sitting on the lawn with Shakespeare asking him how Richard III should be played. When we were rehearsing, if there were a new idea or a new thought he'd say 'Go ahead, try it.' And we'd try it, and he'd say, 'Gee, I never saw that done before', or 'Gee, that's kinda interesting.' He was always open to it. If he didn't agree he never said no, he'd say, 'Now I'll tell you why that doesn't work, because if you do that then . . .' It was a very logical thing. But it was as if he had never seen the play before.

He says you always know when you do this play right because when it's over they don't applaud right away. And apparently opening night when they did it originally that's what happened. There was this silence, and then slowly it was like Orson Welles from *Citizen Kane* or something, one person applauding and then another person, and then it just slowly started and just didn't stop.

When he directed it in China, Inge told me that they'd wondered how it would go there because this is about how capitalism can ruin a human being and they didn't have capitalism in China, so what relevance would it have there? But it went off so well. Inge, knowing that they were going to China, learnt Chinese, and a woman came up to her after the play, I think knowing she was Arthur's wife, and she was in tears, and Inge looked at her and said, 'Why, is your dad like Willy Loman?' And the woman said, 'No, my *mother* is like Willy Loman.' And that's the answer. It doesn't matter if your father is like Willy Loman, or if you're a Chinese woman who has a mother like Willy Loman. It just goes past, it transcends.

You can usually tell if a writer loves actors or not by the parts that he gives them. He gives you tap dances, he gives you arias.

He's what I look up to as an artist. He's my artistic father. I can't imagine a purer life form to lead, than he has led, in relation to one's work.

Warren Mitchell

I've played Willy Loman three times, the first time with the West Australian Theatre Company in Perth. We had few resources and only three weeks rehearsal, so learning the lines was a problem. That and persuading the director not to cut the last scene – the Requiem.

'It's so long, the play. The ending is so downbeat, the audience will be exhausted; they'll miss their last bus. Let's finish on the car crash.' I hadn't met Arthur Miller at the time but I pleaded his case with some eloquence, more than I could muster at the first preview. I was very nervous.

I entered wearily, dropped my sample cases as the author suggests, and opened the bedroom door where a worried Linda waited. I got through a page or two and then BLANK, 'gur nicht,' as my Yiddish grandmother would say. My tongue clove to the roof of my mouth. I couldn't think, move or spit. I ad-libbed something brilliant like 'er'. Play your action! my 'Method' training urged. 'Who are you? where are you? and what do you want?' 'I want to run away and hide,' the inner, very frightened, real me replied. I stumbled to the door. 'I'll take some milk' (one of Arthur Miller's lines, actually), I gasped, exiting fast.

I stood outside the door, thought about fainting, 'no', I reckoned I was not a good enough actor, thought about having a heart attack, thought I probably *was* having a heart attack. 'Christ' I thought, 'I've left out all the plot'. I re-entered. 'Linda', I said 'I erm . . . Biff erm . . . did he? . . . erm . . . I . . . I'll erm take some milk'. Out I popped again and stood there shifting from foot to foot, thinking furiously, trying to remember the bits I'd left out. I opened the door again, mewed another impotent 'Linda', then fled down the stairs to the kitchen. I slumped over the table grateful for the darkness as Biff and Happy played their scene. I wiped the play from my mind. I was Ken Rosewall. I'd just played the first set atrociously, lost deservedly, now I would win the next three. Hm! Some method preparation! I got better and the play took over. There is a scene when Charley, the nice guy next door, offers Willy a job. At the end of the scene Willy says, 'Charlie, you're the only friend I got, isn't that a remarkable thing?' In the black-out as we exited the actor playing Charlie whispered to me 'Did you hear that silence?' We were home and hosed as they say in Australia.

After the show the director, all smiles (no one had rushed for the last bus, during the Requiem), came round. 'Wonderful! Wonderful! But, what about your dry. Wow! Do you know what one of the audience just said to me?' He giggled then gushed in imitation of one of the blue rinse matrons. 'You know that moment when Willy hovered around the bedroom door in the first scene was quite brilliant: the nervous exhaustion, the heart wrenching indecision, the frightening weakness of the man, it was all revealed in a flash.' Thank you Ma'am, nevertheless I didn't repeat my magic moment at the second preview or when I played Willy again at the National Theatre in London and in Sydney for the Nimrod Theatre.

I returned from Australia and my friend Michael Rudman invited me to play tennis:

M.R. (*Back Hand x Court*) How was *King Lear*, Warren?

W.M. (*Back Hand Down the Line*) Great. Wanna see my notices?

M.R. (*Fore Hand x Court*) No thanks!

W.M. (*Fore Hand x Court*) You should see my notices for Willy Loman.

M.R. (*Hitting the ball over next door's fence, and advancing to the net*) You played Willy! I'm probably going to direct *Salesman* at the National.

W.M. Really.

M.R. I thought of casting it Jewish.

W.M. Really!

M.R. I didn't think of you, Warren.

W.M. Thank you Michael, you're a real friend.

M.R. No, well you'd better read for me.

W.M. Read! I've just finished playing it.

We played three sets. I lost as usual and I did a scene from the play. Weeks went by – no news. I imagined there was much debate at the National. Michael Rudman pushing my claims others wanting more establishment actors and not one associated with a TV comedy success. I'd like to have been a fly on the wall and privy to that debate. Of course maybe they were all too busy and just didn't get round to making a decision.

I played tennis with Rudman again. I won against a surprisingly uncompetitive Rudman and he was untypically generous with his line calls. Hello! Hello! I thought, what means this? I was right. I got the part.

Now Rudman was a director I'd admired for some time. His work at the Hampstead Theatre Club and the National was exemplary and I imagined I was in for a pretty exciting time, fierce debate, lots of intense creative direction opening me up to new pathways. With Rudman's help I would rise to unexpected heights. At the first rehearsal Rudman in that laid back Anglicised Texan Drawl addressed the cast: 'This is a play about Willy Loman, his real life and his fantasy life, so everything we do in the play has to suit Willy. Now Warren is playing Willy, so everything we do must suit Warren, not just because we're friends and play tennis together but because it must be so.' 'Hello,' I thought, 'not bad for the first day: carte bleedin' blanche.' From that moment on Rudman never took a blind bit of notice of anything I said.

Me: Michael, when we did the play in Perth . . .

Rudman: Just a minute Warren. David you must practise throwing that ball. Stephen I don't think that move is a good idea. Honey, get me a coffee. Sorry Warren, what was it? . . . oh never mind let's run the scene.

Smart operators these Texans. He only directed me once.

Rudman: Warren are you crying?

Me: Yes.

Rudman: Well don't, they'll cry.

Seemed to work though, this minimal direction. I felt free and entirely confident in the role and everyone seemed to like it.

I started this by saying that learning the lines was my main problem and really it is the only problem if you are me playing Willy Loman. I knew the man. My Dad was a commercial traveller. I am a father and have dreams for my children. I really can't schepp any nachas (see Arthur Miller for translation). For my performance it was easy. As others before me have noted 'The Play's The Thing'. *Death of a Salesman* is a great play and actor proof, if you just remember the lines.

At the time I was doing the play I was laying some paving stones in my garden (I'm a happy man with a batch of cement). Next door a professional stone mason was working. He could stand it no longer. 'Oi, Alf (my TV character's name), you're doing that all wrong. I'll nip over and show yer.' He did, too, and hired me his stone cutter at half price. Well, I was grateful and, keen as always to bring 'Kultur to the masses', I invited him to the show. 'What's that, then, Alf?' 'Well it's a play, *Death of a Salesman*, great production.' Modesty forbade I go any further. I met him and his wife in the Green Room after the show. We talked of cards, soccer, tabloid politics, no mention of the play, Me, nuffink, till some twenty minutes and two pints later in what he thought was a suitable moment and not wishing to embarrass me, he leaned forward and whispered, 'Bit 'ard on the bum ain't it!'

John Malkovich

My first personal contact with Arthur Miller came when I was cast to play the role of Biff Loman in a revival of *Death of a Salesman* on Broadway in 1984. I remember many articles and reviews being highly critical of the play, and its venerable author – it was not a tragedy in the Aristotelian sense; it was cloying, maudlin, dated, and did not accept its Jewishness. The criticisms sometimes infuriated me, more often amused me. People are entitled to their opinions, and fortunately I'm entitled to call them stupid. And I do. And I will continue to. Arthur's plays have always addressed the principal feelings and dilemmas and morality of his time. More often than not, they have addressed these issues in a manner which was involving and intelligent, and sometimes in a manner which was cathartic and prophetic. It seems to me we can't ask more of our artists (though we do, for we also ask them to be fashionable). His plays will be performed and enjoyed for far longer than his detractors would care to admit. Over the course of a lifetime, he has taught, in the true sense.

A few years ago I introduced Arthur at a PEN conference in New York. I made an offer to the people critical of his work to please, please write something better. The offer stands, but something tells me it will be a while.

Cliff Burnett

Extracts from Director's Rehearsal Journal, Dundee Rep, 1990

Monday 15th January, 1990
A cold day and a dismal rehearsal space – thankfully only temporarily. 'Readthroughs' are normally a waste of time. Few actors can shake themselves free of the inevitable pre-readthrough sleepless night . . . self included. The consequence is twofold. Either actors mumble

through in a dazed state or overcompensate by trying to offer a full blown performance. Both are unsatisfactory. And yet I'm reluctant to relinquish this first collective 'sharing' of the play. Even that proposition founders in those circumstances where, for the first week, I only have half the cast – the central core of the two families. Were it a comedy I'd have tried to take one sting out of the situation. When we did *Blithe Spirit* I actually did a 'runthrough' rather than a 'readthrough' on the first day. Anything to stir some life into that tired old beast and blow the cobwebs out of the actor's preconception about Coward. But with Miller things are different. Such a dense text deserves a formal approach. It begs all the respect we can afford it.

Anyway, despite the fact that the actors had to contend with me filling in several parts – and in Miller there are no small parts (Stanley is an extraordinary, three-dimensional character) – the text came to life in a highly engaging manner. Bobby MacIntosh brings a warmth and vulnerability to Willy that is deeply touching. Less of a blusterer and more of a little man lost in a morass of confusion. Pat Starr simply *is* Linda. She sat quietly and just allowed her life and breath, her compassion and humanity to bring Linda to life before us. Pat is so full of ease and grace. It's so strange. Bobby and Pat have never met before, yet by the end of the read one would have sworn that they'd lived together for years. There's a real sense of the right kind of bonding. All the appropriate elements of character are being generated, transmitted, solicited and assimilated by the actors. They treat each other with the right level of non intrusive respect. One can almost see their unconscious filtering processes at work as each tries generously to meet the other half way. This is not really a conscious process, but they are trained, if they are worth their salt, to accommodate each other, to be 'sympatique'. Graham McTavish brings great warmth and humour to Happy. He can so easily become a tiresome, unlikeable shit. But not in Graham's hands. John Cagan looks every inch like a young and deeply pained John Garfield. Oh God I wish I could play Biff.

The read passed in a spirit of gentle vigour. It was actually extremely moving. I was unable to resist the welling of tears at the deeply affecting moments. I've not known this at this stage since I worked on *View from the Bridge* so its a good omen. On a more objective, technical level I'm conscious of certain actors, especially Bobby and John, resisting the obvious rhythms of certain sections. These are clearly indicated to the point of certain climaxes being almost orchestrated. In the 'Beijing' book, Miller himself talks about *drilling* the actors into supporting the rhythms.

I hope I don't have to go that far. It was disastrous when I tried that for the Orton plays last year – yet his style, the old fashioned high definition farce, has long since ceased to be part of the actor's vocabulary. And you can't reach Orton's truth in simply naturalistic terms. But then again we are talking chalk and cheese. I know that we can trust Miller. I know that if we create the truth of the character in the given circumstances, the rhythms will spring to life automatically. We will spend the week bringing the family together. When I say 'we' I'm not sure who I mean, but it was interesting to find all four sitting together and *being* together in the afternoon tea break, as if they'd all known each other for years. Maybe I'll leave it to Miller to bring the family together. I count myself a very lucky man at the moment. Opportunities to work with wonderful actors on a text of these dimensions and richness is all too rare these days.

Monday 22nd January, 1990
Now with the whole cast, which is interesting and difficult at the same time. The family are now deeply integrated and this might appear impenetrable to outsiders who were not around last week. Maybe I'm being over-sensitive, but I'm conscious of a gulf between the family and the rest. It's perfectly understandable and perhaps we can make a virtue of necessity. Miller himself mentions the notion of the family as a kind of outpost in hostile *enemy* territory. Last week we concentrated on the reality of the family in the present . . . . where each stood in relation to their lives and each other. Today we looked at the past – by Miller's own admission, and that of other directors I know who have worked on the piece, the most difficult nut to crack. What was clear during today's rehearsal was that the past is extremely unreliable – one cannot take it seriously in *real* terms. It is much less a move backward as a move *inward* – or rather a movement of Willy's consciousness *outward*. The events have little coherence in realistic terms. Their ordering overview has much to do with Willy's own psychological processes . . . . especially the first episode, which seems to emerge from a conscious preoccupation on Willy's part. A doubt, or guilt feeling about his treatment of the boys and the values he asserted to them provokes an explosion of unconscious hindsight rationalisation. If one were able to take the old Brechtian method of *unit titles* or even the Stanislavsky equivalent one could call the first unit of the first

flashback 'Willy teaches the boys'. He begins by warning Biff about
girls, continues with a practical lesson on car washing, there follows a
mini history and geography lesson loaded with positive American
values, and finally a eulogy to the cult of the personality. The whole
unit is *so* positive, *so* 'peachy keen' that it begs considerable inquiry.
My feeling is that Willy is creating for his own purposes an idealised
impression of how things were, in a futile attempt to absolve himself
for his guilt. Interestingly enough, his tired psyche is unable to sustain
his efforts – either that or reality is stranger than his psychic assertions.
No sooner has he established his basic standpoint in the flashback, no
sooner has he cultivated the idyllic atmosphere of what he would like
to believe is the past, than *reality* in the form of Bernard intrudes to
undermine the idyll with the reminder that nothing is achieved without
effort. His insistence that Biff must study shatters Willy's illusions.
And reality, once exposed, magnifies as Linda enters to heap upon
Willy the responsibilities of the various payments outstanding. This, in
turn, prompts his self reflection and the re-emergence of his guilt and
self-loathing. After the hotel sequence the disembodied voices of
Bernard and Linda are all that remain to taunt and haunt him. The re-
emergence of the present finds him still questioning the basic
proposition he started with. The episode of fantasy has failed to placate
his doubts.

In the battle of the second flashback Willy calls upon his most
powerful ally – Ben – to add weight to his claims, and having used
Ben's support to stifle Charlie's assertions about the boys – 'they steal
any more from that building site . . . .' – he emerges from the struggle
convinced that 'I was right'. This is interesting. Willy is clearly using
his psychic faculties to obscure the reality he cannot face. Miller is
absolutely right about the pace of these sequences. In the first one
especially the dreamlike pace, the overlapping of incidents and images,
adds pressure to the onslaught against Willy's attempted
reconstruction. Without pace, these scenes will be reflective and
border on the sentimental. We must avoid that at all costs.

Wednesday 24th January, 1990
Understandably there is resistance among the actors to the
orchestration of the flashbacks. It's not easy to grasp the fact that, in
the fantasies, the characters are not the same characters they are in
reality. They are elements of Willy's construction, not the people
themselves. And it's obviously a problem for actors who are deeply

truthful to adopt a schizophrenic attitude where they are *real* in the present and projected images in the flashbacks. It's even more difficult for those who don't appear in the present. Poor Lisa Tramontin, who is playing the woman in the hotel, looked nothing short of apoplectic when I described the 'hallucinatory surrealism' that Miller asserts is the stylistic foundation of the hotel bits. Apparently this just *emerged* in the Chinese production – probably drawing intuitively upon its own cultural/artistic performance norms. But English actors want to have a *real* basis for character. And yet Brian Tully's Ben ticks along with little or no interference from me.

We tried to find a balance today with some rich results – especially for the family. Ignoring for a time the 'artificial' nature of the flashbacks, we took on board the basic proposition of 'the child is father of the man' and looked for moments in the flashback interactions which, especially for the boys, had 'character forming' implications . . . . sort of feeding the present into the past . . . . looking for incidental links between man and boy. The obvious 'significance' of the hotel scene for Biff is mirrored, we discovered, on a smaller scale for Happy. There are clear indications of Happy being neglected and Biff preferred, especially in the first flashback. This is a clue to Happy's thick-skinned, assertive, attention/love seeking behaviour in adulthood. I know it's a kind of *obvious* point but it was interesting to see the text and rehearsal bear it out. It also adds a dynamic to the process implicit in the rhythm and progress of these sequences. For all Willy's attempt to colour the past favourably, the potential for the fantasy deteriorating – reality – is always there. This is an extraordinarily rich balance, affording manifold options for the actors. It certainly solves the 'I am a cipher, an aspect of Willy's dreamworld' enigma for the actors. There is a presence of reality – deep, psychological reality – even in the dreams. I'm not sure that it helps Lisa Tramontin though . . . . how awful to have to produce that laugh, technically. It's so intimidating. Bobby did everything but show her his willy today to make her laugh, but she can't seem to overcome the block. Oh well, two weeks to go!!

Bigsby: *Death of a Salesman* was 1949. The following decade takes us into a different political climate. Your next play was in fact an adaptation of Ibsen's play *An Enemy of the People*. How did you come to write that? Was it your idea?

Miller: No. Frederic March and Florence Eldridge, his wife, came to me and asked me to do this. They were alarmed that some kind of pre-Fascist period was developing in the United States because of McCarthyism, and they were willing to back a new production of this particular play if I would develop an American version of it, because the original had a lot of repetitions in it and the language was quite wooden as far as the American ear was concerned. So I did a rather extreme adaptation of it, here and there, in order to make it something that Americans could listen to and clarify some of its themes, which even at the time were a little muddy. And that's how I developed it.

Bigsby: *An Enemy of the People* is very much a play in which the public world and the private world interact. But that is equally true of all your work is it not? You can't conceive of the individual outside of the public context.

Miller: The metaphor I like is that of the fish. The fish is in the water but the water's in the fish. You can't extricate individuals from society and hope to create a rounded picture of them.

Bigsby: Now, producing a play like that, at that time, in the early 1950s, was somewhat sticking your neck out, wasn't it?

Miller: Well, yes. It was greeted with, how shall I say, doubt as to its artistic value. There is a line in the play in which the one ally that the doctor has in town says: 'Maybe you ought to go to America where you'll find there's more freedom.' One critic was so hysterical that he accused me of sticking in this line in order to make this bad joke about America, which at that time obviously everybody sensed was growing less free, but of course it was in the original Ibsen play. Anyhow, then I decided I would write something that would heat up the atmosphere a little more, and I wrote *The Crucible*. That took place, of course, in Salem, Massachusetts in 1692, and the reason I think that I moved in that direction was that it was simply impossible any longer to discuss what was happening to us in contemporary terms. There had to be some distance, given the phenomena. We were all going slightly crazy trying to be honest and trying to see straight and trying to be safe. Sometimes there are conflicts in these three urges. I had known this story since my college years and I'd never understood why it was so attractive to me. Now it suddenly made sense. It seemed to me that the hysteria in Salem had a certain inner procedure or several which we were duplicating once again, and that perhaps by revealing the nature of that procedure some light could be thrown on what we were doing to ourselves. And that's how that play came to be.

Bigsby: The characters in *The Crucible* are pressed, not only to confess, but to name names. And that, of course, was going on at the time and involved some of your closest friends and associates. The writer who you admired most in the 30s, Clifford Odets, named names, the director of *Death of a Salesman*, Elia Kazan, named names, the man who played Willy Loman in the original production of *Death of a Salesman*, named names. Don't I recall that you actually heard Kazan naming names as you drove back from Salem. What was the impact of all of that on you at the time?

Miller: It was rather like a dream, because the people these men were naming were of course all known to the Government, and they made a point of saying, 'We know who these people are'. Then why did we have to name them? Well, you had to name them in order to establish your credibility as a patriot. In other words it was a ritual. It had no practical meaning. It wasn't as though someone was committing treason and had to be exposed. These were all actors, anyway, and they usually had no political clout of any kind, or importance. All this had happened fifteen to twenty years earlier, their involvement in politics. So this spectacle was now purely to feed the endless appetite of certain politicians, and to scare people, and it just seemed so absurd and maddening, that people were being torn apart, their loyalty to one another crushed and that common decency was going down the drain. It's indescribable, really, because you'd get the feeling that nothing was going to be sacred any more. The situations were so exact it was quite amazing. The ritual was the same. What they were demanding of Proctor was that he expose this conspiracy of witches whose aim was to bring down the rule of the Church, of Christianity. If he gave them a couple of names he could go home. And if he didn't he was going to hang for it. It was quite the same excepting we weren't hanged, but the ritual was exactly the same. You told them anyone you knew who had been a left-winger or a Communist and you went home. But I wasn't going to do that. I didn't know that these people had committed any crimes, and I had known a lot of them in the 30s, twenty years earlier. The farce was too much to stomach. So I had to go through a federal trial and was found guilty of contempt of Congress for refusing to answer some questions. Then the case was thrown out of court by a higher court, the Court of Appeal. But it cost a lot of money and a lot of time, a lot of worry, publicity and so on. It seems impossible but that was over thirty years ago. The reason it seems impossible is that I'm only thirty-eight! I'll tell you a quick interesting story that somebody told me just the other day. He had directed this play in Russia recently, with Russian students, and at the third act they didn't see any point in going on with it. They said, 'Well, here's the whole play'. But in the fourth act – they were playing it in four acts – when Proctor says he will privately confess that he trafficked with the Devil but that he wouldn't give his name for use in public, he felt it was a disgrace, they said: 'What is the point of that?' The director said, 'What do you mean, what is the point of it? Your name is important to you, isn't it?' But they didn't think it was important to them because in their system it was so long since they had had any pretensions in this direction. They thought that the whole thing was pointless.

Bigsby: Well, as you say, it is all over now. It's a long way in the past. McCarthyism has faded into memory. But that's not true of *The Crucible*. *The Crucible* continues to find audiences. Isn't it actually the most produced of all your plays?

Miller: By far, yes. In Latin America there's almost a ritual to it: it's produced when they expect a dictatorship to be taking over shortly, or when a dictatorship has just been overthrown.

Bigsby: I wonder if there isn't a sense in which *The Crucible* is not only dealing with what was going on in the 50s in America but with what had happened in Europe during the war.

Miller: Yes, most definitely, yes. I was quite aware of that. I had known *The Crucible* story back in college but it never occurred to me that I would ever deal with it. It didn't occur to me because I had never formulated an aesthetic idea of this tragedy. It never occurred to me as a form until the McCarthy time which in turn was replaying some of the early Hitler garbage. They were talking the same talk but our American amnesia had completely forgotten it and I began to see that there was some age-old business going back and back and back. It's always happening, this placing holiness on a government, the government being a holy entity and the individual being an unholy one unless he conforms spiritually. You know, people used to say of the Un-American Activities Committee, 'Why do they insist that people testify about something that they know already?' Ninety-nine per cent of the time they were asking somebody for the names of persons when they already had ample testimony about those persons, but they wanted you to say it. It was kind of a mystical transference in which you gave them your soul. It wasn't the name. They had to degrade the person, that's what it was about.

Bigsby: Is that why you once said that you regretted not having made Danforth more evil in that play?

Miller: In a way, I suppose. I didn't know how to do it but I do know that in some cases in Salem, and for sure in the Un-American Activities Committee, these men simply had a lust and a love for viciousness, just on its own, set apart from the ideology. They enjoyed seeing these people hanged and they enjoyed on the Un-American Committee seeing the suffering that they were inflicting on people.

Bigsby: What did you think of Sartre's film adaptation of *The Crucible*?

Miller: I thought it was Marxist in the worst sense, quite frankly. I thought that anybody who had the least sensitivity to history would be just embarrassed by it. He gets the simplest things wrong. He has a crucifix hanging on the wall. That was exactly what they revolted against in Europe. You couldn't have a crucifix in one of their houses. Also, they were imposing a simplistic class interpretation so that the witch hunt was supposedly devised by the upper class against the lower class. Well, for God's sake, probably about thirty per cent of the victims were people of property. Now that's more interesting, you see. Rebecca Nurse was one of the largest landholders in the whole area.

Bigsby: Sartre's version ends with almost a revolt.

Miller: Well, there is some truth in that. What had actually happened was that the community had gotten more and more alarmed because of the wildness of the accusations. They thought it was going to go on for a few weeks and they'd clear the devil out and then go back to the way we used to be. Well, it kept going on and on and on and on. There seemed no end to it and finally they hanged Rebecca Nurse who had an immaculate reputation in the town; she was a loved woman, who had given away a lot of her worldly goods. When she stood up there and they put a rope around this ancient woman's neck there was a surge of people to get her down and the soldiers held them back and they hanged her. But that was the end. They didn't want any more to do with it. But it wasn't the people in Salem so much as it was the people in the next town who resisted. When the so-called court started to come in they lined up on the road and wouldn't let them into the town. They wouldn't let them hold the court there and said they wanted no part of this. They turned around and went home and that was the end of it, really. It wasn't so much a revolt as people not wanting any more to do with it. As usual in the United States it sort of evaporated like McCarthyism did. There is no date on which he fell; it sort of got boring, repetitive; it lost its charge and its charm. People were on to something else.

Margot Leicester

An Enemy of the People, *The Young Vic Theatre
Company 1989*

I was struggling inside the cramped portakabin which housed a very
hot phone box on a very hot Greek Island, holding two struggling small
boys and shushing them to be quiet, when I first heard that we were
going to be doing *An Enemy of the People*. It was Summer, 1988. David
[Thacker] put down the phone, after what seemed hours of
complicated conversations with people in England and America about
why the Young Vic wasn't going to be doing *Hedda Gabler* (basically
Hampstead Theatre had got in first with the publicity), and said to me:
  'Right, it's *Enemy of the People* then.'
  'Oh, right.'
  'The Arthur Miller version.'
  'Oh . . . . right . . . well . . . oh good. Now can we *please* get these
children on the beach.'
  And as casually as that began one of the happiest and most creative
work experiences of my life.
  Not for quite a while did I have any deeper relationship with this
play than that of interested onlooker and admiring/envious member of
the audience. I was not in the cast during its run at the Young Vic in
the early autumn. But when the production transferred to the
Playhouse (in London's West End), and they needed a quick
replacement, I was lucky enough to go with it, playing the part of
Katrin Stockmann.
  Now I had known, through seeing the play, just how powerful it was,
but only when you step round the edge of a page of text, go through
that pass door and onto the stage, do you ever begin to discover just
how good or bad a play really is. Saying the words out loud, moving it,
simply pretending to be that particular person, gives an actor a
wonderful closeness to a work that no single viewing or reading could
offer. I think Arthur is referring to this in *Timebends* when he says that,
in approaching the part of Willy Loman, the actor Lee J. Cobb
recapitulated the processes that he had gone through in writing it. This
seems true. I think actors are the most accurate assessors of plays. And

consequently of playwrights. Maybe this is why there is a love affair between actors and Arthur Miller.

Actors suffer greatly, at least in this country, from the *ad hoc* and unplanned nature of their work. They are always on the receiving end of a set of decisions made outside of their control. As a result genuine development is impossible and it is often difficult to believe that you have real utility and significance. So the best experiences, I think, occur when they hit on a particular moment, a moment lifted out of the ordinary, in which there is a sense of union between the audience and those on stage. Tom Wilkinson hit this moment for us all, night after night, in Act II, Scene 2 of the play when Stockmann finally manages to get a hearing for his case before the people of the town. Fighting through all the barracking and harrassment to tell them that the town's water is contaminated, he realises that there is something larger than this single social issue. Out of his pain, humiliation and anger he discovers something vital about what it is to be a human being: '. . . don't think you can fog up my brain with that magic word – the People! Not any more! Just because there is a mass of organisms with the human shape – they do not automatically become a People. That honor has to be earned! Nor does one automatically become a Man by having human shape and living in a house and feeding one's face – and agreeing with one's neighbors. That name also has to be *earned*.'

Every night Tom nailed this moment for us all. When he came to the words, 'the majority is never right until it *does* right,' you could feel the sense of unity in the theatre.

Of course this play has a history of exciting such feelings. Stanislavski performed Ibsen's text in 1901 in St Petersburg after a demonstration had been brutally broken up and many of the participants thrown into jail. In the evening they were released and many chose to go to the Moscow Art Theatre. An eyewitness recalled a hungry, exhausted, but excited crowd coming straight from jail to the theatre. Stanislavski gave orders for them to be given tickets and when, in the last act, Dr Stockmann, who has returned from a hostile meeting where he has been more or less manhandled, looks at the tears in his clothes and says, 'When you go out to fight for freedom and justice you don't put on new trousers,' there was an elemental explosion of feeling from the audience.

As that eyewitness observed, 'the character of Stockmann had grown at an instant from an individual rebel into a figure of enormous political significance. The Manager and Box Office Manager ran to the theatre . . . the temperature suddenly rocketted. "Well, we'll all be arrested and the play will be stopped" – that's what went through the minds of all us students who were inured to catastrophes of that kind. But the performance just went on to the end.'

Our audiences were not living through such tumultuous times in 1988 but the issue of the poisoning of public water was only too apt a metaphor through which to view the moral struggle of this play, a struggle as yet unresolved both for us and the Stockmann family as they fiercely hug each other at the end of the play. For me, it was ending almost where I began, holding, comforting and shushing two small boys, bracing ourselves for the future, whatever it may hold.

It is rare to meet your heroes in real life. Often they are dead or too famously inaccessible, and perhaps even when encountered are incapable of measuring up to expectations. But Arthur Miller is still with us and still 'wields truth substantial as a sword' at all that stands in its way. As we in the cast discovered he is also so funny and sane and kind and witty that you feel the world is a safer place because he's in it.

David Thacker

in conversation with Heather Neill

When I was directing *The Crucible* at The Young Vic in 1986 I had a strong sense that the play exists on an intellectual level and an emotional one at the same time. It is politically and socially comprehensive while being a powerful – and at the same time accessible – piece of theatre. My belief is that you must always be faithful to the text. You don't need to come up with apparently new and original ideas when directing Miller. It's hard enough to express just what he was trying to express. That is in itself an achievement. *An Enemy of the People*, though, did present a particular difficulty.

Miller's version of Ibsen's text is set, like the original, in Norway, but it is written in American English. The positive side of that is that it becomes a collaboration between two playwrights shaking hands across the century. It has led to a play neither could have written alone. We decided that the specific setting should be kept, that the 'Norwegian-ness' should not be diminished since the exactness of time and place made it more relevant, more vivid and powerful. But this meant that the language had to be anglicised if it was not to jar on English ears. I telephoned Miller with some sense of apprehension but found him sympathetic. In rehearsals we proceeded to analyse the text consulting various translations and going back to the Norwegian. We even suggested changes in the presentation of one character, Petra: Arthur had cut some lines and modernised the part in a way which we didn't think worked. He was extremely generous in his response and endorsed what we were doing. It was the next best thing to having him in the rehearsal room. Further changes were discussed in subsequent telephone conversations – no fax machines being available on either side at the time – and there were two or three things that he confirmed about our approach which were essential to the interpretation of the play, anchors for me, really. One was that it is absolutely crucial that you put up the best possible case for the brother, avoid him being played as any sort of villain. It is also crucial that you avoid any tendency to romanticise Thomas Stockman himself, that certainly in the first two or three acts of the play he is a bit pig-headed and full of himself, blind and gullible, not a hero from the top of the play. It's a basic guideline that if you try to express the contradictions as honestly and vigorously as you can, you tend to have more profound and dynamic productions. I think the same would be the case in *The Crucible*, with Danforth. You would have to try to play the play from his point of view as much as you possibly can if its range is to be expressed. Miller was also clear about the love that exists between the two brothers in *An Enemy of the People* – it is a great cause of pain and agony that they are split in this way.

John Arden

When I was a young man, and very conceited – that is to say, when I was already writing plays but had not had any of them accepted for professional production – I knew more about Arthur Miller by reputation than actual experience of his work. All I had seen of it was at the cinema, Frederic March in *Death of a Salesman*; and an extraordinary parody of the same play, one of the items in the revue-movie *New Faces*. I had also read a rather devastating critique of *All My Sons* by Walter Kerr, in his book *How Not to Write a Play*. Kerr was on about the apparent inability (or at least unwillingness) of modern playwrights, particularly on Broadway, to tell a simple, strong, swift story of variegated dramatic action without cluttering it with Emotion for its own sake disconnected from Plot, with Plot pre-determined in the interests of an Ibsenite Social Issue, with Character regarded as *being* rather than *doing*. He thought (if I remember his book correctly) that *All My Sons* was a classic example of the first two tendencies. I thought that *Death of a Salesman* only too clearly represented the third, and that between the original play and the *New Faces* buffoonery there was very little difference. How could I have judged a writer on the basis of what a movie-company had done to his script? For, despite Frederic March, it was not a very good film; its half-hearted playing about between stage-conventions and cinema ditto all but debased it into another of those Hollywood father-and-sons sob-stories (a sentimental genre still going strong today): I really believed this was Miller.

And then I saw *The Crucible*, at the Royal Court in London, one of the first productions of George Devine's new venture there. 1956, was it?

I don't know what I expected when I bought my ticket. It was conventional wisdom that transatlantic writers had a difficulty with period drama. 'No historical sense', people used to say. (People? Cambridge undergraduates, at any rate, and it was not long since I had been one myself.) Only compare, say, Olivier's Shakespeare films with the Hollywood *Romeo and Juliet*, or David Lean's Dickens adaptations with the American *David Copperfield*. The Russians, on the other hand . . . or the French . . . I am appalled when I remember the cultural snobbery of those days, and I was as bad at it as anyone.

We did not of course regard westerns as 'period drama': their stories were more or less within living memory, and the vernacular had not changed much. A good script for a John Ford could be trusted; cowboys, cavalrymen, and itinerant medicine-show proprietors really had talked and acted like that.

But what would a New York playwright make of events in Massachusetts in 1692? Was it really at that date *American* history or a sub-division of *English*? Everyone knew it was supposed to be a parable of McCarthyism, but that was not reassuring. I was, am, desperately interested in historical plays and tales for their own sake. The idea of thrusting seventeenth-century personages, a fascinating brood of cultural ancestors, into protest against mid-twentieth-century political

89

abomination, disturbed me rather. I did not know very much about the Salem witch-trials, but what I did know made me feel that I needed to know more about them (and draw my own conclusions from them), not have them *diagrammed* at me with subliminal nudges – 'Say, this is just what's going on in Washington: watch that judge, he's McCarthy; note that witness, he's Ronald Reagan; hey, see *this* one, he's got to be Miller himself . . .' etc. I very much disliked the idea that someone in the play would have to be 'Miller himself'. I regarded, and still do, such identification to be the curse of twentieth-century theatre.

In short, could the knife-edge balancing act between history and modern times be convincingly held, and how would it be held? There was no proper style for historical plays in England, just a choice between over-ritualised *Murder in the Cathedral* poetics, if the writer was 'serious'; or (more popularly) conversational looseness with a few over-modern, over-regionalised locutions carefully omitted, inspiring no confidence in the hearer, however persuasive the decor and the dynamics of the performance. (Contradiction here, of course, with our vaunted British 'historical sense', but never mind . . .) Rattigan's *Adventure Story*, wherein Alexander the Great conquered the east with the vocabulary of a Guards Brigade subaltern improbably in charge of an entire desert army in World War II, was the sort of thing one might expect – and alas within American terms of reference.

Let me say, at that time in my career my own attempts at historical writing had been embarassingly bad. I knew (roughly) what I wanted, but had been unable to find a technique for achieving it.

The Crucible, quite simply, showed me how it could be done (and it has never done better since). It was a play that was cold, detached, hot, immediate, seventeenth-century, twentieth-century; and all at the same time. I have not seen it performed since that production at the Royal Court. I took the book out of the shelf to refer to it for this writing. I can hear the very voices of the actors as I look through it, see the grey-brown-blue bitter sets, the dark puritan costumes, the deliberate pacing of the dreadful story up and down the depth of the small Sloane Square stage. It stuck in my mind like no play I had seen since I was twelve years old and was taken to *Hamlet* on a wartime night in York; and it was the *language* that made it stick.

I won't involve myself here and now in analysis, merely remind myself through some short quotes of the sort of words from which the whole was made up.

Judge Danforth is exhorting an unhappy witness:

No, old man, you have not hurt these people if they are of good conscience. But you must understand, sir, that a person is either with this court or he must be counted against it, there be no road between. This is a sharp time, now, a precise time – we live no longer in the dusky afternoon when evil mixed itself with good and befuddled the world. Now, by God's grace, the shining sun is up, and them that fear no light will surely praise it. I hope you will be one of those.

Proctor tears up his false confession:

And there's your first marvel, that I can. You have made your magic now, for now I do think I see some shred of goodness in John Proctor. Not enough to weave a banner with, but white enough to keep it from such dogs.
(*His wife ELIZABETH is weeping in terror.*)
Give them no tear! Tears pleasure them! Show honour now, show a stony heart and sink them with it!

They take him out to hang him, and Elizabeth concludes the play:

He have his goodness now. God forbid I take it from him!

It was not just the monosyllabic Anglo-Saxon strength of the words chosen so much as the rhythms that impregnated the speeches. Avoiding mush of sentiment on the one hand and throwaway casualness on the other, he never fell into the trap of rhetorical emphasis over and above the probabilities of an archaic Bible-based culture.
Miller writes in his published notes to the play:

No-one can really know what their lives were like. They had no novelists – and would not have permitted anyone to read a novel if one were handy. They believed . . . that they held in their steady hands the candle that would light the world. We have inherited this belief, and it has helped and hurt us. The Salem tragedy . . . developed from a paradox. It is a paradox in whose grip we still live, and there is no prospect yet that we will discover its resolution. (Salem society, like all self-protective organisations) was grounded on the idea of exclusion and prohibition, just as two objects cannot occupy the same space. The witch-hunt was a perverse manifestation of the panic which set in among all classes when the balance began to turn toward greater individual freedom.

That's about all he has to say directly on the matter of McCarthyism. He did not need to insist further, for by saying it specifically within the terms of his understanding of the seventeenth century, and – outside the preface, on the stage – by means of the *sounds* of the seventeenth century, not tediously imitated, but (as the above quotations show) imaginatively re-constructed to shake hands with the sounds and speech-patterns of the twentieth, he also shook hands with the horrid politics of the twentieth. John Proctor's courage became Miller's courage in face of rabid anti-communists, without reliance on the knowing nudge, the irritating 'lemme tell it like it is, man' of so many intense playwrights whose works serve an instant purpose and are then forgotten.

Miller on witch-trials is as historically intelligent as was Shaw on St Joan's trial, but Shaw attempted no such verbal feat. I have long thought it to be the chief weakness of *Saint Joan* (or, to take a lighter but culturally closer example, of *The Devil's Disciple*) that he did not.

Miller, in short, with *The Crucible*, moved the theatrical re-creation of history forward in one great stride of English language, and thereby made it as important a vehicle for enacted ideas as were Brecht's not dissimilar and roughly contemporary plays (*Mother Courage, Galileo*).

Except that we had to hear Brecht in translation; we could not know what he felt like to German ears. To me, in those days, that made all the difference.

Howard Davies, Bill Dudley, Tom Wilkinson, Zoë Wanamaker, Clare Holman, David Burke

The Crucible, *The National Theatre, June,*
1990

HOWARD DAVIES (Director)
When somebody interpreted one of his plays in a particularly eccentric way Arthur Miller remarked, 'Why can't you do it the way I wrote it?'

In this production we are trying to work as closely as possible towards what we perceive to be his wishes. We want to be true to the characters and the political and moral commentary that runs throughout the play, from beginning to end. But that still leaves decisions. One possible approach to the play is to see it as a rebellion of youth against age and any production is likely to stress that simply because the girls don't have anybody of their age group (the nearest of them are a collection of men in their early to middle age, and that age difference is quite marked). But what we have done is to make sure that the people who are the main contestants in the fight for the moral and political future of this community, for its life, for the heart and soul of that community, are people roughly the same age, in their middle age. So in this production Danforth is not the authoritarian figure in his sixties that he is described as being in the stage directions. He's one of that age group. The reason for casting like that was to make sure that it did have some pertinence to the kind of debate that exists in England at the moment, to the way we conduct our society, to the manner in which we've all participated in it over the past ten years. Do we want a major change or to turn back? How do we look at ourselves? And those questions, by and large, have been thought about most acutely by the people who now find themselves in a position of power by their early forties. And of course in any power struggle, within any society or community, what you name to be real, or relevant, or significant, if you're in authority, is what becomes significant and relevant. It then takes a major upheaval, the sounding of a common voice, before that reality is changed, those names are re-named or re-defined. McCarthyism is central of course but it's only one example of a more general truth. The fact is that this play is eternal and timeless. It is relevant to a Chinese community or a community in any part of the world. To reduce it to McCarthyism would be a mistake. In a sense it is a play about power, about people who find themselves forced into playing roles which they had not asked for and which they play either heroically or corruptly. Elizabeth Proctor's life is an attempt to assert herself in the face of her own education, upbringing, beliefs. It becomes necessary for her to contradict what she has believed to that point in her life in order to retrieve the situation. She has to revise all her beliefs, the beliefs that have sustained her. And she fails. But she never asked for that role. Nor, in a sense, did Danforth. He conducts himself badly but he didn't ask for a set of circumstances quite so epic, for a situation so critical for the society. But that's the way it is.

93

BILL DUDLEY (Designer)
In approaching the question of design I was interested in the plight of
the early settlers. Howard and I tried to look at the reality and the
predicament of these settlers, how hazardous their life was. There was
real danger. They nearly all got wiped out by the winters in the early
days, and I think that the folk-memory of that would have been very
strong in the 1690s with the children and grandchildren of the 1620s
settlers. We felt that some of their actions in seeking to stabilise the
community had some real basis. It's too easy to judge the actions of
characters in history by our standards. So in designing the set I tried to
emphasise the day-to-day lives of these people. We made the building
and the erection of their shelters a communal act. So we started with a
fairly simple structure having to do with the building of houses, and
ended up with the more municipal structures, the accretion of power.
The final image is of a gallows. They started to hang people for
deviancy, out of fear and superstition, the emotional luggage that they
brought out from England and which they thought they had left, like
the Plague, on the quayside. It turned out that they had brought too
many old ideas with them, especially intolerance. Miller, as absolutely
an American writer, understood, like the best spirits of the seventeenth
and eighteenth centuries, what America could be, and what it was in
danger of becoming. Faced with the possibilities of America they chose
to act like mean-minded English people. In design terms we start with
a bare stage, and then enclose it. People may have gone to America to
get away from enclosures, but they brought the enclosure mentality
with them. So we try to pen the characters in. Walls and posts appear,
and we show a much bigger space outside, which is mysterious and full
of potential, and possibly hidden dangers, whether it's Indians or
climate. We've put one small window in. I think it's the only window in
the piece, and these small enclosures are a kind of reflection of what
they haven't freed themselves from. It isn't a natural play for an open
stage like the Olivier; you would think it would be better at the
Lyttleton, or the Cottesloe, where it was last played by the National
Theatre about ten years ago. But, given that we had to do it in the
Olivier, we tried to make a statement about America as they saw it, an
early settler's view of America. We took as the other central image the
barn-raising sequence from the film *Witness*, which is based on the way
the Amish people raised the barns. That seemed central: they raise this
edifice, this construct of a village, a community, and a canker comes in

94

because they haven't go a clear enough vision of what it could be. They haven't left behind old European values.

TOM WILKINSON (John Proctor)

I think John Proctor has a sense of morality which sees his betrayal of his wife as being amongst the lesser crimes. I think that had the action of the play taken a different course, if he hadn't been placed in the crucible which will reduce him to seeing the world in terms of this morality, he would have been able to reconcile this sense of sexual betrayal to an overall moral structure, which necessarily must be vague, as it is with all of us. It's very rare for people to be asked the question which puts them fairly and squarely in front of themselves. He's a dissenter but he feels that his dissension enriches the community. I don't think he wants to opt out of the community. The first act of the play shows all the various factions in Salem fighting for a certain view of that society: they are in the process of making their society and Proctor has his commitments. The problem is that if you're going to bring with you greed, and all the things that go hand in hand with a burgeoning society, then you're not going to build the kind of society that you want your children to live in. Proctor is quite conscious of this, of the need to get things right. Of course the fact is that most people do not make decisions as if it were life and death; most people drift along through their lives, and only at various times do they have a chance to look round them and take some kind of stock. And even then it's probably an imperfect business. Proctor is just a man, a man more good than bad, who one day betrays his wife with Abigail Williams. Now, in the scale of things, that's not a great offence. That kind of thing happens. But I don't think he would have stood by and watched people hanged if the court had not reached out and touched his life. I think not. But of course it does reach out and touch him and I think the moment he sees what he must do is the moment he sees his own name written on a piece of paper. I think it's then that he comes face to face with John Proctor reduced to his quintessence; the crucible has burned off the flabby bits of John Proctor and he's left with his own irreducible moral self, the person he is. And he knows then that life wouldn't be worth living if he gave in and signed his name to save himself. It would be like seering part of his brain. I don't think he would be able to live after that. He'd kill himself. He's not defending an abstract principle. He's defending an idea of himself, or rather he thinks he's defending a principle for a good part of the play but is finally confronted with who he is. And that's not something that one ever wants to happen to oneself.

ZOË WANAMAKER (Elizabeth Proctor)
Elizabeth Proctor is a Puritan. She is fundamentally motivated by religion. But she goes through a development, a self-development, though she can't really admit to it. After all, it's not easy to know what you want, what you believe. Faced with a life and death situation she learns to read her heart and discovers that she has been lacking. At the beginning of the play she suffers from the sin of pride. Her pride is very hurt the first time we see her. But there are many layers to her character. When we first meet her she's a very strong person, but there's also another layer, because she suspects that she's going to die, and she has to deal with that as well as the past relationship, the infidelity. Elizabeth cannot lie. But she does in order to save her husband. I think that's the beginning of her self-discovery, in a way the beginning of her humanity, because part of her discovery about herself, part of what she must come to terms with, is her emotional and sexual coldness. Because she's so tough and moral she cannot 'give' of herself: 'I kept a cold house.' I think that's because she has this steel around her which is her religion. She's married to a man full of energy who is feared because he says what he thinks, but she can't respond to him. She says what she thinks but she does so with her hand on the Bible, metaphorically, which is a bit more frightening, a bit more threatening because she's so unbending. I don't think this play is only Proctor's story. I think it's everybody's. That's why the play is so epic. In the same way the McCarthy trials were everybody's story. None of us would like to be in that situation.

CLARE HOLMAN (Abigail)
What drives Abigail before the affair starts, and what drives her after, are probably different things, though linked. She's been terribly hurt; she's been taken out of a kind of sleep and given knowledge of what she considers to be love. She's been shown a different world from the one she's known before. Then she is dumped and she can't accept it. I think she's probably always been a free spirit; she's always been slightly an outsider. She has no parents, and though she's obviously in the community she's not quite of it. And as a result she fights. I don't think she feels she has anything to lose, because she's already lost an awful lot, by losing John Proctor. At the beginning of the play she's not sure

of that but pretty soon in the first act she has her confirmation. There's a crucial moment in the one and only scene they have together in the play, when he rejects her, quite definitely. What follows is a kind of revenge but it's also a struggle for survival for her. The irony is that she gains a kind of power, which she misuses. She is seduced by that power. She is very manipulative and very conscious of most of the things that she does. At every point in the court scene, when something is going badly wrong for her, she turns to the spirits. That's very conscious. But, having said that, what I discovered was that in playing hysteria, something else began to happen. There's very much an unconscious side as well. Once you get into it, you can't actually control it. And you feel right about it; you start to believe in it. So, although on one level she is very conscious of what she's doing, I think she also starts to believe that there are spirits. I think she does believe that something's happening. I don't think that Abigail is evil. She's somebody who misuses power and gets carried away with it. But if she gave it up, if she suddenly admitted to lying, if she confessed that her motive was revenge, she'd be lost. It is the key to her survival. And therefore part of her has to believe what she is saying.

DAVID BURKE (Rev. Hale)
As far as the Rev. Hale is concerned I think the seeds of doubt are there almost in the first scene. Certainly, as the play goes on, he begins to look back and realise with horror that he has made terrible mistakes. He can see exactly where he made them. For example, the pressure that he puts first of all on Abigail, and then on Tituba, are the triggers that start the whole tragedy. It is the pressure that is put on Abigail that makes her point the finger at Tituba; it is the pressure that is put on Tituba that leads to the others. Parris is merely following the leader. It is the pressure put on Tituba which makes her say 'The Devil has other agents.' It's rather like a child at school: 'Did you do that, Tommy?' 'No! He did it.' And he suddenly becomes the focus of attention. And that's where everything starts to go horribly wrong. It is conceivable that in different circumstances that interrogation in the first act might have ended up quite differently. One of the things that fascinates me about Arthur Miller's plays – and I felt this especially reading *Timebends*, his autobiography – is his belief that we all have to bear responsibility for our actions, or lack of actions, throughout life. As you get older you are haunted by the things you did twenty or thirty years ago. You have relationships and then you pass on, and you think

97

they've gone but they affect people, they often affect people terribly. And they come to haunt you. I believe that happens to all of us. *Timebends* is not written in a straight time sequence: he tells a story about some incident or some character in his childhood, and then he'll pick up that character twenty years later; he'll turn a corner and he'll meet this person and it's his way not merely of bringing the two people together, but bringing the two moments together. And it's the same in his plays. Willy Loman does things to his sons which he doesn't mean to do; he does them, as he thinks, with the best of motives, and they turn out to be terrible things that he has done, and done to himself. And in *The Crucible*, as far as Hale is concerned, as he says in the last act, 'I came into this village like a bridegroom to his beloved, bearing gifts of high religion; the very crowns of holy law I brought, and what I touched with my bright confidence – my bright confidence – it died; and where I turned the eye of my great faith, it died.' Bright confidence has to be blended with that blood flowing out. If he hadn't had such bright confidence, if he had had more self-doubt, maybe it wouldn't have happened. And his progress throughout the play is the awful dawning realisation of his responsibility. He was an innocent man who walked into that village: he didn't start the so-called witchcraft but in the end his responsibility for what happened is awesome. At various points in the play he does try to stop this juggernaut, but he can't. Hale is torn apart because, in the end, he has to go against what he perceives as his religious tenets, to try and stop this thing. He has to ask people to tell lies. Lies are what rot life. When people tell lies, very basic lies, about themselves and life, it actually rots them, and makes everything go wrong. That's what makes everything go wrong in this play. It's the lies which Abigail tells and which Tituba tells. The play could be called *Lies*, because it's all about that, but the irony is that eventually this man has to ask people to tell lies in order to put everything right. And he is torn apart by that, and torn apart by responsibility. Miller's plays are tragedies, tragedies in the classic sense of the word, in the way that Shakespeare's plays are tragedies. They are about the big things, they are about life and death, good and evil. But beyond that, and the thing that I'm always moved by in this play, there is always an enormous compassion for people, for the characters he's creating. It's like Othello says to Iago: 'The pity of it, Iago.' Because when you read his plays, or act in his plays, what strikes you is the pity of what happens to good, well-intentioned people, broken on the rack of life. And they are broken, very often, by the consequences of their own actions. In the end, as we all have to, they must take responsibility for what they've done.

Jamie Hayes, Bethan Dudley, Hilary Summers, Andrew D. Mayor

On an operatic version of The Crucible *at the Royal Academy of Music, London, 1990*

JAMIE HAYES (director)
The Crucible as an opera was composed by Robert Ward with a libretto by Bernard Stambler. The work was premiered by the New York City Opera in 1961, and was awarded the Pulitzer Prize for Music and a New York Critic's Circle Citation.

Bernard Stambler's libretto has remained quite faithful to the original play by Arthur Miller. Often when dramatic works become the source of musical interpretation a lot of the narrative becomes lost and confused. Not so here. Added to this, the composer found time and space to add to his adaptation a scene from Miller's play which had been cut after only a few performances. This scene began Act III, the forest becoming the arena for a confrontational scene between Abigail and Proctor. Miller felt that the dramatic tension and pacing was lost and chose to discard it. In operatic terms it gave the composer a freedom to write in a musical vein different from that of the rest of the text, which by its nature is very conversational.

For our design we required a basic acting area which became a wooden disc, sloping and set in the centre of the stage with a semi-circular back wall which closed around the top of the wooden floor and contained several hidden doorways. This allowed us to move, at will, a pelmet door-surround to any of these hidden doorways, thus suggesting a change of location. The floor and back wall were then surrounded by the 'forest', tall, real trees which were dense and painted in a rather surreal fluorescent green. The stage was then covered in peat to give a general 'rustic' quality. The players were dressed in period puritan costumes.

We were interested in featuring the forest, as Salem Village (unlike Salem Town), where the witchcraft mania began, was surrounded by white pines, an area feared by the puritans as it was inhabited by pagan

Indians. In turn, this gave the production a claustrophobic atmosphere adding to the tension of events. Sections of our 'forest' were placed on movable rostra which were wheeled around the front edge of our performing floor. Though all of the play takes place inside different locations we played the first act of the drama beginning inside and then moving outside with the arrival of the Puttnams. This gave us the possibility of still seeing 'inside' Rev. Parris's home while action continued outside, and permitted us more scope to develop the character of Abigail as she could be seen as an individual behaving in a clandestine manner with Betty Parris. It also allowed us to play a 'mimed' scene between Proctor and Abigail (a scene from the play not featured in the adaptation for opera) while the other players are discussing them outside. By having Proctor step off the wooden floor onto the peat we were able to continue a theatrical entrance of some surprise.

For our semi-circle structure of doors we managed to compartmentalise the protagonists for the court scene by placing them within the recess of the doorways. Above them, on the roof of the door structure, stood the witches, giving the court a gladiatorial atmosphere which again highlighted the paranoia.

BETHAN DUDLEY (Abigail)

It is interesting that the Abigail of the opera has no direct dramatic contact with the other girls in plotting their evil games. Instead, she interacts with the adults of the community and is not seen as one of the children, playing with fire. In the opera, Abby is not playing with fire, she is stoking it.

Abby's dramatic language in the play is youthful, playful and deceptively simple as she toys with the lives of people. In the opera, her musical language is far more strident, sensual, sexual, mature. It leaps from one extreme of pitch and dynamic to the other. For example, when the Rev. Hale questions Abby in Act I, his tone, in the play, is relatively gentle and patronising, as he speaks to a child. Her replies in turn are suitably childish in nature.

Abigail: That were only soup
Rev. Hale: What sort of soup were in this kettle, Abigail?
Abigail: Why, it were beans, – and lentils, I think, and . . .

However, in the opera, the Rev. Hale's questioning is menacing as his repeated notes stress his emphatic quest for the truth. He treats

Abby, in musical terms, as an equal. She is an adult, in his eyes, deserving mature understanding. It is interesting to note that in the play Abby blurts out, 'She makes me drink blood' as she attempts to blame Tituba for the devilish deeds. However, in the opera, Abby's line is more sinister as, with a minor key colouring it's evil connotations, she sings, 'She made us drink babies' blood' (Act I, Fig. 44).

The opening scene of the opera's third act is not found in the play. The music depicts the longing Abby feels for John Proctor with its blues style and sensual harmonies and suspensions. Her love for John is as clear as the mature sense of destruction within her power. Abby knows her own value as a woman in Proctor's eyes, and as a menacing force in the village. The rich orchestration, combined with her sexual vocal line, depicts Abby as a fearless woman weaving in and out of Proctor's consciousness, thereby shattering the image we might have conceived of Abby as a dissembling girl making mischief. This seductive quality is combined with a decisive declamatory style towards the end of the scene, as she tells John, 'If your snivelling Elizabeth dies, remember, it is you who killed her'. This dark message is not communicated via a broad Pucciniesque line, but by means of a direct quasi-recitation. As a result, the whole scene ensures that we are completely aware of Abby's motives in the Courtroom, and able to see her maturity in the evil games she plays. In the play, Danforth addresses the 'children' as children, explaining in simple terms the dangers of the devil. In the opera, no concessions are made. The music is characterised by relentless rhythms as Danforth questions Abby.

In Act IV of the play, Abby does not appear. The opera, however, presents a scene in which Abby visits Proctor in jail, in an unselfish attempt to free him. She has plotted an escape, has the transport arranged and offers him material assistance (clothes and money). This foresight and cunning makes Abby appear a grown woman facing the realities of an adult situation. Proctor is concerned with ideals; she deals with reality. This addition to the play ensures that Abby is not only seen as a woman of strength in the face of adversity, but also as a sympathetic character. So, in contrast to the play's Abigail Williams, Robert Ward's Abigail combines many adult qualities in the adult world of Salem.

ANDREW D. MAYOR (John Proctor)

The most interesting first impression of Proctor as an operatic character rather than the Proctor of the straight theatre in Miller's original was how little he had been altered in the transition. An ordinary, hardworking, conscientious man, labouring under the guilt of a sexual liaison outside marriage, Proctor displays an awareness and sense of personal responsibility and moral integrity that eludes all his antagonists. These characteristics appear in both the play and Ward's opera. At important dramatic moments Ward and his librettist preserve Miller's lines virtually intact. Proctor's final statement is such a case and it is for me the moment that shows the importance of self-knowledge. There are many figures in history that could have said such words in the face of oppression. Perhaps Nelson Mandela is the most recent example:

> I can, and there's your first marvel that I can. You have made your magic now, for now I do think I see some goodness in John Proctor. Not enough to weave a banner with but white enough to keep it from such dogs. Give them no tear! Tears pleasure them! Show honour now, show a stony heart and sink them with it!

HILARY SUMMERS (Rebecca Nurse)

I first encountered Miller's play as a belligerent teenager, forced to view an elder sister's Tituba with a local drama company. Apart from the adolescent gales of mirth at the sight of one's kin covered in boot polish and sporting her grandmother's carpet slippers, I was quite overwhelmed by the whole thing and it was with considerable interest that I learned that Mr R. Ward had made an 'opera' out of it and that we were to be performing it at the RAM.

The role of Rebecca Nurse frankly did not hold enormous appeal at first; a seventy-two year old crone, she meets an unpleasant end with little to do in terms of dynamic activity. I soon discovered, however, that musically Mr Ward had treated her quite kindly with a mellow 'aria' in Act I and a powerful 'tune' in the final Act. I was then faced with the physical challenge of transforming my 6′2″ well-built and robust self into a little old woman with a will of iron.

Having re-read the play I found that the Rebecca of the opera was much more vacillating than her original, at one moment a staunch and real believer in good, the next reduced to rattling her tambourine in the Pentecostal psalm along with the Puttnams and Paris's. And her poor husband! What a non-entity Mr Ward has made him! But then, as fringe characters perhaps they were adequate.

Barry Kyle

The Crucible, *Royal Shakespeare Company, 1984*

In 1984 I embarked on a production for the RSC of *The Crucible* in collaboration with Nick Hamm which was designed to tour England and Northern Ireland in unconventional theatre spaces: cathedrals and agricultural showgrounds were among them. I had been exploring free-form theatre with peripatetic audiences in my work, and wanted to approach a great naturalistic masterpiece in the same way. Witchcraft and mass hysteria would break out amongst the audience, behind them and over them. The design (Bob Crowley) was dominated by a huge mural of the American wilderness, the audience had to move to avoid Hale's arrival in a covered wagon, the trial was conducted over huge distances, the actors raised up on innumerable kitchen tables – the tables emptied by the arrest of the women of Salem. Alun Armstrong and Lynn Farleigh gave blazing performances as the Proctors, and the play, massaged into a shape its author could never have intended, stretched, expanded, and filled even cathedrals with its excitement. 'Do you think they're trying to tell us something?' said one Northern Irish Protestant lad to another as they left at the end of a performance in Belfast. In Ripon Cathedral one cold Saturday night in November, Alun Armstrong roared the great line 'God is Dead' and I thought the stones would crumble. 'A great spiritual experience' opined one of the clergy after the show. We went to Poland with the production. 'We must play in churches not theatres,' I declared after the British Council had secured our invitation there just after the lifting of martial law in 1985. Churches, however, were packed with solidarity activists barred from performance in state theatres and TV by their government. The RSC could not perform in churches we were told; it would be tantamount to turning up at the airport with '*solidarnosc*' badges. We came to an agreement. We would perform in Warsaw Technical College's Student Union, and a film studio in Wroclaw. 'Will they understand English?' queried the actors. 'Have they heard of McCarthy?' Our performance had a few chairs for the disabled, but if the audience wanted to sit, they had to sit on the carpeted floor. The Polish Minister of Culture came and sat on the floor. To our even greater amazement so did the British Ambassador. Quiet attention throughout the performance. Politeness? Then something extraordinary. As Proctor was faced with the paper to sign his supposed confession, sudden stirring, whispering, laughter among the audience. A real drama was breaking out amongst them. The tension intensified throughout the fourth act, and the play received an ovation. In the dressing rooms a British official, deeply excited by the show, told us that 'the stir' was because Solidarity actors, artists, directors had recently been asked to sign a paper disclaiming their Solidarity views as a condition to re-employment in state theatre and TV. The cast were mobbed in the bar by members of the audience keen to communicate *The Crucible*'s new secret meaning for the oppositional artists of Poland. Our production had set out to explore a new form in the play, and found a new message. Seventeenth-century America was not just a metaphor for 50s America, but also Eastern Europe in the 1980s. *The Times* of London reviewed our performance as a political story.

Gerald Freedman

Roundabout Theatre production, New York City.
March 1990

In many people's minds, this play is connected to the McCarthy hearings, since it first premiered in 1953 during the height of the red scare. Yet it has a much broader application. It's not really about witch hunts, it's about something much greater, and it will always be truthful and pertinent.

For me, the play is about one's choices in regard to one's moral actions. In all of his plays, Arthur Miller is concerned with your responsibility – both to yourself and society. And he comes down heavily on the side I'm on, which is that each individual must feel responsible. Miller doesn't dictate morality – but he does say that you have to wrestle with your conscience, and that you have to live with it.

I realise that the 'witchcraft' label is going to be difficult to transcend. In this production, I'm trying to treat the environment more abstractly, to focus on the argument. And I'm trying to strip away the sentimentality that I think accompanies old New England artifacts – real mantlepieces, and spinning wheels – all the things which identify the period, but clutter the mind even as they clutter the eye.

Arthur Miller's plays are not realistic, they only seem to be. So for the setting I envision a box, because the characters' feelings of repression and of not being able to escape are very strong. They are literally boxed in. So when I need a door or a window, I'll punch an opening in the box. It's an environment – it could be anywhere at any time. The thing to remember is that his plays are elevated; the questions, the passion, and especially the language are elevated.

Language is particularly important in *The Crucible* since the play relies on the structure of truth and lie. Just yesterday listening to auditions, I wondered, 'Does Abigail know that she's lying? Or has she lied so much that she can't tell the difference between truth and a lie?' Sometimes a lie may be the way to the truth, which is one of life's paradoxes. And when is a lie even more important than the truth? Illusion – structures which keep our dreams together and enable us to face reality – is another word for lie. And isn't it a matter of degree as to when an illusion is destructive and when it helps energise. It's a balancing act which I'm constantly investigating – and which *The Crucible* deals with in a most challenging way.

Notes for the actors – first day of rehearsal of *The Crucible* at the Roundabout:

1 What is the objective truth and does it matter?
2 Is your life more important than your soul, your sense of yourself, your integrity, your name (*Crimes & Misdemeanors*, the movie, examined some of these issues.)
3 Is the illusion enough? keeping up a front? can you live with yourself?

The answer seems to be different with each of us. Where do you draw the line?

The emotional crux of *The Crucible*: Reputation defines a Person from the outside. Integrity defines a Person from the inside.

4 Webster Dictionary definitions. I thought I'd examine these words:

Integrity – soundness of and adherence to moral principle and character; uprightness, honesty. (2) the state of being whole, entire or undiminished.

Reputation – the estimation in which a person or thing is held especially by the community or the public generally; (2) a favourable and publicly recognised name or standing for merit, achievement.

(I didn't know what I was going to find when I went to the dictionary. But doesn't that tell you everything about the play?)

Crucible – a vessel of metal or refractory material, employed for heating substances to high temperature; (2) a severe searching test. (Danforth and the Trial.)

Refractory – a material having the ability to retain its physical shape and chemical identity when subject to high temperatures. (Proctor.)

5 I want to take your mind off of the McCarthy hearing. I want you not to be seduced by the exotic information surrounding witchcraft and the seventeenth-century belief in them. Your work on this play must come from specific character needs, not general principles. So for our purposes you must not think of the Salem witch trials as political and they were not about civil rights. They were about *conscience*. The accused would not say they were witches when they were not. They lived in a universe of Puritan beliefs where each was saved or damned by him or herself, and what happened to one was personal.

Characters are motivated by greed, lust, materialism, reputation, so as to maintain a false illusion of integrity, righteousness and sanctimony. The trials represent a devastating and morally indefensible exercise of law over common sense.

What is your secret guilt? We all have them. What have you buried? What have you covered over?

Ruth Nelson

Directed by Gerald Freedman, within days the play began to take shape and with such ease it would seem to be magic, until one realised it is only necessary to listen – the words will tell you what to do. And they will keep on telling you, refreshing your mind as you reach out from day to day. Gerry made this clear not by speaking of it but 'by letting it happen'. Each day we would run through scenes or run through the whole with a few precise and simple notes at the end. And so we grew with the life, the vitality, of this wonderful play, with its powerful parallel today.

Gordana Rashovich

Elizabeth Proctor is a woman who struggles with her individual needs and transcends them because of her faith in a higher order, a greater responsibility.

The catalyst for the re-organisation of her world is her husband's adulterous act. This forces her to be outside the relationship as she has known it, and create a new bond with him. I've learned something inexplicable from the way she loves – I'm grateful for that. This continuum of questioning is the best of what a play provides.

The play also forced me to experience what it means to be 'outside the law', an expression I heard from a Jewish family who recited their exodus from Vienna in '39 each Passover. A Pillar of Society – bound by its ideals and laws – becomes an outcast. What is this 'poor rabbit' after she is stripped? That is one of the questions I must give credence to every night, viscerally. One could not ask for a more compelling task.

Bigsby: I think we probably tend to think that all of your plays were extremely popular in American and with American audiences, but that's not really true, is it.

Miller: How I wish that were true. The receptions change over time. For instance, *The Crucible* was fundamentally rejected the first time around, but, within a year or so, there was an Off-Broadway production, with the same script, that was welcomed. Of course Senator McCarthy had died in the interim so that made it a little easier to appreciate the play. In fact, *Salesman* was the only play of mine which was universally received in a positive way, all the others were debatable: hated, by some, put down by others and welcomed by some.

Bigsby: What is your explanation?

Miller: I must be irritating people in some way. It may also be that there is a presumption, in some of these plays, that these ordinary people – longshoreman, salesman, farmers, or whatever – have tragic dimensions and that seems pompous to some people. Then again, many critics favour reportage of one kind or another and I've had an impulse which is, may I use the word, poetic. I've wanted to create a symbol, an image, that is more than merely white bread and butter.

Bigsby: There is an irony about your appearance before the House Un-American Activities Committee in that it came three years after *The Crucible* and what you had to say was almost a paraphrase of what Proctor says in *The Crucible*.

Miller: Well, there's only one thing to say to them. You don't have much choice, you know, but that wasn't in my mind at all. I was just trying to stay out of jail.

Bigsby: Did you have any personal doubts about how you would stand up before them?

Miller: Not really. I had invested too much of my mind in my contempt for the whole procedure. I just didn't believe them. I didn't believe what they were doing. For God's sake, the Head of the Committee, a man named Walter from Pennsylvania, a Congressman, a day before my appearance, (and you know I was supposed to be a very dangerous man, otherwise I wouldn't have been asked to appear), made an offer to my lawyer that if a photograph could be taken of him and Marilyn Monroe he would cancel my hearing. That's how dangerous he really thought I was. When I heard this, I said no. He then got back on his horse and acted as though I really was a danger to the country. They were headline hunters, that's all. They'd made their livings by scaring the great unwashed who would then be caused to run around in circles looking to them for salvation.

Bigsby: You must be aware of how intriguing and, I suppose, in a sense, how baffling that marriage with Marilyn Monroe seemed to people, partly because they were dealing with public images which had been developed by the media anyway. Given the extremes of the publicity machinery that was brought to bear, was that a relationship that could ever have survived?

Miller: God knows. You never know, because there's no scientific test that you can apply to it. That it didn't means that it probably couldn't, I suppose. I have all sorts of reasons to think that it might have and equally heavy reasons that it could never have succeeded, given what I was and what she was.

Bigsby: Looking back from this distance, is there something baffling about it to you as well?

Miller: There is something baffling about all my relationships, with whoever. I can't say I understand more than a fraction of them, quite frankly. I seem to drift through life touching whatever comes up and trying to find out what it's made of. So I can't say that I really understand what happened but I have a pretty strong idea, I think, of what happened. It's impossible to answer that question.

Bigsby: Did the image in some way come between you and the person even then?

Miller: I think it's fundamentally simpler than that. Marilyn would be sixty now. This comes as a shock to people since she is always supposed to be twenty-five or six or seven. And the reason it is a shock is because she is not a human being who you can visualise as being sixty. It's impossible with her. That's why the myth goes on. But the thing she would want to say now, I think, is that you ought not to abuse your children and you ought not to become addicted to over-the-counter drugs, that's really what they ought to be talking about in relation to Marilyn, that's really what she 'meant'. She was an example of somebody who was kicked around once too often and it ultimately killed her. She couldn't deal with it and it got worse and worse as she grew older, the traumas of her childhood. You couldn't go on with that intensity of life and those drugs and survive. I knew Marilyn before she was famous, of course. She was not a big movie star. She was a young and ambitious actress but she wasn't a star by any means. I knew her as early as 1952 and we didn't get married until '56 so my first affection for her was long before she became a public image and she never was a public image to me. But I understand why she would be to everybody else.

Bigsby: I presume that you find Norman Mailer's account of that relationship something of a travesty?

Miller: Well, it's Mailer in drag really. It's what Mailer would have been like if he were Marilyn. I don't know how else to put it. It had very little to do with her but he was using her, as he said, as a figure of fiction, putting a real name upon her as he did to all the people in that book that I have any knowledge of.

Bigsby: There was a twelve year difference between you and Marilyn Monroe. You are enough of a Freudian to notice something in terms of what you say in your autobiography, that she used to refer to you sometimes as 'Pappa'. Does that imply that she was looking for something, a husband and a father simultaneously?

Miller: Yes, maybe, that's the common thing with anybody. But in her case it was that way.

Bigsby: Do you resent the fact that people who interview you, the media, have this concern about that relationship, which after all was a very, very small part of your life.

Miller: Well, it's a distortion, of course, but I can understand it. I mean I don't have to contribute to it very much. I have never gone on about her but she was in my life.

Bigsby: Ironically, you followed *The Crucible* with a play which offers a compassionate account of an informer, in the form of *A View from the Bridge*, a play, moreover, in which the law is helpless. It has nothing to say.

Miller: Because Eddie Carbone, in *A View from the Bridge*, is obeying an ancient law which predates the laws we know. That's one of the points of the play, and the reason for the title. It takes place beneath the traffic on Brooklyn Bridge, and the modern society we live in; down in a little neighbourhood an ancient tragedy is being worked out. It is an attempt to look at informants informing as a tragic act, as an act which finally is unavoidable.

Bigsby: Even when he informs, of course, what he's technically doing is simply his civic, legal duty.

Miller: Yes. This is another side of it. In other words what the play is pointing out is that there is an ancient, immemorial ache in the event of informing on someone. Though it has something to do with the external circumstances, they don't control it. The ancient ache controls it. And it's beyond rationality, I think; and that's why it's a tragic circumstance.

Bigsby: What was the origin of *A View from the Bridge*?

Miller: That story was told to me when I was around the waterfront in those days. I was told about a waterfront longshoreman who had squealed on his family and a tremendous outpouring of fury against him had forced him to leave the area. No one knew quite where he had gone; he had to leave his family and he fled. In ancient times he would have gone out into the mountains, vanished amongst the wild beasts. Well, this particular area, Red Hook and the waterfront, stands right under Brooklyn Bridge and it always struck me oddly that here is this commuter traffic going over it night and day, people going out to nice neighbourhoods somewhere else, passing over the area where this Greek drama was taking place and no-one ever thought about it. No one, of course, knew about it; the whole area, the different culture that was down there, was unknown to the people on the Bridge, so it was a view from our culture, which is up on the bridge, down into their culture. The narrator's view is the view from the Bridge or, rather, he is looking at it all from both the point of view of American civilisation and that ancient one that is really down there.

I started out to write an extremely direct work in the way that Greek dramas also tell their story quickly. They tell us what is at stake. They don't waste much time. Sometimes a narrator, or what we would call a narrator, comes forward and tells us that the king is coming toward the city and his wife is in bed with three other guys. So something has got to happen here. In *A View from the Bridge* I wanted to eliminate all the usual machinery of playwrighting which spends the first act in a rather long and involved explanation of where we are. So I introduced a narrator who could set up what I call the moral situation. This was an immigrant community. The solidarity in that community was very important, more so than in the general American public. The reason was that they felt themselves separated from the vast majority of Americans by language, by background and, on the waterfront, by the kind of work they did, because the waterfront is a special place. A lot of people had come over as long ago as the 30s from Italy, from Calabria, from Sicily, and they had never properly entered the country. They had no papers, but the

Organisation protected them, in return for which they would give a piece of their pay to the Organisation, but at least they got into the country, instead of slowly starving in Italy. You see, America was all there was. America was the light and Europe was the darkness. America was where all the action was, where the hope was, and I grew up with that. There was never any question: it was better here than it was anywhere else. The whole idea of life was a development toward a higher level of existence. The idea of repeating what your father had done was completely unknown, the idea of your family being in the same financial or social condition as the previous generation. As I was growing up, it was taken for granted that you were on some inclined plane that was rising higher. I found to my surprise in Europe at that time, in the late 40s, that a lot of people were surprised at this; they presumed that the good thing to do was to snuggle into some job where nothing would change and you would be a bug in a rug.

That element in this play, of Eddie Carbone's desire to see his niece improve herself, was at the heart of the immigrant idea. So, part of his motive for resisting her wish to marry an illegal immigrant, a man who worked with his hands, was understandable. But of course there is also an element of incest in that play, although oddly enough there strictly speaking isn't. For years I unthinkly thought of Catherine as his daughter. In fact she isn't, so there was no incestuous feeling but in my mind there was, in my imagination there was, in my instinctive reaction to it there was. And this incestuous line, of which I was not conscious when I was writing, emerged one day in a later production when I suddenly saw relationships in my own family that were reflected on the stage. The stories had no real connection but suddenly I saw, My God, I was writing something I didn't even realise I was. His instinctive desire is to fend off sexuality for the objective reason that the folkways of the area would make her life dangerous if she proved too attractive to the young guys around there, but, basically, he is trying to defend his own innocence so that at the end, when his wife says, 'You can't have her', he is genuinely outraged and shocked. He is simply horrified that she could think that of him. He defends himself against this sexual accusation to the end. But if there is a sexual guilt operating in here it is, of course, combined with, and threaded through, the social situation he is in. In other words, there is simply nothing as horrifying to the general public in that area as betrayal. It menaces the whole fabric of their

Arthur Miller outside the Royal Exchange Theatre, Manchester.

left Jamey Sheridan,
Frances
McDormand and
Christopher Curry
in the Long Wharf
Theatre production
of *All My Sons*,
New Haven,
Connecticut, 1985

below In rehearsal:
Arthur Miller with
Christopher Bigsby,
producer of the gala
performance of
Miller's work at the
Theatre Royal,
Norwich, May 15th,
1989.

right Tony Lo Bianco and Saundra Santiago in the Long Wharf Theatre production of *A View from the Bridge*, New Haven, Connecticut, 1981.

below Arthur Miller talks to Warren Mitchell about his role as Willy Loman in the gala performance of Miller's work at the Theatre Royal, Norwich.

left Trevor Peacock and Carmen Rodriguez in the Royal Exchange Theatre production of *Death of a Salesman*, Manchester, 1985.

below John Cagan, Robert McIntosh and Graham McTavish in the Dundee Rep production of *Death of a Salesman*, 1990.

right Rosalind Bennett, Natalie Abbott and Kim Benson in the Royal Exchange Theatre production of *The Crucible*, Manchester, 1990.

below The cast of the Royal Academy of Music operatic version of *The Crucible*, London, 1990.

left Maryann Plunkett
and Frank Converse in
the Long Wharf
Theatre production of
The Crucible, New
Haven, Connecticut,
1989.

below Zoë Wanamaker
and Tom Wilkinson in
the National Theatre
production of *The
Crucible*, London,
1990.

Pat Hingle and Arthur Kennedy in the original production of *The Price*, New York, 1968.

Nick Simons, Ric Morgan and Arnold Yarrow in the Dukes Theatre production of *The Price*, Lancaster, 1990.

Marjorie Yates in the Young Vic production of *The Price*, London, 1990.

Bob Peck, Alan MacNaughtan and David Calder in the Young Vic production of *The Price*.

little society there. It destroys their protection. And there is a political side to it, too, because we were in the middle the McCarthy period, the so-called Congressional investigations of the Left in this country. The idea of a person who informs on his former associates and friends was in the air and I was very much opposed to it. So that's in the play, too. You see at some point, particularly when he is about to put the coin in the telephone to call the Immigration Department and inform on the two young illegal immigrants he's been hiding, that's an option he accepts for himself. He is going to cross over; he is going to turn against his community because that's in him. The most important thing for him is his own instinctive need. He is not a very nice fellow but I think humanity is enlarged by knowing this man and what he did far more than if he were a careful little fellow who didn't go over the edge like that. There is also, in a perverse way, something fascinating about somebody who pursues his obsession, right down to the end. That's the engine of that play. The idea of a man fulfilling his destiny is absolutely compelling. For me the play represented an experiment. I wanted to see whether I could write a play with one single arch instead of three acts in which it rises to some kind of a crescendo before the curtain comes down, then another crescendo before the curtain comes down again, then finally an explosion before the curtain comes down for good. I wanted to have one long line with one explosion, which is rather the Greek way. We have all forgotten that the Greek plays were all one-act plays, a continuous action. I just aesthetically liked the idea. It was simpler and more direct. But also, when I heard this story for the first time it seemed so perfect the way it was made, I didn't want to play around with it. On the one hand, it was obvious, it was obvious that Eddie Carbone was going to get in trouble if he kept doing what he was doing, but, on the other hand, he was so obsessed he couldn't stop it, nobody could stop it. It was obvious to everyone around him that the trouble was coming. And it came, so it was a play with no surprise really. One knew in the beginning more or less what was going to happen by the end and I liked that a lot because what was really involved was not *what* was going to happen but *how* it was going to happen, which is a much stronger way of telling a tale.

But there are two versions of the play. I wrote it originally as a one-act play, then Peter Brook wanted to do it the following season in London and by then I had learned one thing in watching it and that was that I had not really sufficiently allowed into the play the viewpoint of the two women. So I added material which strengthened their roles. Also, I guess in the final version Eddie is closer to being a suicide than in the first. What I was after was that the audience should achieve self-knowledge. They might want Eddie to realise what has happened but I wanted them, as a result of experiencing the play, to understand where it had gone wrong, how it had gone wrong, even though I think that, implicitly, Eddie knows. It's this understanding that gives us importance, gives a human being importance, gives someone who is watching it the feeling that life is not just a lot of chaotic impulses pushing us this way, pushing us that way, most of them unfulfilled. Most of the time nothing happens that we want to happen, or too much happens. In this play it begins here and ends over there and it's a pleasure to see that even though it involves terrible pain and anxiety, what we usually think of as negative elements, they may be the lasting ones.

I wrote that play in 1955 and about seven years later a marvellous production was done with Robert Duval playing Eddie. I went down there one day and saw it and loved it. I thought it was marvellous. Then I went back again and Duval had gone; an Italian actor had taken his place. He told me the following story. This was a small theatre and with about three hundred seats he could see everyone out there; they were right at his feet. And one evening, when the audience had gone, one man was left who was in tears and he saw him and the guy looked like an old Italian labourer, with his heavy shoes on and work clothes. Well, he thought nothing of it but about three or four days later he was taking his bows and he sees the old guy there again, and again he was weeping. And he thought, I really ought to go over and talk to this man, it's interesting to come back twice in the same week; but he didn't. About a week later he looked out and there that guy was again, so this time he went out and he talked with him. The audience had left the theatre and he said, 'Why do you keep coming back here?' He said, 'Oh, I knew that family'. Of course I invented this family but he knew this family. 'Really?' He said, 'Oh yes, they live in the Bronx', which is a part of New York I have had no experience with. 'And it's all true. That's exactly the way it happened, except the end, the end was different'. 'What was the end like?' 'Well, at the end, in real life, the girl waited for Eddie to have his nap and then she went in and stabbed him through the heart'. I thought, God, I'm not sure I wouldn't have used that if I had heard of it.

Richard Eyre

Artistic Director, the National Theatre

To grow up in the 50s was to be willingly, indeed eagerly, colonised by American culture: rock and roll, jazz, movies, fiction – even the theatre. It wasn't just that it was something other, something not British, it was simply better than anything we had. We invoked a litany of secular saints – Elvis, Buddy Holly, Jerry Lee Lewis, Little Richard, Fats Domino, Charlie Parker, Miles Davis, John Coltrane, Billy Holliday, Brando, James Dean, Grace Kelly, Ava Gardner, Marilyn Monroe, J. D. Salinger, Kerouac, The Beat Poets, Saul Bellow, Norman Mailer, Tennessee Williams . . . and Arthur Miller. Few have survived this 50s epiphany either in their life or their work.

Arthur Miller seemed to me to be the opposite of everything that the British Theatre in the 50s stood for. His work was ambitious, dense, political, poetic and heroic where his English counterparts seemed merely petulant. He touched the heart as well as the brain. I don't feel that the power of his work has diminished; in particular, *Death of a Salesman* and *The Crucible* seem to me as powerful fables for the twentieth century as can be found.

I am proud that the British theatre has so consistently celebrated his work in the only way that means anything to a playwright, keeping his plays in the repertoire. He has repaid the British theatre by becoming its vocal champion. He is, in every sense, a man to be listened to.

Alan Ayckbourn

Director, A View from the Bridge, *the National Theatre, February, 1987*

I've directed two of Miller's plays. The first was *The Crucible*, which I have to say, modestly, was quite a success here in Scarborough.

And then there was *A View From The Bridge* which I did at the National Theatre with Michael Gambon which was very popular indeed. I remember we rehearsed that when the snow was deep and crisp and uneven. The National Theatre had dispatched us from the greenhouse conditions of their own rehearsal rooms (overcrowding, I think) to the coldest church hall I've ever been in.

Consequently, we only rehearsed for about two hours a day or we'd have frozen to death. We didn't talk to each other much either in order to conserve energy.

But then *View*, like most of Miller's work, is so well written that, as it turned out, this was the ideal way to tackle it: swiftly – and with the minimum of irrelevant chat. All this director needed to do was keep open the lines of communication between cast and dramatist, then climb aboard and enjoy the ride. Money for old rope as they say.

With a dramatist as eloquent, coherent and technically assured as Arthur Miller – and there are few more so than he – you do well to allow him to speak for himself.

Michael Gambon

Acting in Arthur Miller's *A View from the Bridge* was rather like being on a high-speed train – a terrific sense of forward movement, with the world outside being a blur through the window. We could control the speed ourselves as an integrated group. Sometimes, when a sharp bend was coming up, we would shout: 'Hold it! Slow down or we'll come off the rails.'

Finding the accent and the costume were major factors in finding Eddie. Joan Washington, the dialect coach, lent us all tapes of *Mean Streets*, *The Godfather* and *Raging Bull* to help with the accent and we spent all our time in the canteen talking like Robert de Niro and Marlon Brando. Lindy Hemming, the costume designer, found me some wonderful heavy boots, which gave me Eddie's walk. And I used to make sure the dresser didn't take the shirt and vest away each night to wash them because the longshoreman's dirt and sweat were a help.

Like all great parts, Eddie is one you inhabit. His actions are all instinctive. He doesn't understand why he's doing what he does, and he can't express himself very clearly – so the actor playing him has to get inside him perhaps more than with other parts where the words tell the audience what the character is thinking.

It was never an easy journey, being in the play, but then of course it shouldn't be. When we got to the end (the station?) it was very peaceful and quiet with a great sense of achievement.

Christopher Hampton

When I was fifteen or sixteen, my English teacher persuaded me to enter an essay competition, the subject of which, rather grandiosely, was 'Tragedy'. The quite short list of plays he suggested we should read ended with *A View From The Bridge*, a relatively adventurous choice at the time, since not so long before, in the theatrically portentous year of 1956 to be precise, the play had fallen foul of the Lord Chamberlain, whose strictures had made it necessary to turn the Comedy Theatre into a club before Peter Brook's production could be displayed to the public. Another book on the list was the recently published *The Death of Tragedy* by George Steiner, an exuberant and wide-ranging survey of the topic, which arrived at the conclusion (and here I oversimplify) that for a variety of reasons including the decay of religious belief and the shadow of the Holocaust, tragedy was no longer possible. This was perhaps my first experience of what was to become a familiar pattern: a critic argues a passionate and authoritative case for, let us say, the second-rateness of Shakespeare, the demise of the Novel or even, latterly, the perfect irrelevance of the author except insofar as he or she provides fodder for the dazzling insights or profound ruminations of the critic; all of which may be entertaining enough in its own right, but collapses like a pack of cards in the face of a page of *King Lear* or a couple of paragraphs by V. S. Naipaul. I read *The Death of Tragedy*, very likely in the school library, and found it immensely stimulating and convincing; then I went home and read *A View From The Bridge*. If I vividly remember the contours of my room in a flat temporarily rented by my parents (street and town I can scarcely recall), it is no doubt because I read Arthur Miller's play in that room. In short, the corpse, whose obsequies had been so eloquently performed by Professor Steiner, suddenly sat up.

Not long after this came the movie, black and white, directed by Sidney Lumet, which I watched, alone and enthralled, in a cinema in Richmond, now defunct or twinned. No doubt for some entirely fortuitous contractual reason, it never seems to be shown on British television, but I can still see, across nearly thirty years, the incoherent anguish of Raf Vallone and the frightened eyes of Maureen Stapleton, whose performance was heartbreakingly sympathetic, without being in the least ingratiating.

Time burnishes these memories and adolescence is notoriously more disposed to emotional surrender than to discrimination; as an adult I was dismayed to find that *A View From The Bridge* was far from universally admired. People (or John Lahr, to be more exact) spoke of 'turgid naturalism' and there seemed a general consensus (contradictory to Lahr's lazy assertion) that the Lawyer/Chorus, Mr Alfieri, was in some way an aesthetic misjudgement. I can remember anxiously rereading the play in the light of these criticisms, but my admiration remained undented. Alfieri seems to me an entirely justifiable link between the audience and the world of the play; some plays require narrators, Choruses, persons who will intercede in ways necessary to the audience's complete understanding. If memory serves, the film omitted the choric aspect of the piece: but this only goes to prove it is a quintessentially theatrical device – and the two scenes in which Eddie goes to visit Alfieri are among the finest in the play, providing an indispensable glimpse of Eddie's baffled dealings with a world of authority and abstract theory. 'You mean to tell me that there's no law that a guy which he ain't right can go to work and marry a girl and . . . ?'

This leads me to another lesson I absorbed from the play at a time when I was trying to decide whether I could possibly find a way of writing for the theatre myself. Most of the admired playwrights of the day (generally admired, as well as admired by me) had an unmistakable personal style, a voice of their own. Clearly this was a desirable, not to say unavoidable phenomenon. But the language of Eddie Carbone, the language of Alfieri pointed in a slightly different direction. For here was a dramatist whose respect for his characters was so absolute, that he paid them the ultimate tribute of allowing them – seventeenth-century Puritans or Brooklyn longshoremen – not simply the dramatist's voice but their own individual turn of phrase, thus granting them a more authentic presence and a fuller life. This is not a matter I have ever seen discussed in a review, but it seemed to me a consideration very close to the heart of our profession.

Finally, in 1987, some twenty-five years after my first encounter with the play, I saw it in Alan Ayckbourn's production at the National

Theatre, with Michael Gambon, Elizabeth Bell and Susan Sylvester. My ear lacks the experience to discern whether the Brooklyn-Sicilian accents were accurate or whether they were (as Arthur Miller said of the 1956 London production) 'an accent never heard on earth before': it scarcely matters. For here was a magnificent ensemble, dominated by Gambon's towering performance; and here, one after another, were the familiar scenes: Eddie's fear of Catherine finding a job, the singing of 'Paper Doll', Beatrice warning Catherine, the boxing match, the raising of the chair, Eddie's discovery of the lovers, the reckoning with Beatrice and the sickening lurch of the climax. And, miraculously, all this added up to one of that handful of revelatory evenings that rewards the life-long theatregoer. I was profoundly shaken and exhilarated; and the ghost of my fifteen-year-old self put in a posthumous claim for vindication.

I have chosen to write about this play in particular solely because of the personal circumstances which made it of special importance to me: there are a number of other Arthur Miller plays I could equally profitably have considered. In this century and, come to think of it, in most centuries, there are very few playwrights of which this can be said. Salutations!

Arvin Brown

Director, A View from the Bridge, *Long Wharf Theatre, New Haven, 1981*

One chilly fall night during the rehearsals of my 1981 revival of *A View from the Bridge* I went to dinner in Brooklyn with Tony Lo Bianco, the Eddie Carbone of that production. Tony's uncle lived two blocks from where Arthur Miller had set his play, and Tony wanted me to ingest the atmosphere, along with a meal that went on for hours and featured every dish his aunt had ever learned to cook. I will never forget that apartment, nor will Arthur Miller ever let me, for it was exactly the apartment he describes as the home of the Carbones. When Tony's aunt filled in her husband's stories with all the neighborhood detail, I heard Beatrice and Eddie at the table. And after dinner, as Tony and I explored the streets around the tenement, people appeared in doorways and on stoops to smile at the local boy who had become a star, but who respected the code by which he had been raised as if he had never left home. Grey-suited elders, dining in a restaurant, were not to be greeted unless they indicated they wanted acknowledgement; otherwise Tony's celebrity might detract from their status and face would be lost. A certain dignity was everything in that world of the docks, and it wasn't hard to imagine that the penalty for betrayal in the 80s would be the same as it had been thirty years earlier: humiliation and death.

I have directed a number of the recent American revivals of Arthur Miller's plays, and, during the preproduction and rehearsals for each one, I have had experiences like the evening in Brooklyn to confirm Arthur's uncanny ability to capture a specific time and place and thereby give a concrete shape to his moral preoccupations. For the Long Wharf 1990 production of *The Crucible* I spent some time in Salem, and while I had been warned that I would look long and hard to spot even a shadow of the seventeenth century, I found once again that Arthur's imagination had caught a scent in the air, and that the spirits of his Proctors, his Hale, his Parris, were everywhere. This dark, small bedroom could easily be the one where Betty lay in bed possessed; that house on the hill could be where Rebecca Nurse's loving family reburied her after stealing her body from its witch's grave. In Salem, I discovered that a man of conscience named John Proctor had truly existed, a simple but intelligent farmer who had grown slowly and reluctantly into his heroism, and who had disturbed his own time as much as he troubles ours. Arthur had got him right and had been able to reproduce with total conviction the world that had contained him. Whatever its enigmatic mysteries, Arthur's Salem happened, and in its reality lies the parallels he sought for his portrait of our age.

Specifics of time and place are building blocks for directors and actors, but people in the theatre also love a plot (although they only admit this sometimes, to close friends) and storytelling is another underappreciated aspect of Arthur's art. When Arthur's plays are done with skill and respect, audiences re-experience their childhood hunger to know what happens next. Events in Arthur's plays are startling, yet inevitable. We toured *A View from the Bridge* from New England through Florida before our Broadway run, and nowhere did we encounter an audience too sophisticated to keep from gasping audibly when Eddie kisses his rival Rodolpho on the mouth. No matter that we have seen for years on our stages every kind of sexual encounter; that moment, charged with one man's attempt to humiliate and castrate another, shocks and threatens an audience as few theatrical moments have ever been able to do. The trial in *The Crucible* contains in a single scene a perfectly constructed and complete courtroom drama, as the clash of spiritual belief, political ambition, and sexual hysteria creates a spin of events that leaves the audience breathless. Arthur helps his director and his actors rediscover the pure joy of narrative and reminds us that one of the compulsions that propelled us all into the theatre was the desire to tell a good story and tell it as well as or better than it had ever been told before.

If narrative excitement has been diminished in much contemporary theatre, another pleasure has become so devalued it is practically furtive: that of living for two or three hours in a moral universe. Arthur believes that human actions have a certain ordered consequence, that bad deeds will out, that man pays for his evil in countless unforeseen but inevitable ways, and is even occasionally rewarded for his good by some hope of spiritual well-being. Self-knowledge is all. Eddie Carbone has none, and is therefore destroyed; John Proctor discovers his, and though he loses his life, he regains his soul. I watched audience after audience come to our 1985 revival of *All My Sons*, fresh from the battlefields of Wall Street. Filled to the brim with news of Ivan Boesky, and junk bonds, and secret arms to the Contras, they were desperate to believe that there might be a world where pragmatic self-interest did not hold absolute sway over human conscience and responsibility, where if a Joe Keller sold faulty airplane parts in war time, he would find a terrible retribution when peace came back once more.

I've done five Arthur Miller plays, and every one of them has been like a gulp of fresh air, a respite from moral and political relativism that clears the head and makes breathing easier. Arthur's is an American sensibility, increasingly threatened on all sides, and I take a welcome pride in this commitment.

Tony Lo Bianco

I first met Arthur Miller in 1954, when I went to the Dramatic Workshop, an acting school in New York. He was teaching a playwrighting class and inspiring us, giving me a foundation and purpose for being in the theatre.

A View from the Bridge was a play that I loved from the first moment I read it. In summer stock, I got to perform the role of Eddie Carbone. I knew then that Mr Miller's words were my thoughts, which made it inevitable that I should speak them. One night, at a performance, the power and reality of the play struck so deeply that a young lady ran from the theare, sobbing, at Eddie's death, and could not be consoled until I spoke to her after the show. I promised myself that one day, I would play that role on Broadway.

When the Off-Broadway production was planned in the early 1960s, I saw Mr Miller and told him I wanted to play Eddie. He thought I was too young. I told him I was not. He suggested I play Marco. I told him I did not want to play Marco, I wanted to play Eddie.

In 1981, my friend, the wonderful director Arvin Brown, and I put on a production of *A View from the Bridge* at his Long Wharf Theatre in New Haven, Connecticut. Arthur Miller and I met again in his home for dinner. We spoke of Eddie Carbone as I lay on the living room floor. Arthur told me of the nakedness of the man and how out-front he was: a man with no cover, a good man, trapped viscerally by his emotions. His conversation was organic and compelling. He thought that commitment to the role was imperative, and asked me if I was ready to throw myself on the knife.

In 1982–83, when that production moved to Broadway, America's greatest playwright and I walked down the street one night after dinner, looking up at the marquee of the Ambassador Theatre. It had been a long trip, but it had also been a promise I had to keep – one that has given me the greatest fulfillment of my theatrical career.

Bigsby: *A View from the Bridge* was produced in 1955, but it was going to be another nine years before a new play of yours would be staged in New York, or indeed anywhere in America. Why the nine year silence?

Miller: Well, I don't know. I wrote *The Misfits* in that period. That took forever to get on. Shepherding that through production must have taken – oh, the whole thing must have taken three years – which is not abnormal with a film, if you get as involved as I was. And the theatre was changing in a way that kept me off. It was the time when the theatre audience began to fragment, at least in New York which was where I had always worked; it simply exploded. Some of them, the more hip and alienated, went to Off-Broadway, which was then beginning. Indeed *The Crucible* was produced a second time Off-Broadway after it had all but failed the first time. On Broadway the audience was self-satisfied, quite rich, not really interested in what I was interested in. And I felt that I was no longer part of that theatre, if I ever had been. So I was really trying to find my bearings and I simply couldn't find my way through the new American morass. All people were concerned with was getting rich as quickly as possible. I think that what happened was that the morale of the war time period and, paradoxically enough, the morale of the Depression period had finally vanished. What was left behind was simply opportunity without social concern. The idea of a community had vanished. And it wasn't just me. Tennessee Williams, who had a quite different orientation toward things, felt the same way about it: people weren't caring that much any more about the feelings that we were dealing with. They were being ironical, distant, rather cold, unmoved about life, and you either wrote that kind of play or you weren't welcome, it seemed, and so the welcome wasn't there. That's basically why I think I moved into film where there seemed less hostility.

Bigsby: So you felt you had lost an audience?

Miller: I was just out of synch with the whole country, I think. I would have had a long period of that type no matter, whether I'd married Marilyn or not. I simply couldn't find a way into the country any. more. This was the great American century, or so it was declared by Henry Luce. It is what somebody has called the twenty year century.

I never believed it would last. I didn't believe in the values that they were espousing. I didn't think it had a future and I thought we would pay for it, one way or another, which we did in Vietnam. And I couldn't begin to speak of it. It was as though I were living in a different world. I couldn't speak of it as an artist. I didn't know how to do it, quite frankly. At the beginning of that nine-year period, I had the sense that the whole thing wasn't worth the candle. Also I had a sense that the time had gotten away from me, that I didn't really understand or sympathise with what was going on here. Not that I knew very much more about what was going on in any other place; I had just seen that it had all become rather pointless, which indeed I think it was, in a way. There was a lot of milling about in that time, and I'm glad I didn't write. Well, I did write a lot of stuff and tore it up, and I'm not unhappy that I didn't turn out a lot of stuff just to keep my name in front of the public, which I could have been tempted to do, and probably would have done, incidentally, had I had a theatre. If I'd had any kind of a company of actors and a couple of directors, you know, an active theatre, where you didn't have to produce on the so-called grand scale for Broadway where everything costs a quarter of a million dollars, I probably would have written and completed a lot more, just sowed it into the hopper to see what would happen; but production was very formal and you were risking the fortunes of people with money.

Bigsby: Why not Off-Broadway?

Miller: Well, by that time, it had started, to be sure, and I finally did do that with the Lincoln Centre. I grasped that opportunity because it seemed to be a way that I could operate. Indeed a play like *Incident at Vichy* I probably would have thought of but never written on Broadway, because there would have been no place for that. But they came to me – the Lincoln Centre people – and they said, how about another one. Well, I knew all the actors by this time and we were beginning to get the feeling that a real theatre was starting to emerge. As a matter of fact, many of the actors in that company later became great stars: Faye Dunaway, Jason Robards, Jon Voigt. Everybody said that company was terrible, but it wasn't. There were more future stars in that company than any company in the city of New York for a hundred years. So I did *Incident at Vichy* because they were all saying, 'Well, come on. You have a home'. Had that continued, which it didn't, or had I had that in, say, 1958 or something, it would have been a different story. I am quite convinced of that. I'm very much moved by an environment. I've always hated Broadway theatre. I don't know why a play has to run two years. If you look back, it's so stupid, it's beyond all belief. If Ibsen ran ten days in Germany, that was an event. If Chekhov ran three weeks in Moscow, that was something. They made their reputations and their livelihoods as much from the printed versions of the plays, as from the productions. But on Broadway you have to have people come every night for two years if you are going to call it a success. I never liked it, and gradually grew really to despise it. Then again the nature of the audience changed. They seemed to be absolutely brainless. They didn't share any of my concerns. It started to become a musical comedy theatre. All of which shouldn't have mattered, and wouldn't have mattered if I had had some support around me. So I finally found myself in a little corner writing for myself. I wrote a lot of stuff. Finally, I didn't know whom I was talking to. It was as simple as that. Then I wrote *The Misfits*, and somehow I saw a way back into some kind of an arena that mattered to me, with a mode of speech that could connect with a bigger public, not the theatre public. After all, that's a movie, and was written for the great unwashed, everybody who was out there. And that sort of broke the ice a little. But, I don't know, I go long periods without being able to finish anything.

Bigsby: Do you feel now that the gap between yourself and the public for which you're writing has closed at all?

Miller: I think so, yes. This is my illusion, anyway. I rather think that there is a public that I can address. It's just that I ceased giving a damn about it, finally. I suppose that relaxation helped.

Bigsby: Your work in films hasn't always been entirely happy has it? There was a script that you wrote that was never made into a film because of changes that they wanted you to make.

Miller: *The Hook* you mean?

Bigsby: *The Hook.*

Miller: Yes. *The Hook* is one good reason why at that time I never went back to pictures excepting that one film, *The Misfits*, which I could do fairly independently.

Bigsby: What happened with *The Hook?*

Miller: Well, I wrote *The Hook* based on my life in Brooklyn and my knowledge of the waterfront there which was run by a corrupt union whose chief went to prison for a long term not a few years after I got wind of it. It was about longshoremen who were being victimised by this gangster union in combination with the ship owners. I wrote it as a film because I thought it would be best as a film – an original film – meaning that it was not derived from a book. We started to try to get backing for it in Hollywood and got Columbia Pictures interested in it. Then Harry Cohn at Columbia decided that it would be the better wisdom if he asked the FBI what they thought about this film, quite simply because the blacklisting was beginning in Hollywood. I wasn't on it. Neither, at the time, was Kazan, who was supposed to direct this film. And Cohn brought in the FBI man from the area, in Los Angeles, as well as the Head of the Unions there, a man named Roy Brewer, who was appointed, incidentally, by President Reagan, to a very important non-job in the Federal Government. And they decided, first of all, that the whole picture, in which I showed union racketeering, was false, invented by me for radical reasons, and that, furthermore, it would be dangerous to produce this picture because we were in the Korean War. They thought it would create chaos on the piers and our war materials would not flow in an orderly fashion to the troops, so they made a simple request, through Harry Cohn, that I change the scripts so that all the gangsters would become communists. Well, I knew the two communists on the whole of the Brooklyn waterfront and I explained to them that if I did that I would never be able to walk on a Brooklyn waterfront again because I would be pushed into the water. I would be laughed into the water. So that was the end of that. I simply had to withdraw the script. There was no way to do it.

Bigsby: But what you've just described sounds remarkably like a film that Kazan did eventually make, *On The Waterfront*.

Miller: Well that was later after his problem with the Un-American Activities Committee.

Bigsby: Is there a direct relationship between your script and that one?

Miller: I have no way of knowing. Of course they are both waterfront pictures. The one succeeded the other but they were quite different pictures.

Brian Cox

When in 1986 I was asked to direct a diploma performance at the Moscow Arts Theatre School, the choice of play that came very quickly to mind was Arthur Miller's *The Crucible*. An allegory of the McCarthy hearings, it stood equally as an allegory of the Stalinist purges in Russia.

The following year I was commissioned to write a book about the experience. In reliving what was for me a major private and political awakening and chronicling events which had notes not reverberated since childhood, again it was to Miller I turned.

The influence was *Timebends*, his autobiography. To carry his ideas and passionate beliefs, Miller creates organic structures, gossamer in appearance, but with a durability to support monumental themes. In *Timebends* his structure is memory and those memories demonstrate the philosophic pattern of his life. Of course, these memories are selective and the process of tapping and shaping them on the printed page may appear to some to be artificial and self-serving but for me the hidden Arthur Miller comes through, warts and all.

While reading *Timebends*, I was also presented with a copy of Elia Kazan's autobiography, *A Life*. Both books inevitably cover similar historical ground; the two men's lives were very much connected, particularly in the early 1950s. It was fascinating to compare the separate views. The difference could not be more extreme: Kazan, while being fond of Miller, at the same time regarded him as priggish and somewhat pompous: Miller, on the other hand, was compassionate and recognized Kazan's great worth as an artist. The split between these two men was caused by Kazan's naming of names before the House Un-American Activities Committee. Nevertheless after a period of time he felt that Kazan's talent as a director must be fully acknowledged in the forming of the possible American National Theatre at the Lincoln Centre in New York.

A further difference that epitomises the two men was the abandonment of Miller's screenplay *The Hook*, about a longshoreman's attempt to overthrow gangsterism on the New York waterfront, which Kazan was to direct. In Kazan's book, he fails to understand why Miller withdrew the project. He merely excuses it as a male menopausal crisis, as resulting from the fact that Miller had fallen in love with Marilyn Monroe and perhaps didn't want to return to California. But the real truth of the matter was that the project that Miller wished to see realised had been compromised. Harry Cohn, who was to produce the film, brought in Roy Brewer, head of all the Hollywood unions, to advise; he had read the script, told Cohn it was a lie and said that if the film was made he would pull out all the projectionists across the country on strike. Cohn demanded that the union crooks and the gangster protectors in the story should be communists, not mafiosi as in fact. Miller until this point had travelled part of the way down the road of rewrites but on Cohn's request could proceed no further and so withdrew his script.

It is quite clear from reading both books that the self-server, and confessedly so, is Kazan. He paints a picture of Iago-like honesty and seems to embrace a code of end-justifies-the-means. At the conclusion of *The Hook* incident, Kazan went to see Harry Cohn:

'"I knew it," he (Cohn) said, "Miller is a Communist." I protested that I didn't think so. Cohn said, "Then tell me what other explanation there could be for what he did. First, he can't face any more questions. Second, he sees that the movie will not say what he hoped it would say. It all figures." I told him I didn't agree. "I could tell just by looking at him," Cohn said. "He's still one of them." "What about me?" I said. "You're just a godhearted whore like me," he said. "We'll find something else to do together."'

In reading *Timebends*, the opposite is apparent. Miller was, and still is, a man who lives and works towards the reconciliation of the private and public life, who awkwardly perhaps treads a path of principle and vision.

On his way to research *The Crucible* at Salem, Massachusetts, Miller visited Kazan in Connecticut. Kazan confided that he would name names at his coming appearance at the HUAC. Miller writes in *Timebends* that, as he drove away from the house:

'I was carrying several contradictions at the same time, my brother-love as painfully alive in me as it had ever been, alongside the undeniable fact that Kazan might have sacrificed me had it been necessary. In a sense I went naked to Salem, still unable to accept the most common experience of humanity, the shifts of interest that turned loving husbands and wives into stony enemies, loving parents into indifferent supervisors or even exploiters of their children, and so forth. As I already knew from my reading, that was the real story of ancient Salem Village, what they called then the breaking of charity.'

Bigsby: Can you tell me why you have so seldom turned to film?

Miller: I think it's basically that the writer can't control film, where you can a play, and it gives you a feeling of futility therefore when you start working on something in which you feel so provisional. You are dependent on the whim of a director and that takes the heat out of me. I don't know how anybody can do it for very long without getting depressed.

Bigsby: You've said that a screenwriter on location is like a guilty conscience arriving on the scene.

Miller: Yes, well he's walking round there reminding people what the original vision was when nobody can remember. The truth is very simple, really. The picture is basically a director's work and the screenplay is one of several elements going into that work. The forces are going toward the director and away from the screenplay and away from the cinematographer and away from the actor. The director has to make it all coherent. It's directly the opposite of the theatre in which all the forces are going toward the stage play. There, ideally speaking, the director is trying to interpret it, as is the actor and the scene designer. And if there's music, it all goes to enhance the interpretation of the stage play.

Bigsby: So what is the role of the writer in the cinema?

Miller: He is really only one of four or five different elements. He's more important, perhaps, in that he gives the whole a certain structure but, apart from that, his vision is severely limited by the director's use of it. The director can change anything in the film simply by casting. The stage actor does not dominate the play – at least not my plays – in the way that a screen actor dominates the screen and the audience's consciousness. The audience only knows what the actor is telling them and what the actor is saying becomes his own. A good performer eats the screenplay. He makes it his own and there's nothing left of the autonomy of the written word. It becomes part of the actor's image. Now that's fine; that's the way it ought to be. I have no complaint about it. It's just that I don't want to be part of it. It just doesn't suit my temperament and I think that this is why writers in general, that is writers from another medium like the novel or the play, either overtly or secretly feel a little bit ashamed to be involved in the movies. It's because the art, in the literary sense, is being prostituted for another. It is being used instead of standing there as some kind of a unified choice of the writer.

Bigsby: You once suggested that screenwriting doesn't require you to write very well.

Miller: It doesn't. Some of the best screenwriters are not necessarily very good writers, that is in their use of the English language. When I was a boy there were two fellows, twins, living on our block in Brooklyn, who never finished high school. They were very good football players but they weren't very much good at anything else and they went to Hollywood and became two of the best screenwriters in the history of Hollywood. They wrote *Casablanca*, among other things. But those boys wouldn't have called themselves writers in the conventional sense of the word. They were proud to be, and rightly so, writers of screenplays, of stuff for actors on the screen to say, and they would have been amused and aghast at my making any complaint about all this because they had been brought up in the art of the movies. It was just a different kind of hearing.

Bigsby: Presumably the process of film-making tends to be one of paring back language?

Miller: It's skinned alive. You've got to do that. If you don't do it, it's probably not as good a movie. This is a totally different medium: it has only a tenuous connection with conventional ideas of what literature is and what writing is. The screenwriter's fundamental contribution is the organisation of the material. He is making the story in blocks. I'd liken it to the Bayeux Tapesty, a series of pictures, stills, of the invasion of Britain by the Normans. Somebody laid out a scenario for that before they put all those stitches in. He was a screenwriter.

Bigsby: He had a storyboard.

Miller: He had a storyboard. That's what that is. That's a movie.

Bigsby: But 'story' has never been the most important element in your work has it?

Miller: No. It's important, but it's really only a means to an end. In a movie, it's the end. I think it's all got to do with the nature of film. It resembles, as has been often said, dream, and that means that the dreamer is practically supine and has no powers over what he is looking at. He is passive in the face of the dream and the dream is fundamentally, images. There's an occasional word in a dream, or a few words, but you don't need many. Indeed, sometimes people speak in dreams but no words come out. It's as though the sound track is cut off. I think movies are attempting to reproduce the dream situation.

Bigsby: But images are also important in the theatre.

Miller: Yes. It's just a question of emphasis but the emphasis is everything. The emphatic truth in the theatre is that the words are carrying the story. They are carrying everything, more or less. We are waiting for the actor to *say* something. On the screen you are waiting for him to *do* something and that change of emphasis is vital. If you watch a movie carefully and really begin to become conscious of how much time is taken up with silent images and how much with speech, you will be amazed at how little of the time is taken up with speech. If it is, as I say, an attempt to reproduce dreams, that's as it should be.

Bigsby: Presumably there is also a different sense of space in films from that which operates in theatre?

Miller: Well, clearly, yes, and that has to do with the editing. The audience in the theatre edits, to a certain extent, what they see. When you have two/three/four people on stage you have to decide who to focus on. In a movie that's all decided for you. The close up and the cut make you listen to this one and not the other one. And the relationship between the foreground and the background is vital in film. It's less so in the theatre. Everything in the theatre is in the foreground. You try to see to that. There's a vital triangle of interest in the centre of the stage, that spreads backwards and widens out, and anything of importance has to be within that space. You can't be putting somebody in a corner and ask him to deliver a key line. That's all done on the screen with a lens; they do it for you. You are made more passive in the movies. There's no doubt about it. That's why you can tolerate bad movies more than you can bad plays. A bad play irritates you because it requires some effort: you have to interpret language which relies on a far more developed part of the brain than visual impulses. A baby of two months of age can discern images and be affected by them. It takes a long time before language can do that to a human being. So we are using a higher part of the brain when we have to listen to language. You only have to sit there to enjoy a movie. It is a seemingly more contemporary form because it doesn't require active participation.

Bigsby: But couldn't you argue that in theatre you have to do in words what you can do more easily and just as subtly perhaps in film?

Miller: I would question the word 'subtly'. You see, I think that language is the most subtle thing we've got, the most subtle means of expression. I don't think images are as subtle as that. It takes longer to convey something in images, oddly enough, than with a few words. Those images have to be carefully composed and that takes longer to do than it does to say something. Any relationship between people, I think, takes longer to do on screen if you want concision and subtlety.

Bigsby: How far is the importance of the actor in the cinema a factor of the size of the image on the screen?

Miller: Overwhelmingly. That nostril is six feet tall. It's another reason why the word loses some of it's importance because a shift in the gaze of the actor on a screen that size tells you more than anything he's going to say. That's why casting in the movies is really the most important part of the picture. The picture lives or dies the day you cast an actor. If he's right for what you want to express, you're a long way towards your goal. If he's wrong, you're probably never going to make it, no matter what you do. You're working against a human being.

Bigsby: Does film have a bias in favour of realism?

Miller: Absolutely. Film, reduces everything to what it is. On stage, things can take on a metaphoric meaning or significance. They can have an implicit poetic quality. On the screen, it seems to me, they become more of what they are in real life, the longer you look at them.

Bigsby: And this is why American actors are particularly well adapted to film.

Miller: Sure. I think it may well be that that whole style of acting came out of the movies, rather than the stage. The movie has been the dominant form in America for ever, not just in recent times. The stage has been an elite form at least since the mid twenties. The masses didn't go to the theatre; the acting, consequently, suited the climate in which it existed.

Bigsby: But isn't that bias in favour of realism, which you find in the American cinema, equally strong in American theatre, too?

Miller: Yes, our form is realism, there's no doubt about it. It's the native American form. It's partly, I think, because theatre, at least in the last half century anyway, has been minimally based on poetry and language and mostly on street realism. The British actors, and to some degree the French and the German, spring out of the classics. That's what their training is, so they come with a different tongue into the theatre. They are capable of handling poetic language and taking on a style of behaviour, a stance and bodily movements which are far from realistic. Our actors are unhappy with it. It doesn't suit the democratic tastes of the country and I think it has got to do with democracy, which is a style, amongst other things, and not just a political philosophy. They're supposed to come on the stage and look like anybody and behave like anybody. We've got a classical American speech which has never been aristocratic. It's been essentially middle class.

Bigsby: Isn't there a curious paradox, though, in that if the cinema favours realism, the process of making a film, from an actor's point of view, works against that. You shoot the end before the beginning – you shoot things out of sequence – and that must make it difficult to build a role. In the theatre, despite its obvious artifice, it is sequential, and presumably, therefore, easier to build a kind of realism into character.

Miller: You know, the shooting out of a sequence, despite the complaints of actors, doesn't affect it all that much because the imagination is powerful. I remember Clark Gable telling me that in the old days, when he worked for MGM, he used to start a picture every three weeks. Every third Monday he'd be there but since he'd been at a party at the end of the previous picture he had usually been unconscious for about two days before he arrived on the set and he didn't even know what the hell the movie was that he was doing. They'd give him safari clothes and tell him, 'You're in Africa'. Then he'd look around and say, 'Where's the girl?' 'She's over there.' 'What's her name?' 'Judy.' 'Oh! Hi Judy!' and 'OK, what do I say here? Where am I?' 'Well, you're in a tent and it's raining.' 'OK, who talks first?' That's the way it went. Even at the end of the movie he didn't know how he got there, why they were there. Yet if you look at the picture, it made perfect sense. It didn't bother him. He never thought that you had to make things in order. As long as the scene made sense, of some kind, within itself, he was perfectly happy with it.

Bigsby: There is another fundamental difference between theatre and film, surely, and that is that while there are many productions of a play it would be a fool who wants you to remake *Casablanca*.

Miller: Sure, right. It's words again. You see that image is fixed. You can't inflect it any differently. You can't reinterpret that story. In the theatre you can bend words, you can inflect them differently, get different interpretations out of the same sentence. Both theatre and film tell stories. Both come off a typewriter. But they are very different. They're very different arts. And they often forget that when they try and adapt stage plays for the movies. When they horse around with a play and try to make it into a filmic event, namely by breaking out of scenes, expanding them into outdoor scenes, cutting and splicing dialogue, they suffer. It doesn't work. Where they attack the play intensively, rather than trying to extend it out, they succeed more, and it may be that my plays are so integrated that you can't break them up. It takes longer to do the same thing, that's all. One of the best productions of a play of mine was *All My Sons* done on American public television a few years ago. It was marvellous. They didn't change a line. They used the camera brilliantly. It was all in one place. There was no real shifting around and you didn't object for a second. It didn't seem like a stage play at all. It seemed like a film and yet nothing was changed. In the original movie version of *Death of a Salesman*, though, they moved it all over New York City. As a result they had to cut out pieces of dialogue and then create filmic devices to bring them back in, because the story is so intense you can't drop it out. It's a botch, that's all, because of some convention that you can't do a play intensively. If Willy Loman comes back from work, you've got to show him on a subway, for some reason, I don't know why, but that's what they think they have to do. So that wastes five minutes. He's got to take a little walk down the street and meet somebody when there is absolutely no point to it. It's just that they want to vary the scene. It's stupefying and they are all doomed to fail. You can make a different kind of film if you retain the intensity. It will work, most of the time, if the play is good. If the play involves too much dialogue, though, then I would say you've got a problem. I love films made as films. I think that that's terrific. I enjoy movies, but they have got to be conceived as movies. I have always said that I don't know why they have to adapt plays. The movie is more like a novel than a play in that novels usually find it easier to shift scenes around. I am not pessimistic about movies or hostile to them. I love them. But the misuse of the film is awful. Why do we have to shift focus so many times? Can't they do a scene and let us rest inside the scene and build up steam inside the scene instead of puppying all over the place? The ideal thing to me is a director writing his own screenplay or a screenplay writer directing what he's done. Then you get a unified piece of work.

Bigsby: Have you ever been tempted to do that?

Miller: I have. I should have done it but it takes a year or two to make a film. I'm not sure I'm ready to spend a year or two like that. I'd much rather write a play and figure it will stay on the stage for as long as it lives. That's good enough. Let somebody else worry about making a film of it.

Bigsby: In terms of theatre you reacted very strongly against the *avant garde* experiments of the 1960s and 70s. Why was that?

Miller: A lot of my feeling toward them was almost the resistance of someone who is observing a culture being torn apart with nothing being put in its place. So much of the acting was so terrible. You went to an *avant garde* so-called play and they couldn't act. But they could be brash and abrasive and so on and this got forgotten so that fifteen or twenty years ago I said that the problem about critics is that they have never seen anything good. I saw Sara Allgood and Barry Fitzgerald. If you see Sarah Allgood and Barry Fitzgerald you can't accept this garbage as good theatre. It's ridiculous. They wouldn't be allowed into the same theatre as those people. The standards simply got blown away. I was treated to some of this myself with a group called the Wooster Group, in New York. They did a production of *The Crucible* in which everyone spoke at a rate of speed like an automaton, and this was celebrated in the *avant garde* circles as being the wave of the future. Of course it's a form of graffiti; they simply take a work and scribble on it, like children often do, and cut up the pages and so on. It's creating nothing excepting the excuse of not being bored. You see, since you can't understand quite what the characters are saying it becomes interesting simply to try to make out what's going on. Running a phonograph record at twice the speed, as we all know, is funny, it's amusing, but what that has to do with the investigation of human beings and society escapes me.

Bigsby: But you also reacted against the absurdist drama of the 50s.

Miller: I thought it was a cop out, quite frankly. You see, at the end of absurdist drama you have to say, 'Why do you write this?' If it's all as hopeless as you are making it out to be, why bother communicating anything? How are you going to run the world at all. You see, I am the father now. It's perfectly alright to act like a kid, provided you don't drape around your shoulders the philosopher's mantle, as though you had the key to freedom. I didn't see this as having the key to freedom; I saw this as something like game playing, and that bothered me.

Bigsby: But isn't the writer always trying to shore up the world with

136

language, to create his own form for a situation where there is no form? Isn't this what Beckett was doing?

Miller: Except Beckett was a very formalistic writer. Beckett was not part of that *avant garde* at all, in my opinion. Beckett was a vaudevillian and knew all the tricks. He was technically very adept at telling jokes and using actors. This is not the same thing at all.

Bigsby: When you returned to the theatre, in 1964, it was with *After the Fall* at the Lincoln Centre, which is I suppose as close as America has got to having a National Theatre, although it patently is not that. Do you think that if you had had an institution in America like the National Theatre or the Royal Shakespeare Company or the Young Vic, that your career might have had a different shape.

Miller: I have no doubt about that. In effect one had no friends any more. Everybody was off making his career. There was no Group Theatre any more. There was no art theatre any more, that I knew about, and the morale of people had collapsed. We were part of a generation that no longer had any relevance, it seemed. And there was no way I could find a metaphor for that. I wasn't interested in simply showing man slipping on a banana so that the play could, in effect, say, well he slipped on a banana and he fell down. But beyond that it was very difficult to project any kind of significance for human beings. We were quite content with ourselves, you know: these were the Eisenhower years. He was a very nice chap, but he had left us, morally, it seemed to me, with no bearings that one could really conccive. Of course the Cold War was moving through everything, then. That was the meaning of life. The meaning of life was defeating the Russians. Well, if you can get excited about that, that's fine, but I couldn't.

Bigsby: Now, both in 1964, with *After the Fall*, and 1965, with *Incident at Vichy*, you wrote plays which were in part addressing the question of the Holocaust. It had taken a time to assimilate that kind of darkness.

Miller: Oh yes. I'm still assimilating it. You know, still, if you look at it objectively, it's simply an inexplicable human circumstance. On the other hand, if you want to be totally despairing, it's the most natural thing in the world – people killing each other for power, and out of stupid prejudice and the rest of it. But the structure of that event in the human mind was too terrible to really try to deal with, and I think by the early 60s it seemed possible to attack it from a certain angle.

Bigsby: But you had something of a problem with *After the Fall*, didn't you, in that one of the characters was based on Elia Kazan and he ended up directing it.

Miller: Well, you see by that time a decade had passed and the only hope we had at that moment was the Lincoln Centre. That was Bob Whitehead's baby and he assured me that it was really going to work, that we would get a company together, that there was funding for it and there would shortly be buildings for it and so on. And the Artistic Director that he had hooked up with was Kazan. There was no question in my mind that he was the best director in America and I simply felt that he was also the best man to have such a theatre because he had had all that experience with the Group Theatre. He had worked in a similar group and all his training years were in such a group. There was nobody better suited. In fact there was literally nobody else, in my opinion, who could possibly pull that off, and therefore the issue became do I kick over what is maybe the only possibility there will ever be in the next decade for an art theatre because of my differences with Kazan, or don't I? And I felt that I had a greater responsibility than that. I felt that I was in a situation where I would have to perpetuate a blacklist, quite frankly, if I refused him. Anyway it was undeniable in my mind that nobody was better prepared than he to run a theatre like Lincoln Centre. I hadn't even seen him in all those years, and I thought, well, do I feel that someone has a right to his artistic life or not? I still don't approve of what he did. I never have. But I understood his situation as I had that of Odets and Lee J. Cobb. You see, they were very vulnerable people. Of course I blamed them but I have to say, for good or ill, it made me more despairing and more angry at the Government. I mean, why does everybody have to be strong in order to be an artist? A lot of wonderful artists are not very strong. Why do they have to go through this hell, from their own Government, in a democratic society? I felt toward them as probably Czechs in Prague felt toward similar situations. That is, they see past the individual to the Government, toward the regime. I couldn't let myself be deflected from that.

Bigsby: How did he respond to the portrait of himself in the play?

Miller: I have never known. I have never discussed that with him because actually the basis of that character is somebody else, too. It's not quite him.

Bigsby: It's a play that seems to be a critical one in a number of ways. That's to say it seems to deal with a number of public and private issues, almost as though you were trying to come to terms with those elements in your own life. Was it psychologically an important play to you?

Miller: Tremendously, yes. You see the way I see life is that there are no public issues; they are all private issues. We have gotten divided. We are political men or private men. I can't see the separation. The President of the United States is a man to whom you are giving the key to your house. He'll come in and take your son. He comes in and takes your money. This is private business, when you decide to elect this guy as opposed to the other guy, because the one that comes into your house better be the fellow that you want to be there. So it's all one thing to me and the attempt, in *After the Fall*, was to unify both worlds, to make them one, to make an embrace that would touch the concentration camp, the Un-American Activities Committee, a sexual relationship, a marital relationship, all in one embrace, because that's really the way it is.

Bigsby: So that betrayal on one level is of a piece with betrayal on another level?

Miller: Yes.

Bigsby: Isn't there a problem of proportion there, though, the disproportion between an act of personal betrayal (in one incident a child is deceived when the family is going off to the seaside) and a public betrayal on the scale of the concentration camp.

Miller: There is, of course, a disproportion. No question about it. But the underlying principle of taking up a commitment and betraying it, if not the same, is pretty close.

Bigsby: There is a line in the play that says that we are all born after the fall, that, in other words, there is a degree to which all of us are guilty, nobody's hands are clean. But isn't that another way of saying that all our hands are innocent. In other words you have destroyed the basis of moral distinction.

Miller: No. It's quite the opposite to me. I think that the basic thrust of the play is that the enemy is innocence. That's what it's saying, in so many words. That is, until you can give up your innocence, you are very open to crime, to becoming part of the crime. The problem with crime is that the people who commit it cannot conceive themselves as the ones who committed the crime. In one way or another we are all victims, one man of his family, another man of society, another man of, whatever, and if that's going to be the limitation of the vision then we are really finished because everybody can justify anything on the basis that he is only paying back the world for what it did to him. If there is an enemy, so to speak, of man, it's the idea of innocence. Incidentally, I can't tell you how many letters I've gotten from psychoanalysts since that play was published who tell me that this probably is essentially the closest to a moral evaluation of psychoanalysis that they have ever come upon. It is an unbroken record of refusal to confront the dilemma of that play.

Bigsby: The dramatic structure itself seems to be based almost on psychoanalysis.

Miller: It is in a way, yes.

Bigsby: You have been accused in that play, though, of yourself naming names in that Kazan was partially behind one of the characters, while Marilyn Monroe was identified as another. Do you think that there is any justice in that?

Miller: Well, the only comment I can make is that I didn't read about any of this in a newspaper. This happens to be involved in some of the great struggles of my own life. If I can't refer to my own life in my own work, then I might as well give up.

Bigsby: And there is a character in the play who seems remarkably like your present wife who plays a kind of redemptive role. It's almost as though you had come to an end of a period of your life and wanted to clear the decks before moving in a new direction. Is there any sense in which you felt that to be so?

Miller: That probably is the case, yes.

Michael Blakemore

Director, After the Fall, *National Theatre Production,*
June 1990

In 1987 I was directing a new play for the Manhattan Theatre Club,
Don De Lillo's *The Day Room.* The designer was an old colleague and
friend, Hayden Griffin, like myself working in New York as a visitor,
and leading the same distinctly unglamorous life, walled up in our
basement theatre until eleven at night, then returning to a hotel room
to flick briefly through thirty indifferent TV programmes. This was the
week of technical rehearsals, and we usually kept each other company
during the dinner break. One night we had chosen a restaurant that
supplied its patrons with a tumbler of coloured crayons so that they
could doodle on the paper tablecloths between courses. Hayden idly
drew a rectangle and asked me if I knew what the Golden Mean was. I
thought I knew. Wasn't it an ideal proportion dreamt up by the ancient
Greeks, and illustrated by the shape of the old Academy movie screen?
That was true as far as it went: 1 to 1.618. Hayden then drew a vertical
line off-centre through his rectangle, creating to one side a square and
to the other a new and smaller rectangle, with the peculiar property of
having identical proportions to the first. Another line through this
second rectangle repeated this effect on a reduced scale. Theoretically
it was possible to create an infinite number of squares, all diminishing
in a spiral to an infinite point.

This spiral, rather than the original rectangle, was at the heart of the
Golden Mean. It was not, as I had thought, an invention of the Greeks,
but an observation by them, an intuitive understanding of a form found
constantly in nature. The same spiral is everywhere, most evidently in
the structure of a sea-shell or the cross-section of a breaking wave, but
in many case disguised, as in the organisation of the petals of a rose or
the relation of the ends of the fingers when the upturned hand is
relaxed. Hayden went on to explain that this spiral, and what can be
derived from it, is endlessly repeated and reinforced in the
masterpieces of Greek architecture.

I was astonished. It is not every day one is told something worth
remembering. I understood now exactly what it was I responded to in

classical buildings, and also what I had always found alien in modernism; why the Parthenon, for instance, notwithstanding its modest size, presides so effortlessly on its rock above modern Athens; not only *on* the rock, but somehow *of* it.

Two years pass. It is summer and I am visiting Arthur Miller in Connecticut to discuss the National Theatre's forthcoming production of *After the Fall*. There is quite a large group around the lunch table under the trees, attesting to the undiminished social energies of the Millers: Inge's mother, on holiday from Austria, a sprightly 90-year-old whom it is impossible to restrain jumping to her feet to serve and clear away, their actress daughter Rebecca, watchful and ethereally beautiful, and a young visitor from Russia who has been staying for three weeks, and who exercises her excellent English in cadences which veer from earnest scholarship to shrugging and rather sweet self-effacement.

Lunch over, Arthur and I repaired to his workroom, which is a hut at a distance from the house. We settled down to talk about the play, and agreed at once that there were two particular problems that had to be solved. The first was how to divest the play of its biographical associations with Marilyn Monroe. Most of its English-speaking productions had become so mired in celebrity speculation that the meaning of the play was simply overlooked.

Maggie, the character identified with Monroe, is not an actress but a very successful popular singer. Illegitimacy, child abuse, and educational neglect have shadowed her childhood. It had occurred to me that it was the kind of background shared by some celebrated black performers. Somewhat hesitantly, I suggested to Arthur the idea of a beautiful black Maggie. I saw him mentally ripple through the play before answering. 'Say, that's not a bad idea,' he said with one of those cautious, dawning smiles that herald the solution to a puzzle. Any anxieties I might have had about the inflexibility of America's most distinguished playwright melted away. Indeed, in our discussions then and later, in all intellectual or artistic matters, Arthur exhibited exactly that quality of 'Now' that his character Quentin most reveres in Maggie. The door of curiosity or laughter was always ajar.

The second problem concerned the set design. Kazan's original production had followed Arthur's description of a series of levels, but hadn't taken into account the necessity for instantaneous entrances and exits. The play, a mosaic of memories, runs the danger of breaking down into its constituents, unless one piece is glued tight against the next. Arthur thought the most effective set had been the one Zeffirelli used for his Italian production. From the auditorium it was like looking into the inside of an old bellows camera – a progression of squares retreating to a central 'lens'. Within this nest of boxes, as it were, actors could appear and disappear within seconds at different levels and in different perspectives.

The following day Arthur took me for a drive to see the lovely eighteenth-century villages in the neighbourhood of Roxbury, white clapboard buildings of neo-classic design harmoniously disposed under trees to which they related (I now knew) not only in scale but in form. As we left the car to stock up with provisions at the local supermarket, dumped down like a concrete crate at the edge of town, I had good reason to remember Hayden's spiral. It suddenly occurred to me: could this be our set? I recounted the conversation in the restaurant with the crayons to Arthur, whose knowledge of the Golden Mean had been as sketchy as my own. He now added something of great interest. On a visit he had once made to Epidaurus, the guide had shown his party a curious construction adjacent to a Temple of Asclepius, the god of Medicine. A flight of steps led down to what was essentially a cave but carefully shaped to resemble a vortex, and at the blind end of which there were the remains of ashes. No one knew exactly what purpose it served in the life of the ancient Greeks, but there was a theory that it had been used to minister to mental distress: the sufferer would be left inside the cave, which would then be closed while he contemplated by firelight the spiral twisting around him. *After the Fall* traces the journey of the leading character from a profound doubt about his own life and human nature in general, to a cautious, qualified, but nonetheless sturdy, hope.

Back in London I conveyed all this to Hayden, whom I'd asked to design the play. Then a few weeks later, on holiday abroad, I bought on impulse a copy of the Saturday edition of *The Daily Telegraph* – not usually my newspaper. I opened its colour magazine to find myself staring at a double-page spread of our proposed set. Except, of course, that it wasn't a set. It was a colour image arrived at by computer graphics. The caption read, 'Order out of chaos. With powerful computers, scientists can highlight the movement of molecules involved in a chemical reaction. The resulting picture shows how they spontaneously organise into a spiral. Could this throw light on how life began?'

I sent the picture to Hayden. Had we found our set? As is so often the case in artistic quests, it was more as if the set had found us.

Many problems lay ahead. Though the spiral was easy enough to draw in two dimensions, it was virtually impossible to model in three – a bit like trying to freeze a whirlpool. Hayden was now working in Los Angeles, where he had a friend at the LA Music Centre who had access to the Autocad computer software. This extraordinary machine enabled them, after much trial and error, to explore the spiral in its third dimension. Back in London and armed with this information, Hayden was now able to model the logarithmic cone that occupies the space enfolded by the spiral. The process was as contradictory as using a jelly to construct a jelly-mould, but eventually we had our miniature spiral sitting in a model box of the Cottesloe stage.

Next we had to devise modes of entry in and out of the spiral, and also a way of tilting the entire structure backwards so that its surfaces were not so steep that they couldn't be acted on. However, every alteration threw up unexpected problems: of access to the lighting rig, or diminished headroom for the actors. At one point, as we tilted the spiral, its outer perimeter threatened to slice through the side wall of the building.

I write this the day before we start rehearsals, and I daresay our spiral has a number of other surprises in store. It is a very ticklish structure and has many aspects, sometimes the rose, sometimes the whirlpool.

David Rabe

Several months ago, while doing an interview with Toby Zinman, Arthur Miller came up as we talked and when I was approached to contribute to this book, I thought back to my comments on that day. The following is a modified version of our exchange. It began with Toby Zinman referring to a comment I had made once about feeling influenced by Ionesco, Genet, and Arthur Miller. She was intrigued by the three and wondered at the details of their differing effects.

But you see Arthur Miller is a deceptive playwright. People act like his early plays are the only ones he wrote. I mean, that's the way it's gone down – the critics have praised him for a certain kind of play and dramaturgy of moral ideas and then they have maligned him for not growing when in fact what has happened is that they have refused to admit that he has grown. When he wrote plays that broke out of or expanded his original approach to playwriting, these plays, such as *After the Fall*, *The Price* and *Creation* etc. were dismissed, and then they – the critics – could just go on and view him as they had been, as this guy who wrote these few great plays that were historically situated and outdated. I mean, *All My Sons*, I've always felt it was creaky in its dramaturgy, but, on the other hand, if you face where we are today, it's prophetic. I mean, it's shockingly sound with a truth at its core that's amazing about things like the Challenger Space Shuttle blowing up because of the O rings and the rush to launch – things like Agent Orange in Vietnam. I mean, there was that Admiral and his family who played it out – they played out *All My Sons* with the Admiral being instrumental in the deployment of Agent Orange in a certain area and then his son, who served in that area, dying of leukemia. So even in that play, which is not my favourite, there's something at work, a mind you, have to take seriously. No, no, he's a wonderful writer and in the later plays his work is quite amazing. He's been mistreated by the American critics, though he has done well in the rest of the world, I'm thinking of England in particular, while he's been unappreciated here in recent years. The plays I most love are the ones that haven't done all that well here, like *The Price* and *After the Fall* both of which are, I think, great plays – plays in which the remediable world began to disappear in cogent and dramatic emotional terms. In *After the Fall*, he said 'this is not, things are not – '. And they've never forgiven him for *After the Fall*, and that is very strange. They attack that play; it's a great play. I've seen it several times and read it several times. I saw it recently with Frank Langella and Diane Wiest and I said again, 'This is an amazing play'. And they all get kind of huffy about his treatment of Marilyn Monroe, when it looks to me that – if it is Monroe, which it probably is to some degree, on some level – well then he treats her with more dignity than anybody else ever treated her in her career or life. Maggie is a character of great power and dignity – not the ditz Monroe was made into by the media, her directors, other writers and critics. But somehow they've never forgiven him for that, though I suspect sometimes that it isn't writing about her that he hasn't been forgiven for, but marrying her. Anyway, when I see the play, it's a

145

mystery to me why it isn't recognised. *The Price* also is woefully mis-perceived. To me it's a cunningly open-ended play. I mean, the moral issues do not close in that play. The whole thing just evaporates right in front of you, that old dead man laughing at you and your concerns, your whole need to understand mocked by that laughing ghost. You have nothing left but the people and a lot of pain and wit. So it seems to me his reputation is set on his earlier plays, *All My Sons* and *Death of a Salesman*. They're all valuable, of course, the product of a unique talent and mind. Putting them into any kind of hierarchy is a little nutty, but a kind of reflex against which we all seem to be somewhat helpless. But what is really insane is not to recognise the value of the later plays, the development of the writer, the evolving struggle of his relationship to the idea of a moral position. He goes from: 'I have a moral position and this is it and it's clear,' to 'This is really difficult, how the hell do I do this?' to 'Maybe I shouldn't be trying to do this, maybe it's impossible and harmful and I am wrong to even think about it' to 'And yet, here I am. Alive. How do I do it?' That's what *After the Fall* is about to me. It's a struggle to be honoured, unless we've all turned into that old man, that ghost at the end of *The Price*.

Bigsby: Yours has always been very much a moral drama, not just in its subject but in the way that it insists on causality, responsibility, the pressure of the past on the present. And yet, in *Playing For Time*, which was your adaptation of Fania Fenelon's book, one of the more painful moments comes when the main character realises that evil and cultural sensitivity actually can co-exist and do co-exist. That being so, what is the value, what is the function of art? Can it deflect history? Can it actually be a moral force?

Miller: I think it can. I don't think that I have managed to deflect history in any way but, you know, whatever you say about this age, we are probably one of the more poorly educated, as compared with some ages, in terms of our literary background but we are under the pressure of images which are artistic images to a greater degree. In a way we have got more primitive. The way the modern mind is formed is on the basis of television images, information through television, information through the movies, and the theatre, to a degree, a much less degree and even orthography, painting, sign painting, advertising. That's the way we know where we are. It's not by reading Browning or Keats or Shelley or Yeats or something like that. The world is being made by images. Therefore, if these images move in a certain direction, presumably, since man is paying intense attention to them, his brains will be partially formed by them. Now if you take the state of some of our conditions it means that the art has been pretty sinister. I'm not really ready to go that far but I do think that it has an effect, yes. I'm not quite sure what it is. It's not an arithmetic one; in other words if you set up a so-called positive hero, it doesn't mean it makes people more heroic. It could also bore them to death. It can make them decide that that's not what they want to be, but it certainly does have an effect. It tells people, young people especially, how to behave or how they ought to behave toward their girlfriends, towards their parents etc. I think that as a young person one looks at how other people in a similar situation react. It's part of your education. It's your initiation, in a way, into society. You go to a movie and see the way a fella treats a girl or a girl treats a fella. Oh, that's the way it's done! Well that could change behaviour.

Bigsby: Towards the end of the 1960s you wrote *The Price*, which, apart from anything else is an extraordinary, funny play. It also treads very dangerous ground in that it has a central figure who is an elderly Jew who comes close to stereotype and I wonder if you would have actually been able to write that play had you not previously dealt, in *Incident at Vichy* and *After the Fall*, with the question of Jewishness and the experience of the war?

Miller: Probably not. I probably wouldn't have felt relaxed enough to do it. Yes. I enjoy that character more than anybody I ever wrote, incidentally. But I probably wouldn't have. I hadn't thought of it that way. I tell you, I thought of that story for twenty years or more. Actually, I'd thought of it since the 30s and I never could find a way to tell it. But I think what happened was that in the late 60s and early 70s, the whole question arose in the States as to whether any kind of a life was possible that wasn't totally self-serving, totally cynical, that wasn't truly false and insupportable. So this play came out of that, finally, but the people had been with me for many years. You see, Victor, the policeman, is an idealist of sorts. He can't help it; he can't kick it. In a sense the world depends on him. It's got nothing to do with him being better than anyone else. It's that he's carried that weight of his idealism through his life and his strict code of justice and injustice. He's all we've got. It's a thin reed. I wouldn't say he's my representative. I'd say that I wish he would win but I have my doubts. I don't know that he can win in this world, the way human beings are set up. In other words, there are creators, like his brother Walter, a surgeon, who are very cruel and destructive. But without them we are going to stand still. He does save lives. It's part of his ruthlessness that he can do what he does. He is a great surgeon. He takes risks lesser men wouldn't dare take and he cares enough to do that. We need that guy. But Victor is much more careful about life. He doesn't want to risk himself or others. He's got to hold back this creator or one day he'll probably blow up the world with his creating. So there's a dialectic. There's a Ying and a Yang in there.

You see I get very depressed when people raise serious subjects in the theatre or the movies and then sentimentalise them. That means that they really can't face the facts. That saddens me. That's pessimism. This play does face the facts and it turns out that neither of these guys is 'wrong'. What the play does is run through all the rationalisations of their lives, both the ones they have for themselves and the accusations of the other. And the inevitability of this conflict is laid bare and we take it to its ultimate statement. And I think that that's exhilarating, not depressing. You really feel, if you've done it right, 'My God, we've really done what we rarely do in life, which is to exhaust the possibilities'.

But of course part of the pleasure of that play for me was the delight I felt in writing the character of Gregory Solomon. He's a real vaudeville act all by himself.

Vanessa Redgrave

Playing For Time, *CBS Television, September, 1980*

In 1956 George Devine founded the English Stage Company at the
Royal Court Theatre. The objective was to have a permanent repertory
company of actors to present the works of contemporary playwrights
both English and foreign, at this time a revolutionery programme.

The Crucible by Arthur Miller was the second play of the season. The
House Un-American Activities Committee hearings were in full swing
and American intellectuals and trade unionists were being persecuted
and blacklisted, especially the Jewish artists, whether they were
socialists, communists or liberals with an open mind. The play made a
big impression on me, especially the scene where Elisabeth Proctor
begs her husband John to sign a false confession and save his life, and
he refuses and goes to the scaffold. I decided to attend a Sunday evening
Symposium 'What is Wrong With The English Theatre' organised by
George Devine with Arthur Miller and some English writers. Basically
they said the problem was that English theatre refused to be concerned
with anything but the narrow interests of the English middle-class at this
time. The American theatre, on the contrary, was in a renaissance of new
creative writing. Miller, Tennessee Williams, Carson McCullers and the
artists working at the Actors Studio with Elia Kazan and Lee Strasberg –
full of passionate concern with the problems of the time – racism and
bigotry being number one.

It was not until 1979, however, that I was able to meet and work
with Arthur Miller in his masterpiece for television *Playing For Time*. In
one scene the women of the Auschwitz orchestra are arguing about the
Nazis. One woman says 'They're not human!' Fania Fenelon replies
'They *are* human! Don't you see that's the whole problem!'

Television and cinema have shown films which depicted the
horrendous bestiality of German Fascism. Only Miller went beyond
description to the essence of this problem. He showed us *how* Fascist
ideology operates in and through human beings and just how difficult
it is for human beings to struggle against being dehumanised. His deep
concern and thought on these questions make him and his plays really
great and truly universal.

Pat Hingle

The Price, *New York, February, 1986*

Arthur Miller took over as director of *The Price* when we were out of town in Philadelphia in 1968. I can't remember (or probably never knew) why the original director was dismissed. I do clearly remember that until Arthur took over I did not feel I knew what the play was about or where my character, Victor Franz, was coming from. If the original director knew, he was not able to communicate it to me; and I was unable to figure it out for myself. I'm reasonably sure the other actors were in the same boat. (Maybe not David Burns, who I feel had a special genius for playing Soloman.) Arthur did not restage anything. He did not re-do the show in any way. For me he answered two questions I asked him.

1. What is 'the price'? He believes there is a price you pay for everything you get in life. The 'price' and 'what you get' varies greatly in each individual. And each person has to honestly look into his own soul to know 'the price' and 'what you got'. He alone really knows.

2. What is Victor looking for? Victor knows the price he paid taking care of his father, but he doesn't know what he got from it. And that's his main problem in the play. It took almost the entire play for him to find out. Once Arthur answered these questions, I could do the rest. I assume he did the same for the other actors. At any rate, when he took the helm, the ship righted itself, and we had a hit.

The Price is the only play of the twenty-two I've done on Broadway where I've communicated directly with the playwright. In all others the director was the conduit.

Arthur Miller is a special person to me.

Richard Dreyfuss

BBC Radio Production of The Price, *1989*

I like playing Victor. Ultimately he's a man of good character and sacrifice and nobility. But what he does to himself and to the people directly around him is a puzzle.

I feel a connection to Miller. Completely. He is *my* playwright. There are similarities in the experiences between his family and my own. They differ only in detail, not in the thrust of things. He could easily have been writing about my family. And there's a whole culture that exists, what you might call the New York, Jewish, left-wing progressive, CP, Socialist Party Brooklyn-type of the 30s and 40s, whose gods were destroyed during the McCarthy era. This was where I grew up and where Miller came from.

Timothy West

BBC Radio Production, 1989

In 1989, Richard Dreyfus, Amy Irving, Harry Yulin and Ed Asner, as members of the L.A. Masterworks Company, were to come to London to record Miller's *The Price* for BBC Radio. At the last minute Mr Asner was delayed in California, which is how I came to join these distinguished Americans to play the 89-year-old Lithuanian used-furniture dealer Gregory Solomon.

I'd never seen *The Price*, only read it, years before. Now I read it again. Apart from being bowled over by the play, I fell flat for Gregory Solomon. Every so often – well, not so very often – you come across a character in a play who seems to spring to life on the page simply by virtue of the way he uses language. His way with words tells you everything about him. And it's as though the text were written out on a musical stave; the key and time signatures are there, the bar lines and dynamics – all the actor has to do is follow the instructions.

I don't believe it was until I was actually listening to the broadcast, months later, that it properly dawned on me what an extraordinarily complex character, dramatically, Solomon is. He'd seemed so straightforward when I played him, and now here was this amalgam of moralist and pragmatist, hero and con-man, victor and victim, Father Confessor and Jewish Comic. I'd been seduced by the clarity of the writing into playing with complete confidence someone totally outside my experience.

Afterwards, Arthur Miller said, 'I love the accent, but what the hell is it?'

Ian Forrest with Ric Morgan, Nick Simons, Anny Tobin, Arnold Yarrow

The Director and cast of the Dukes Theatre,
Lancaster's production of The Price *1990*

It is a very daunting play to come in and rehearse, particularly with a short time-scale. To make it clear to an audience you have to penetrate its various layers and you have to be so specific at which point you let the audience move on to the next stage as the characters slowly learn.

We did take it apart in very small chunks each day of rehearsal; we never rehearsed without quite a lengthy discussion of what we were trying to achieve in that half page, of where everyone was coming from and going to. That's why it's such a joy for actors and directors to take material like this, because, without that attention, no matter how wonderful the language, no matter how beautiful the play, to bring it to life you have got to get the dynamics right. It's a play that's full of language, of confrontations and long speeches. There is not a lot of action so it has got to be about those people and how they have accumulated all their resentments and then how those resentments are gradually demonstrated to each other and to the audience. Simply in terms of action, you have four people in a room who talk about old times and selling the furniture. But those people bring on years of history. It's a multi-levelled play. One's initial reaction was an emotional one, perhaps sentimental. The fact of two brothers confronting each other, struggling to come to an understanding and then solving a relationship, could touch you very much on an emotional level. But, as we worked on it, so many other levels emerged. It's a huge play in a chamber format. That's what is so deceptive about it.

Our production was in the round, with the audience on all four sides, and whilst that was a terrifying prospect it only added to the discomfort which emerged from what was happening to these people. The fact that you were being observed on all four sides had a claustrophobic effect. You couldn't go anywhere; you had to face those problems and deal with them. That really did help.

I think what is brilliant about the play is that alongside the dispute between the brothers we have the character of Gregory Solomon, who is the supreme kind of realist who lives from moment to moment and has a capacity to believe only what he sees. He is there as a kind of emotional safety-net, I think, for the audience who are watching it. I think if there were no Gregory Solomon in the play you could end up being torn apart by watching it.

The joy of Gregory Solomon lies in the richness of the character and the colourful nature of the language. A survivor, he never gives up; whatever the reverses he bounces back, sees the worst, doesn't flinch from it and deals with it. He has a belief: not a religious belief but a belief in humanity. He wouldn't put it that way. He just likes people, cares about people, which gives him a code. You strike a hard bargain, fight your own end, do the best you can for yourself in your business dealings and in your personal relationships, but within defined limits. You can be crafty, cunning, elaborate, exaggerate – but then all his language is exaggerated. You don't lie, you don't cheat, you can conceal your true feelings but you mustn't pretend to their opposite. If you're offered a piece of Chippendale you can say it's a lousy piece of Chippendale, 'Mr Chippendale must have lost his glasses the day he made that'. But you don't insist that it's a nineteenth-century repro. His language is colourful and marvellously witty.

Putting the character into the context of the play it's fascinating to pick out the thematic elements which occur. There are echoes which cross over from one character to another, of themes, of near-identical phrases. And these are surely an expression of Arthur Miller's philosophical view of life.

When Miller talks about the play he seems to see it as ending on a note of the impossibility of reconciliation, but that's not really how we felt. There seems to be tremendous hope in the fact that a relationship between two brothers can be of such intensity and complexity and that they can reach these points of huge rage and anger with each other and yet at the end of the play still both be intact whole beings. They haven't been diminished or destroyed. They are going on. They are still giving and they are still going on and that is wonderful because so many people are convinced that if they speak the truth that is going to be the end of the family. Everything is going to fall apart, be destroyed. And he is saying, no, this doesn't have to happen.

So much has happened between them, in that brief time, that their relationship, their non-relationship almost, has changed irrevocably. In the heat of what happened there appears to be no way they are going to get together. When Walter goes for a moment it is as if that's it, but when that has subsided, given the knowledge of what each has said to the other, and the revelations that each has made to the other, there is no way that they are not going to meet, somehow or other start to come together.

And there came a moment when Victor heard Esther for the first time. He had been made to realise, for the first time, what Esther had thought. Everything that she had done to that point had been to support the road he took and the decisions he made. There was great disappointment in many areas but she repressed that because of the love she had for him. She went along with everything, until this extraordinary realisation that in fact he had lied to himself and he had not faced the truth about his father and his brother. Suddenly she realises that she has sacrificed years believing her husband to be someone else. But even so there is some hope for them. Certainly they are going to continue but it is going to be different, whatever else it is, it is going to be different; the journey has opened up the possibility for that relationship to be better. It can never be the same. As Miller says, she walks out with her life.

What has happened in that room for two hours has irrevocably changed those people and they have had to come to terms with what they have learned from that experience and evaluate it. It is there, in their head, like baggage which has to be sorted through.

But those characters have to decide whether they take that and actually make the possibility into something which is specific and definite for them which will actually alter their lives. It's been an exorcism.

David Calder, Alan MacNaughtan, Bob Peck and Marjorie Yates

The Young Vic Production of The Price,
February 1990

CALDER: T. S. Eliot says that humankind cannot bear very much reality and that remark came up all the time in rehearsals. It's quite clear from the play that nearly every character has that problem in one way or another. Truth has to be adapted to reality in order to survive. So they avoid certain truths and hang on to others. But truth and memory clash, dynamically and tragically.

PECK: My first reaction to Walter was that he was a man who was trying to have his cake and eat it. After a couple of weeks I began to resent this man because he seemed to have had all the benefits and not paid any price. I think my appreciation of the price he had paid, and how very real and human his situation was, became more and more evident as the rehearsal went on and the run continued. I think he is a man who has come to terms in his own way with the history of events and is not going to shift on that. He is being true to himself at the time you meet him in the play. I think he believes he has got rid of a lot of surplus baggage and got down to something approaching a proper working relationship with himself.

CALDER: When I first read the play I saw Victor as being exceedingly flawed. When I was playing it, however, I was absolutely and totally convinced that Victor was right. I had completely forgotten my first impression of it because when the clash takes place it is between two people who absolutely, honestly believe the position that they assume. They don't doubt it. The doubts are generated by the clash that takes place in the process of the play itself. When his brother, Walter, offers him a job, a possible future that will release him and his wife Esther from their predicament, it confuses him profoundly. He has to hang on to the belief that there is deceit in it, that Walter is trying to get himself off the hook. As an actor you have to play the belief, not the doubt. It's up to the audience to make assessments as to what is actually going on. By the end of the play, though, he has had to face a central truth about himself. He has to cut away all the rationalisations as to why he stayed with his father and just say 'I stayed because I stayed'. And that is a crucial perception. Victor has always responded to Esther's encouragement to 'snap out of it', 'stop your paralysis', 'make independent decisions in life' by saying that he can't make those decisions because the past has disallowed him. They are not of his making and neither is the future. It's really all down to that bastard of a brother that I have. It is quite clear by the end of the play that that rationalisation is stripped and destroyed. But what is revealed by this moment of truth is that he couldn't walk away and it was as simple as that. There is no reason for it and no explanation for it.

YATES: It's not until the very end that Esther comes to a crucial understanding about her husband Victor: he stayed because he loved his father. And she comes to realise that that is excusable. That is the only answer that can be excusable. In certain respects they have wasted their lives but their relationship is good. You might say they had something that the Walter character didn't have. Esther might seem to sit on the sidelines but she is a vital character. She has got to be there one hundred per cent in my opinion. Most of the time, the play is filtered through Esther. She is not just an observer. In fact David Calder and Bob Peck felt it essential almost to get the best out of the acting. It became very important that she was there and I think that helped me to feel very much that I was as important a character, not only as Esther but also as an actress. It is important also to remember that her life is in just as much a mess as theirs but the psychology of it doesn't go quite as deep and she knows that the answer to her problem is for Victor to move because their marriage is that kind of a marriage.

PECK: It became more and more clear that Walter and Victor present two different attitudes to life and nobody is ever going to change that. Their response to the way they are, the way they handle what they are, can alter but what they are can't really alter. They are two different people and they are animated in two completely different ways and those two different attitudes don't seem able to exist in one person or be reconcilable. And that's what Arthur said he found in the construction of the play as he was writing it; he wanted a resolution but couldn't arrive at one. If those two attitudes can't co-exist in one person, it seems, or the world, and society needs those two different energies to operate, to function, a compassionate one and an apparently selfish go-getter, forward-looking attitude, the character Solomon brings in a completely different energy and

157

attitude which seems to be in some way more healthy than either Victor's or Walter's.

MACNAUGHTAN: Solomon has a total belief in life and that's the thing. They *think* what the future's going to be and he *lives*; he just goes on living. He's eighty-nine years old; he's been through four marriages and a daughter's suicide. He's been through everything and he still loves dealing with furniture, meeting new people, hearing their stories, pouring out his own stories and just living life. And, significantly, the play ends with him alone on the stage, listening and laughing. He's a vaudevillian. His first scene is a vaudeville act. He's been doing it all his life and he loves it.

CALDER: Arthur gave us a great description of Solomon. He said that he's the kind of guy that if he fell off a ten storey building, he'd land on marshmallow. He is a fantastic counterpoint because he's the man who's discovered the simplest secret: that the secret of life is life itself. That's a truth the other characters have not yet understood. To me, the key to Alan's performance was that he played it for real. In a theatre like the Young Vic, where you're really under a fantastic microscope in terms of what the audience see, you have to be truthful, theatrically truthful, and, therefore, even though, as Alan put it, 'this is a man's act,' he acts life, it is the survival kit that he carries with him. It is the fast one-liner that turns the situation round to his advantage. If that doesn't have a root in reality, if it is not seen to be a method of engaging life, then it goes for nothing, it is just a series of jokes. That's what was so successful about the way that Alan played it; the laughs that came were a bonus as opposed to a target.

There's a note in the back of the playscript which says that *The Price* can be done without an interval. Now since one tends to think of Arthur as a radical writer, we assumed he would prefer the radical decision. So we rehearsed in the belief that it was going to be played that way, because that's the way Arthur would like it. Then he turned up and gave his respone to the first twenty-two years of the play's history and at the same time a profound summary of our work: 'By the way,' he asked, 'are you going to have an interval because I did have a pee before I came in – but by God I want another one'. Suddenly we were forced to rethink the radical position on the interval. But I think the truth of the matter is that the structure of the piece is such that you need the pay-off, and the pay-off is that the last moment of the first act is the unexpected entrance of the brother, of Walter, because if he doesn't come on, that is the end of the play. The furniture is sold and we all go home. And so there is an audience which is getting slightly anxious at that moment and then suddenly all is revealed: the brother has made a decision to turn up. What does it mean? There is a fifteen minute interval to think what it means. And then you've got an audience coming back for the second half saying, 'Right, come on, tell us,' and then they are definitely told what it means.

PECK: The audience definitely wanted these brothers to get it together, to stop being so stupid or whatever. When somebody seemed like leaving, they didn't want it to happen. They didn't know, couldn't see, what on earth the next twist would be, because the structure of the piece is that whoever speaks last seems to command the truth. What is there to be said against it? Nothing, apparently, until it's said. And of course more has to be revealed each time as people dig deeper.

CALDER: We all worked with a method, the Method, in the sense of building up enormous biographies and internal lives for these characters. By the time we had got to our first run, which was the one Arthur saw, it was like walking around with the whole of your holiday luggage under your arms, between your legs, on your head. Bags and bags of informational things, emotional information that was informing how you played something. And it was a wonderful moment when he allowed us to dispense with these by pointing out some very simple things. For instance, the actor who is playing Victor, who has been bad-mouthing his brother to a complete stranger and building up this unbelievable head of resentment, is suddenly confronted by the brother who he hasn't seen for sixteen years. Now if you let the head of emotion take its course, then between every line that's saying, 'Hello, how are you, how's the family,' is a kind of question saying, 'Well, what the hell are you doing here, bastard' and it's kind of heavy-handed and slow and cautious and suspicious. Arthur was able to cut through that by just saying, 'Well, you know you haven't seen your brother for sixteen years; it's probably quite nice to see him, isn't it'. And this was suddenly like you were able to put ten bags into left luggage. Suddenly you straightened your back a bit and the weight came off. He used the word 'redundant' which is an amazing word for an actor to hear because it suddenly sharpens you up so much. He even cut most of the pauses he'd indicated in his own text.

159

PECK: He came in at a late stage of the rehearsal and saw us through to the first preview. The first preview was a euphoric occasion. The audience went berserk and he witnessed that but his comment to me afterwards was, 'Bob, I always knew you could do it and when you do it'll be great'. And I think he was right, really; but the first preview we thought, 'Crikey, here we are, isn't it marvellous'. Then we had an awful lot to do after that and frankly I barely got there by the press night and was still fighting when we finished.

CALDER: He came up with that expression which every actor hears, usually from a writer, and something dies inside of you when they say it: 'trust the play'. Now the truth is that trusting a play for an actor is an enormous act of faith, which you have to make anyway but you don't do it with ease. I can certainly say that this is the first time in my life that I really truthfully ended up understanding what that meant. That you don't have to play the play, you don't have to take the weight of the play on your shoulders like four individual versions of the play, that you play the situation, you play the first aspect of the situation, the part which is on the surface. It's governed, controlled and informed by our life, but you play what is actually happening in reality and then the play itself does all the rest of the work that you think you're supposed to do. It didn't matter how much we could genuinely greet each other and be enthusiastic about seeing each other after sixteen years, asking about each other's kids and what was going on in the world and how are things. The play itself was what made the audience say, 'hang on, that's not quite right, something doesn't ring true'.

MACNAUGHTAN: And what was interesting was that I was in the same position as the audience really. I knew nothing about Walter except what Victor had told me. I hadn't heard anything from the other side and I always found it fascinating to be able to feel one's way with this extraordinary brother, about whom one had heard such awful things, meeting him and watching him. It was very, very, interesting because in a sense I was really the audience there.

CALDER: Like my colleagues, I feel that I have been incredibly enriched as an actor as a result of this production; the reason being that it is an extraordinary experience to be in the room playing with the man whose material you put on the level of the great classic writers like Chekhov, which I do. And even if he hadn't been there, the demands the material makes on the actor are profoundly personal; you have to discover things about yourself, you have to discover things about your techniques of expression and you have to change those things and develop them. To have those changes, as it were, articulated by Miller himself was like the best acting lesson I've ever had. If you do achieve what you believe the material requires of you, you then have the joy of experiencing what impact that had on an audience. Because every night we had the same experience: audiences were very, very generous about the acting, but they very quickly got past the acting and the production to the meat and the content of the play and would tell you things about their lives which were very personal. I now know what the relationship between acting material and an audience really is. I think that in Britain today there is an audience hungry for this kind of material and hungry to think about the past, to think about its effect on the present. I think that the rediscovery of the play wasn't just for the audience. I think it was rediscovered by Miller in the process of him being here. I think that he rediscovered its emotional truth. The play spoke back to him and he wasn't fully in control as the sculptor/ dramatist. The play spoke back to Miller and I think that this production spoke back to Miller.

David Thacker

in conversation with Heather Neill

When we did a run-through in front of Arthur Miller he *was* pretty impressed, but he made it clear within minutes that we were miles away. He did it in the kindest way – by telling the truth. He talked about the dialectical nature of the play: every argument posed is matched instantly by a counter-argument and then countered again. Each must be given equal weight and force. He was anxious that the audience should not stand in judgement on Victor or Walter. For three days we went through the play five minutes at a time. Arthur blossomed. It was like a master-class. Sometimes the insights were particular, down to the meaning of one line. When Victor says at the end that he is going to pick up his suit from the dry-cleaners, Esther, his wife, says 'Don't bother'. This is not cynical – it would be easy to play it that way – but loving and generous. She means that he no longer needs to make the effort to be other than he is – a policeman. Victor became a policeman when he believed – this is hinted in the text

– that the Depression would bring the end of Capitalism: if there was chaos there would always be the need for policemen. Sometimes the guidelines were more general. The play, he said, was finally about love. The brothers love each other and want to come together, but can't.

Miller complained of the final section that he couldn't hear the actors, there was no emotional range and they seemed to be doing the play for themselves, adding – the final indignity – 'I don't think anyone would listen to you.' I suppose by the time you reach his age there's no time to waste on bullshit. But he also said some deceptively simple key things about acting. For instance, when you make long speeches, you must not assume that no one else is going to speak. Your acting must demand no other response than that they listen.

Miller expects his actors to achieve 'reality'. The cast of *The Price* did say that, when things were going well (and ultimately this was an extremely successful production), it was as if they were not acting at all but living out the conflicts of the characters. Of course Miller himself is a brilliant actor and it can be extremely illuminating when he gives you a flavour of it himself.

Miller's plays are very personal. It is unbearable for him if they are not expressed in their fullness. On the whole he has confirmed, endorsed what I try to do – in particular that there *is* a right way to play a text. I think there was a tendency, though, to overstate the sub-text, to make the work more dense. You have to know exactly what is behind the line, but learn to play through it, to trust the text.

The thing that marks Miller out as a considerable playwright is his love of human beings and his generosity in relation to their suffering and their pain. There is almost nobody in a play by Arthur Miller who is not a considerable force in their own right – even the people who behave despicably are multi-dimensional human beings. And by expressing these contradictions as fully as we can, we reveal something of the way we all struggle to understand our place in the world.

Bigsby: It seems to me that in the 1970s your career took a radically new direction with works like *The Archbishop's Ceiling* and *Two Way Mirror*. By that I don't mean that there's no continuity with what went before but you seem to begin to get interested in new areas of experience.

Miller: Well, what's been weighing on me for a long time, but I never turned my face to, is the ancient question of what is real, the mystery of time. It's a practically ungraspable subject for mankind, I think, but I could reduce all culture to the question of how it deals with time or how it attempts to deal with it. I'm still involved with this question of memory and self-formation. We're all impersonators in a way. We are all impersonating something, including ourselves. This is one of the drags on our spontaneity nowadays. Everybody feels he is really playing. We have all become actors in this damn thing. The actor becomes the most significant figure, culturally speaking. He's doing professionally what we are all doing as amateurs. It's fascinating.

Bigsby: So that in *The Archbishop's Ceiling* there may or may not be hidden microphones in the room and that of course turns people into actors, performing before some invisible audience?

Miller: Right.

Bigsby: Now it's set in Eastern Europe but it sounds as though it's in part a response to Watergate.

Miller: I hadn't thought of Watergate, exactly. It's rather a question of what is the irreducible in man, in the human being. Is there something irreducible or are we totally adaptable, totally and completely adaptable? One often thinks so. What springs to mind is the story of a guy back in the 30s. I didn't know him well. I just passed through his life for a minute and he was a very left wing guy. We were not good friends or anything. Suddenly he rang me up and came to see me. I couldn't imagine why he would come and see me. Well it turned out he was selling oil stock. And I thought, now isn't that strange. There's this left wing guy and he still had the same enthusiasm that he'd had, let's say fifteen years earlier, when our lives had touched for a moment. The same idealism. And I said, 'I don't buy stock and I don't know where you get the idea that I would but tell me, how do you come to this?' He said, 'Well, it's very important.' I said, 'I'm sure it is but why do you think it's important?' He said, 'Well, when the workers take control we will have to have developed the oil reserves of . . .' He wasn't kidding. See. That's a wonderful comedy in there but it's also very sad.

Bigsby: *The Archbishop's Ceiling* sank largely without trace in America. In Britain though, it had two distinguished and successful productions: one at the Bristol Old Vic and one at the Royal Shakespeare Company. My impression is that over the last couple of decades you've come to feel very much at home in the British theatre.

Miller: Well, you have a theatre, you see. We have shows. There's a difference. In an altogether or semi-subsidised theatre you can do a play like *The Archbishop's Ceiling* because you don't think you have to attract a mass audience for two years in order to pay off the cost of it. In our theatre, the Broadway theatre, you're asking a man to invest his cash in a play which may get very good reviews but probably will not run more than, whatever it is, six months. That's just not long enough any more. That's the reason I have loved to play here. Nobody has a million dollars riding on reviews the next morning. There's no hysteria. I have to say that when I put on *The Archbishop's Ceiling*, a play about Czechoslovakia, people didn't know what to make of it. I don't think that's just America. I think it's anywhere. People aren't aware, really, of what the situation is. I don't know what would make them aware of it. It depends upon a kind of comedic awareness that the State is in the wrong, or it may not be in the wrong. After all it turns on the fact that in the archbishop's palace there may or may not be microphones concealed in the ceiling. As one of the characters says, 'You know, it's just like God. You don't quite know whether he's there or not, and so you'd better speak as though he were there.' So they rebel against it, but they're not sure whether they're being just simply stupid. I mean, what's the point of rebelling against something that isn't there. And so it makes a kind of comedy of this disaster. Well, I think I did not succeed in making the terms of the disaster as clear as I might have done. Because, you see, though we Americans bug everything and everybody for ever, it's not in the consciousness of people. And anyway it's not a social play in that sense. It's really a play about reality.

Bigsby: So now, questions like identity and reality have become much more problematic.

Miller: Oh, yes. Especially in situations where the State or the society tells you that there is no problem in this regard.

Bigsby: But does that also mean then that the moral world has begun to disappear slightly?

Miller: Oh yes, very much so. I think that it's been doing that in my work for a long time. I've been struggling with it, anyway. I think the struggle is necessary. You see, when the struggle is given up, as it is in effect given up in totalitarian places, then we're all up for grabs, and I'm not ready to give up. I mean, then there's no reason why a cop can't come in here and do what he wants to do, which they very frequently do anyway. And you have no basis for complaint against life. You've got to grapple with this somehow.

Bigsby: But, then, from what you were saying, that is exactly the situation in this play?

Miller: Right. But we don't even know in this play whether we're oppressed. We don't even know whether this whole thing is simply our paranoia.

Bigsby: But this is a different kind of humour than one normally finds in your work. It's actually closer to the mode in European drama in recent years, an ironic humour coming out of discrepancy.

Miller: Yes. I've written a television play, called *Fame*, and it has that attitude, I think. It never occurred to me to describe it in that way, but now that you've mentioned that, it does.

David Edgar

By all accounts, Arthur Miller's work is out of fashion in much of eastern Europe. Not only were Miller's early, social realist plays prized by the apparatchika for their perceived exposure of capitalism; he himself possessed impeccable anti-anti-communist credentials, which, with the removal of a double negative or two, imply to today's revolutionaries that he was and is a craven apologist for discredited regimes.

This perception is not just unfair, it is unfair in a particularly specific way. At a conference at a certain fenland university (held in the late 1980s, and chaired by the editor of this volume) Arthur Miller took an equally certain British political playwright to task on the question of the content of political theatre in the West. First, he welcomed the continued muscularity of the political impulse in British theatre, contrasting it with the triviality and domesticity of the American equivalent. (But went on, drawing on the *Salesman* in Peking experience, to note wryly how different politico-theatrical aesthetics look from the perspective of a country where you can't fire actors and polemic is compulsory.)

But most interesting – and most prescient, in terms of what one hears from every newly-vocal voice in the east – was his view of the primary, original socialist sin. For Miller, the highest God to have failed was not so much the command economy, nor the centralised state, nor even the censorship and secret police. It was the emancipatory project of socialism itself: the idea that under a new system people can start again from scratch, can turn themselves into a blank sheet and begin anew. Whereas, for Miller, tradition and the past are 98 per cent of what we are; men and women can change the direction of their lives, but ultimately their future must be written from their past.

It is, on the surface, a fairly conservative perspective. It responds to the darker side of the post-war experience to the showtrials of the 50s, the Cultural Revolution and Cambodia. It is a view that comes well from the author of *The Crucible* (the play of Salem's Year Zero). It accords with at least one reading of *A View from the Bridge* and much of

The Archbishop's Ceiling. Though on the surface it sits rather oddly with the author of *The American Clock* and indeed *Death of a Salesman.*

But, as Miller argues, the reason for the appeal of Willy Loman's story in Peking was not that there is no alienation in the West, but that there is comparable alienation in the East ('they know just how he feels'). His conviction is that the engaged theatre should fix its eye not on systemic questions, but on justice, no matter what its implications are. 'It may be', he said, 'that capitalism is more just'; I think he meant it probably is, bits of it anyway, and I think he's got a point.

But it doesn't follow that there's no injustice and no alienation in the countries of the West. Because, as Miller insisted, alienation is a function not of the political and social system, but of technological society itself. And anywhere the 'eternal values of man's dignity' are threatened, then there the theatre has a role.

'Maybe,' he concluded, 'if we sat back and looked at what the theatre might reveal about this massive enslavement of our hopes in every system that I know about, you could catch fire'. I wouldn't have thought there's that much 'maybe' about it.

Nick Hamm

Director, The Archbishop's Ceiling, *Royal Shakespeare Company, October, 1986*

'There has never been any proof of an installation here. But when so many writers congregate here I've had to assume there might be something.' – Marcus, *The Archbishop's Ceiling.*

When and how can writers work? In what conditions can good art flourish?

The issue of the play was one of truth – who speaks it, how, and if it matters.

Marcus believed survival to be a kind of truth – he decided to survive.

Sigmund decided to throw himself towards the flames – his decision and the degree to which the others become complicit in that decision is the story of the play. What we found most difficult to work out was who was speaking the truth at any given moment. The play became a tangled web of possibilities. The normal process an actor goes through in exploring motive, reason and character – truth, was complicated by

167

the simple fact that what anyone says in the play may be being listened to by someone with a tape recorder.

Is the ceiling bugged or not? Does Marcus work for the state? Is Maya the protector of Sigmund she makes out she is? Arthur was coming over straight from the USSR to attend rehearsal, in fact straight from a meeting with Gorbachev himself. I remember asking Nick Hern, then running the drama section of Methuen books, when Arthur would arrive in rehearsal – both the actors and myself were anxious he should come. We knew that the results of our work up to then could only be sorted out with him present. Nick replied that Arthur must be one of the few writers in the world who could plead the excuse of an audience with Gorbachev for his delay into rehearsal. We were all suitably impressed by this fact and mulled over the unimaginable situation of our own leaders in the West, whether Thatcher, or Reagan, meeting with philosophers and artists as part of their daily work.

Sigmund maybe based on Vaclav Havel – Arthur wrote the play as a response to a visit he made to Czechoslovakia in the late 60s. I've just read an interview with Arthur in today's paper in which he states that Havel would now like to see a production of the play in Prague. What is extraordinary is that the play has had such a varied history and might never have survived at all. When it was first performed in the States, they presented a different play from the published Methuen text and the one we were working on. Arthur was convinced by people associated with the production to include an extra character – I think Maya's husband – by way of explanation. It was felt that the American audience would not appreciate the constant ambiguity of the play and it needed straightening out for them. Arthur duly wrote the other character into the script and the play folded.

It was obvious the play would not work on that basis since any attempt at irony was removed and it requires an appreciation of 'The Ironic' if it is to be understood. In fact because of the failure of that initial production the play might have been forever forgotten had not Chris Bigsby convinced Arthur to let him see the original manuscript and subsequently let Methuen publish it.

Arthur always maintained it is one of his most European works, not simply because of the setting, but because the intellectual jigsaw, that is the framework of the play, is nearer to a European attitude than to an American. It is not without irony that a play concerning the issue of writers' freedoms, will be celebrated soon in some of the new emerging capitals of Eastern Europe.

The arrival of Arthur into rehearsal was an event that few of us working on the production will forget. Was he really going to work directly on the play with us? Or would it be a cursory chat and then we'd carry on on our own? I knew from my previous meetings with him when we'd done *The Crucible* at the Royal Shakespeare Company that he would enjoy the whole process of meeting the cast and going through the problems, but I never expected the kind of commitment he gave to the rehearsal room. He would attend for half a session each day, we would present the options we had arrived at, often more than two or three for any given moment, and he would simply state after discussion, 'Play that'.

The fact that Arthur was able to state the truth as he saw it – clarifying precisely what it was we had to play – enabled the production eventually to work so well. The discussions about a given moment were often intense, mainly funny, but always ended with a line for the actors to follow. I often think that the way we worked on that play was the only legitimate way to tackle it. We had four weeks on our own to explore, confuse ourselves, go through the whole 'What if?' of any normal rehearsal period. In the remaining two weeks the writer was able to use all that knowledge and guide us along a coherent line. (If Arthur had been there from the start, that exploration, that process of 'getting lost' in order to come out the other side, would not have happened. The actors had a reservoir of possibilities to present. They were as pleased as I was to have at last a basis from which selection could take place.)

Selecting *what* to play is what rehearsals are about – not just how but what – the *what* of this play was only solved by Arthur being there. He was direct, witty and very concerned we should get it right. It was a delight to work so directly with him and under the great Baroque ceiling of Fotini Dimiou's design an analysis of freedom and justice took place nightly on the Barbican stage.

He understands in a way few writers do or want to, the internal 'process' of rehearsal. He is not judgemental or cynical in his work. He focuses and gives all contributions their place, helping each individual concerned make the play come alive. He recognises the creative impulse in everyone and demands that it is used. Working with Arthur you have no choice – you give because you want to. He makes the normal frustrations and agony of exploration something you don't mind going through.

John Shrapnel

In Autumn, 1986, five of us were sitting in a Royal Shakespeare Company's rehearsal room, low down in the bowels of the Barbican, apprehensive and slightly nervous. We were coming to the end of the rehearsal period for *The Archbishop's Ceiling*, and Arthur Miller had agreed to be with us during the final ten days or so, and to work with us on the play. Rehearsals were going well, and we were fairly certain we were on the right tracks with it, but it's a difficult piece and each of us had our own problems and personal knots to unravel. He, of course, might well consider that we were not only on the wrong tracks, but in the wrong station. Anyway, today was the day he was due to turn up: we were Waiting for Arthur.

My association with Miller goes back to my student days, and in the sixties he got me into quite a lot of trouble. Indirectly. I was mid-way through rehearsing Willy Loman in an undergraduate production of *Death of a Salesman*, when my college suddenly withdrew permission for me to act. It was an exam term and they feared distractions. Not daring to confess that I was already deeply distracted, I decided to play Willy under a pseudonymn.

So it was as Lloyd Loom (a sergeant on a local USAF base, Miller-enthusiast and keen amateur actor) that I appeared at the ADC, the students' theatre in Cambridge, reasonably sure that my tutors wouldn't attend and blow my cover. But Loom developed in his own right, featuring in press interviews etc. I was discovered, accused of betraying my tutors' trust, but reluctantly allowed to complete the run. There, for the first time, I sensed the power that the play has when it moves towards the final graveside scene, even with a cynical undergraduate audience. I felt it again at the Nottingham Playhouse three years later, playing Biff. Whenever and wherever I've seen the play, I've heard audiences sobbing during that scene.

So, sitting in that Barbican rehearsal room, I don't know who I was expecting to meet: a serious man, seriously protecting his play's integrity, I suppose. What was surprising was his accessibility, and his laughter. Arthur Miller is a big man and laughs hugely. I thought of his stage direction in *The Price* where Victor listens to the Gallagher and Shean record: '. . . He smiles. Broader. Chuckles. Then really laughs. It gets into him . . . now he bends over with laughter . . .' Arthur does just that.

Some time later, working on his early play *The Golden Years* for the radio, I wondered what it would sound like in Brooklyn-ese; those conquistadors could have come straight out of the docks.

He has a New Yorker's ability to make serious points through irony: as, for example, when he was describing the philistinism of American TV Network controllers. '. . . Those guys *like* what's on television – they think it's wonderful! That's what we don't appreciate; they are honestly aiming as high as they can. They are idealists!'

There is a moment in *The Archbishop's Ceiling* where the dissident writer, Sigmund, asks his American friend whether he is carrying a gun, a question which jacks up the tension since it introduces the possibility of firearms into a claustrophobic, domestic situation. Playing Sigmund, I was approaching the moment rather heavily and tending towards melodrama. Much better, Miller suggested, to make this query very natural, almost playful. He described a situation when a man at an airport had asked him the same question, very calmly and pleasantly. The man had then revealed that he was armed: Miller was horrified. A simple tale, but lethal.

Work on *The Archbishop's Ceiling* was relaxed, instructive and hugely enjoyable during the relatively short time we had. Miller has an easy, natural affinity with actors, who therefore trust him completely. Basically, he likes them and admires what they do, and, disarmed by this, they'll follow him anywhere. He hadn't come with the notion that there was a single, inevitable direction for his play and our characters; all possibilities were open. We had been extremely nervous of tampering with his text (thinking of the paranoid obsessiveness of some writers). 'It worries you, cut it' had been Arthur's reaction. Mainly, he opened this dense play up for us, steered us away from piousness, and pointed us to solutions which then seemed obvious; a wonderful and encouraging way of working. I remember thinking at times that it was hard to put the man and the play together: it was as though someone else had written it, but he knew all about it. And there was much laughter.

A year later, I was playing in Vaclav Havel's (then) new play, *Temptation*, again for the RSC. The director (Roger Michell) and I were in Prague, having smuggled a video version of the production out to Havel, then completely deprived of any access to his work. Havel knew about *The Archbishop's Ceiling*, but hadn't read it. He was, however, convinced that he was the model for Sigmund, the character I had played, and was anxious to show us a building up near the Castle, which he was certain was the setting for the play. Arthur, in his preface, is guarded about the location, merely suggesting 'an East European capital'. But it doesn't take a huge leap of imagination, with the play's constant threat of surveillance and the hint of tanks in the countryside, to place it in Czechoslovakia. And so I found myself sipping coffee in an apartment which had belonged to the Czech painter Alphonse Mucha, stacked with art objects, settees, piano, unhung paintings and bits of Bauhaus, with a man convinced that I had recently been representing him on a stage in the West, in a play by Arthur Miller. On my return, I sent him the play.

At the end of *The Archbishop's Ceiling*, Sigmund pays homage (with Arthur) to a list of writers with whom he has communicated from his fastness: Heinrich Böll, Malraux, Bellow and others. As I got to this point during a rehearsal, Miller said 'Hey, lemme see that', and grabbed the script. He sat and thought for a few minutes, and then suggested that he might have some additions which he'd pass on to me the following day.

Next morning, he gave me two more to add to the list. Graham Greene and Samuel Beckett. 'Can't leave those guys out', he said.

Bob Peck

Two Way Mirror, *The Young Vic, 1989*

I think it's peculiar to Miller's writing that the idiom is so authentic that it's foreign. So you have to learn a vocabulary and it affects you physically and emotionally. In *Two-Way Mirror* at the Young Vic 1989 we found it incredibly difficult to assimilate the lines. A couple of days before the play opened we were still breaking down at very short intervals in both plays. Even when we were playing, for the first fortnight we had trouble with *Elegy for a Lady* and had to cover for each other at least once in each performance. What was good about the production was that we seemed to learn more as we went on so that at the end of six weeks we hadn't exhausted the plays at all.

I think that there was one element missing in our production which neither of us could do anything about, and that was that both plays are about relationships between a woman who is significantly younger and an older man. And Helen Mirren and I are of the same age to a month. She was having to age down and I was having to age up and I think that given a real age difference there would be an extra element in the performance. That's because I suspect there is an auto-biographical element in those plays. He wrote it in two and a half days. He's never altered a word since he wrote it and he's said it came straight out of his subconscious.

Helen was aware that *Some Kind of Love Story* possibly takes place in the man's imagination but she had to play against that to establish a reality for herself which she didn't feel was being offered in the text.

The play comes across very strongly as a sort of therapy session for a man who's in crisis. It finishes and a man walks out having been healed or cured; a blight, or weight of conscience, has been lifted off him, for his daring to have a relationship outside marriage. It goes unnoticed, it certainly went unmentioned in the reviews, that both relationships, for the man, are adulterous, and Arthur is saying it's alright, it's human and if you accept it for what it is, see it for what it is, there's no need to carry a burden of guilt about it.

Some Kind of Love Story comes from a different world, a kind of low life world, but again it's about an adulterous relationship. It was based on someone Arthur knew, a specific detective. So there is this dyed-in-the-wool traditional Irish-Catholic American, of immense integrity, who'd got himself besotted with this girl with whom he was supposed to be having a professional relationship, jeopardising his career.

Whereas *Elegy for a Lady* features the man, I think *Some Kind of Love Story* is supposed to offer a *tour de force* for the woman but I don't think either of the plays worked out that way – it's more of a balance in both. The two characters are entirely dependent on each other. They need each other. That's ultimately what's moving about them.

His interests are private rather than professional. He just couldn't give this girl up.

We played in the round and I thought that the plays worked very well except that *Love Story* is shot through with false exits. Because of the nature of the Young Vic any entrance or exit has to be very long. If you're on a normal stage and stand up you're virtually off-stage but in this instance it's quite difficult and the only re-writes that Arthur offered related to cutting out some of the false exits. That recurring aspect of that play was exaggerated by the nature of the theatre. Of course its the only threat that Tom, the detective, can level at Angela. It's the only hold he has over her, apart from physical violence, which is against his principles if not his nature, because there is potentially a violent atmosphere. She, after all, is a particularly volatile and frustrating character.

Perhaps it's an aspect of this real person on whom Arthur based the character that he has a gullibility. He would believe her. He didn't know where he stood with her. Of course he had taken professional psychiatric advice so even though it was a self-deluding device on her part to switch into other personalities, a way of avoiding problems, it nevertheless is a real condition.

We couldn't help but think of someone like Marilyn Monroe. How do you shunt from one self to another without damaging yourself psychologically. I think Helen Mirren has something of this duality. Her public image is of someone sexually provocative. At the same time she has a classical background. It focuses back to her first major performance as Cleopatra – a classical play but a character who is sexually energised, almost juvenile.

The actor playing these parts is required to cry twice but we found that part of the learning process was learning to have confidence in your ability to do the part. You had to allow yourself to be affected by what was happening between you and the thoughts that the words generated. The crying either happened or it didn't, the emotion was either generated between you or it wasn't.

When Arthur was over here I think he was rather surprised and quite probably moved on a couple of occasions in rehearsals of *Elegy for a Lady*. The response of audiences was split. People who were in the business preferred *Elegy for a Lady*, I think because of its strong form and its simplicity, whereas the public seemed to like to have the security of the detective thriller form.

We reversed the order of the plays. David Thacker wanted to leave them with *Elegy for a Lady*. Then we reversed the order every week and eventually every night and never came to any conclusion about the natural order.

If we did *Elegy* first the audience was tuned into a non-realist element and looked for that in *Love Story*. Whereas if we were doing it the other way around they tended to look for some kind of realism.

What he's looking for is a nuance of emotion; it's an emotional journey. The words are a superstructure. He paints with emotions.

Above all, the characters in *Love Story* are human beings and you can relate to them.

David Thacker

in conversation with Heather Neill

In both *Elegy for a Lady* and *Some Kind of Love Story* a man encounters a woman. In *Elegy*, they are ostensibly strangers, drawn to each other as the man buys a present for his mistress from the cool proprietress of a shop. In *Love Story*, a policeman, unable to extricate himself from a sexual relationship with a neurotic hooker, compromises his professionalism. On the first day we improvised around the text of *Elegy*. Arthur Miller sat in a corner at first and I had to invite him to come and join us. He was typically self-effacing. He wasn't going to throw his weight around. That play is the exception to his usual certainty. He had written it very quickly, dragged it up from the recesses of his sub-conscious. He was able to engage with us in a discovery of the play – that it is as much seen through the woman's eyes as the man's almost dream experience. The play was being revealed from both points of view simultaneously. I suppose that it is consistent with his sense of balance, of form.

The policeman in *Some Kind of Love Story* exists. Miller knows him and the play is modelled to a large extent on a case that actually happened. One of my funniest days in rehearsal was when I asked Arthur if he would be Josh, the psychiatrist on the other end of the phone – we only get one side of the conversation, the cop's, in the play – and it was wonderful. You understood at a stroke where the psychiatrist came from. It was very funny. But then Arthur Miller makes me laugh more than anyone I've ever met.

Bigsby: You once said that theatre is a way of changing the world. Does it ever have that power?

Miller: It does, but it's not a direct power. I think that man needs an image; we're desperate. I think that's why people still go to church here. They're looking for an image of themselves in relation to something. If the artist doesn't give it to them, they get it from advertising or some available public means. It changes the person's sense of himself. I absolutely believe that. I was brought up in New York City, in a completely unlettered, uneducated environment, where images of what you were supposed to do and be came directly out of the movies. We didn't have television. They were the popular arts. Later on, I did read books. And I think that people are always setting themselves up in relation to some available image. In that sense you do change people. Because if the image is of one sort, they will be influenced that way; if it's another sort, they'll be influenced another way. And that reminds me not of a book or a play but a criminal investigation I was involved in, a case in which they had clearly got the wrong guy. Before this case you couldn't say anything about the Connecticut State Police, to most anybody here, that was critical. We depend on them, especially in the country. It's a dangerous world, and it's a dangerous job, and, on the whole, they seem to be decent guys doing a good job. In this case, as it turned out, and in others, they were completely wrong. They had put the wrong man in jail, and were persistent about it, even after it became demonstrable that they were wrong. So it wasn't just an error involved here. They were really objectively going about destroying somebody in order to maintain their own reputation. Now this became quite dangerous. The Governor was not about to do anything about it. The only way to get any action was to get the public to see that they were in danger, or their children were in danger, if these guys were running round and didn't give a damn about justice. After all, they were armed. Well, it took some doing, but once they caught on, it totally collapsed. That is a fact. Now all the European playwrights, and the rest of the writers can tell me that it's hopeless, and by and large it is, but it's not one hundred per cent hopeless. That's all I'm about to tell you. Because I have seen where a seemingly impossible thing can be turned around. I talked to people who said, 'Miller, you've been had by some sentimental streak in yourself'. And I would say, 'Look, if I wrote a play like that, with that evidence, you wouldn't believe it. I couldn't make you believe this police case here'.

Bigsby: But in that instance, the meaning is inherent in the action. There was a murder, somebody did it, somebody did not do it. If you enlarge the compass of the discussion, then it becomes much more complicated . . .

Miller: But this is my point. Because it is so complicated, it is, of course, next to impossible most of the time to come to any conclusion about anything.

Bigsby: But doesn't art, therefore, risk simplifying and distorting and becoming another form of a lie?

Miller: If it is not devoted to an ultimate challenge. You see, what we're doing – most of us, myself included – is to take a little piece of that big tapestry and put it under a microscope, and deduce the real nature of the whole from it, hopefully. My initial gods were people like Dosteovsky, Tolstoy and the rest of those giants, who would have sat here and told you, that of course the job is to take chaos and subject it to order. That challenge was the only challenge worth taking.

Bigsby: But that is an order, of course, which you are actually projecting onto the material.

Miller: Right. Finally, I have to admit it, to stand aside and say, 'Yes, that's exactly what I'm doing. I'm projecting that order onto the material, and hopefully coming up with a fascinating and driving work of art'.

Bigsby: But what you are doing, then, is setting up your own fiction, your own version, against other versions. Now what distinguishes you, therefore, from the policeman who invented his fiction?

Miller: I suppose that my fiction is superior, because its internal logic is better, for one thing. It hangs together better than his story. When I punctured it, it collapsed, even though, at the outset, it seemed imperishable.

Bigsby: So it's an art, then, that's not deriving its impetus from morality but from its aesthetics?

Miller: Oh, absolutely. Oh, I've always felt that. You see, the morality comes because I have openly taken positions all my life. People come at me and want some support. Also, my plays often take positions about public problems. But I can't write unless there's an aesthetic influence, unless I really see it as a form, unless I see it as a collage of human forces that are really at each other's throats. And most of the time, I can't find that. I went through this whole criminal case. I know everything about it, but I can't write about it. That's funny. I know a lot of marvellous stories. Occasionally I put them into short stories, works of very limited compass. They are stories, that's all. You come away from it just remembering a few people. Now for me to launch into a play, and all that takes out of me, purely and simply to tell a story, is something I can't imagine. You see, my effort, my energy, my aesthetic is to find the chain of moral being in the world, somehow. It's moving in its hidden way through all my work. If I can't sense that I don't know where to go with it. But I'm not alone in that. I've been reading a lot of Molière in the last few years, and it seems to me that it's right where that age was too, in a way.

Bigsby: I want to ask about this business of imposing order, a moral order and an aesthetic order. You used to write some of your plays in verse originally. I don't know if you still do that? Is that a part of this principle of finding or imposing order?

Miller: Well the musical that I wrote, *The Creation of the World and Other Business*, is really all songs, and of course they're in verse form. It would depend a lot on where a play was set and what it was concerned with. If I were dealing with, let's say, New York, now, with that kind of language, I don't see how I could do it. If I were writing about New England, where the speech is very different, I might be able to do it. You see, what it does for me is to condense language. I might try it that way and then use parts of it. I wouldn't literally just re-type it into a prose passage. I did that with *Salesman*. Where I haven't done it, incidentally, which I didn't do in *The Archbishop's Ceiling*, I regretted it later. If I re-work it, I will go back to my other method. It condenses the scene. You simply drive all the fat out of it. Verse does that; the form does it.

Bigsby: From what you, say about the fate of *The Archbishop's Ceiling* in America it seems that the British theatre might be wary of creating the same conditions.

Miller: When I began to write, the illusion, which was partially based on reality, was that you were writing for the whole people. I never thought that I was writing for intellectuals, though I hoped that intellectuals might be interested in these plays. I never thought that I was writing for 'hip' people. I thought that I had to present in dramatic terms an argument which would draw in anyone of com-monsense: a plumber, a lawyer, a professor, a doctor, a small businessman, really almost anybody who was alive in the United States at the same time that I was. I think Tennessee Williams (without rationalising it any more than I did at the time) felt very much the same way. You felt that you were embracing the whole city, and therefore the whole country, and for that reason the plays we were writing had a story, they had some psychological depth, they were translatable into common experience. Then, for reasons which are quite mysterious and profound, the intellectual side of the audience pulled away and the ordinary folk remained in what was called the professional theatre. The alienation of that first part of the society was extreme, while the part that remained in the theatre was less alienated, if alienated at all. Now, what I was calling for back in the late 50s was some way of holding an audience (a broader kind of audience) together, by some kind of subsidy, or by lowering prices to the degree that anybody could get in. Now, mind you, at that time the prices went from four dollars to ten dollars and it seemed to me a scandal. I didn't know many people who could pay ten dollars to get into the theatre, or who would want to pay ten dollars to get into a theatre. But I didn't succeed. I was even instrumental in getting a meeting going between all the crafts in the theatre in the hope that we'd all take less money, the unions, the playwrights and everybody, and keep the costs down. Nobody was interested. Now we are without an audience at all. We have zero audience, for what you could call significant or serious theatre. Even when plays get good reviews people don't come. They've been driven out by habit and now we've got to start from scratch. Now I hope that the implications are perfectly clear for Britain: if you go the way we went you may well end up in the same place. That is, you aren't going to have a theatre. We don't have a theatre. There's a lot of talk about American theatre. We have shows. That's not a theatre. There is no continuity. I can tell you from personal experience it is next to impossible to cast a top level mature group of actors for a play in New York City today. Why? The good ones went to Hollywood when they made their first hit; they come back when they're exhausted, when their careers are finished. But the ones in the prime of life are very difficult to find. A few stars like George Scott will come back – used to come back – Dustin will do a turn, a few people like that. It came home to me very vividly when we did this movie of mine, *Everybody Wins*, that for a medium-sized part we could call up and get Jack Warden to play it: Jack Warden is a consummate actor, but he'd no more play that part in the theatre than he would stand on his head. He would play that part in a film, and it's not just the money. I despair of casting a play with mature people in New York now because we have dried it up. Britain, with all the trouble you've had, was the one hope as far as I was concerned in the later years, and it was because of subsidised theatre. The theatre of the Bottom Line, as you might call it, meaning that what pays big goes and what doesn't pay big doesn't deserve to live, is a catastrophe. There's an enormous amount of print in the *New York Times* every Sunday, billions of trees go down to publish this newspaper, and you will see 'Entertainment News' that will tell you what this star uses as a hair rinse, how he started or she started as a grocery clerk, and isn't it wonderful? But nobody discusses the central question: where's the audience? I remember the scandal among us when the *New York Times* took the theatre news off the front part of the Sunday paper and put it in the middle, and put the movies and the television ahead of it. That was a shocker! But they were reflecting reality, really. It was gone, the thing was gone. And any discussion in Britain which does not fasten on the question of subsidy is useless. There is nothing to discuss except that, in my opinion, because it's an art that cannot work on a commercial basis for very long. It won't go. The costs are too high. Society has to make a decision. Do we want to have significant theatre? If we do, we've got to pay for it just as you do if you want to have symphony orchestras, if you want to have quartets, even if you want to have opera. Somebody's got to pay. The ticket will not pay for it. The ticket will pay for certain musicals and that's what you've got. You go from one musical to the next. They're not even good musicals most of the time. But you can get enough money in through the box office. You don't need a subsidy for that. But as we all know you can get terrific reviews now of a straight play and it won't go.

So, it's literally the end. If I sound hysterical it's because I can't get anyone to register the news. The critics go on talking as if we had a theatre, they really do. We don't. Not a high level professional theatre. Where theatre is left, where it remains and where it sometimes thrives, is outside of New York City. But there it is usually subsidised to one degree or another. Subsidy is the key. And if you go away with it in Britain you're heading the same way as us. If you let nature take its course then indeed you will have to ask yourselves whether there is a mass audience or even anything remotely like it possible any more. Then you will have to go into the corners of the towns, certainly not the middle of London, New York or Paris, and find a little corner in which to put on your little play. But, in that case, you'd better not write a play with more than four or five characters and, God forbid, a little music. So it's going to narrow that play, and we're going to be a strange little item on the tail of the shirt of history.

In China, in the eighth century, the invading Tartars destroyed the intellectuals; they purged everything, excepting theatre. They loved the theatre. So whoever was intellectual naturally went into writing for the theatre. It was the only writing permitted. And they produced, it is said, thousands of plays. I've read eight of them and they're as modern as tomorrow morning. They're marvellous, short works. But there's an example you see. When they were dri   out of power all that ended. And the reason I mention it at all is .   ne theatre is so dependent upon the political structure of the society, for good or ill. It is not a natural growth. You can't just say, well let's just let it happen. In the circumstances now it won't happen.

I'll tell you another story. About twenty years ago I was at Brandeis University, and I was saying that we needed to consider a subsidised theatre of some kind. A man in the audience raised his hand and said: I manufacture shoes in Boston and I want to know, if I make a product that isn't bought in sufficient quantity so I can come out at the end of the year with a profit, why shouldn't I get a subsidy? Because you're saying that the nature of the theatre is such that it can't make a profit. So I said: You know you've raised a real hard one, but can you name me a classical Greek shoemaker? There is a value here which is not material and if we're going to consistently revert to business nomenclature, you're dead. There is no way to justify this on an economic level any more than there is to justify the creation of a church.

Bigsby: Do you have any hope for American television?

Miller: There's a very rich production company (they're the ones that own all the game shows – they make a billion dollars a week or something unbelievable) and one day its owner woke up and decided he had religion and he was going to do a production of *The Crucible*. They had an enormous amount of money, and I said, 'There's something wrong with this,' and they said, 'You have all the control, control of casting, the director, the way we shoot it.' So I said, 'Well, there's nothing wrong with that – let's do this.' And I said, 'I don't want to write it because I just don't want to go back thirty years.' So they got a damn good script writer, he did *Ghandi*, and a number of other things. He wrote a very good television version of the play. They couldn't get an American network to take it. None. N.O.N.E.

So, this may be a lesson, I don't know, of something. They're now negotiating with Home Box office, which is a Cable Network becoming more and more widespread in the country, and which has, apparently, from what they tell me, put on some very good productions. So maybe that's a way out of the dilemma, but our networks, which still I think purvey most of the television fare in the country, are a desert, and I personally think it's terrible because the guys that run it are really dumbells. H. L. Mencken said, 'Nobody went broke underestimating the intelligence of the American people,' but I think they really have blown it. They're losing their audiences: the networks are contracting. It has to be because they don't have the programming. But those guys are pleasing themselves, because that's their taste, that's what they like. They like what's on television. They think it's wonderful. That's what we don't appreciate. You can't argue with them. They're honestly aiming as high as they can aim. They're idealists. So, it's all over, and I hope you guys don't collapse and fade away, because where the Bottom Line gets in there it's going to take over. It always reminds me of what the economists used to say: bad money will always drive out good money, meaning if I have a printing press that prints dollar bills, and I don't get arrested in time, my fake dollar bills will displace all the good dollar bills in the market place. And the reason is simple. The good dollar bills have to represent some kind of production. My dollar bills simply represent paper, and I can outprint the Government provided they don't stop me. The bad money has driven out the good money in television and they have found that their taste can occupy all the hours of the day, and of course they're losing the audience. But the alternative is to bring in, I don't know what, artists or something. You know we did a television *Salesman* for CBS, that is they put up a lot of money, and they were very impressed with Dustin Hoffman and the whole thing. They were patting themselves on the back. They had a big dinner, and they wanted me to make some kind of statement, and I said, 'Well, you seem to like this programme.' 'Yes, it's marvellous,' they said. And I said, 'You know this was written by one man alone in a room. There was no committee.'

Bigsby: What is the relationship as you see it between the British and the American theatre at the moment?

Miller: There is a symbiosis, a common life, a mutually dependent life between the American Theatre and the British Theatre. The Americans, who are thoroughly commercial theatre people, and generally speaking are not crazy about a subsidised theatre as competition, nevertheless love to come over to Britain and buy into British subsidised theatre, and bring plays at a high profit to the United States. I am secretly hoping that in trying to strengthen your resolve to support such theatre we will make it more possible to establish some such thing in the United States, some day, probably long after I'm gone; but believe me without it the theatre is crippled. I beg you, don't be seduced by the idea which has seduced us, that the botom line is reality as far as the arts are concerned, meaning, don't believe that what does not make a profit is not valuable. We all know the old saying that people who know the price of everything and the value of nothing are impoverished people. You are enriched people because of what you have. Don't lose it. My hope will remain that someday, somehow, the moribund and once thriving New York theatre will once again raise its head from the dead where it now lies.

Malcolm Bradbury

Any writer, British or American, whose work started in the 1950s, as mine did, is likely to have felt the potent influence of Arthur Miller. And in those days in Britain, the new American writers represented world standards in literature in a way that was now almost absent from our own literary tradition. The demise of Modernism, the disordering of thirties radicalism, the chaos of wartime, the devastated state of postwar Europe, the hideous aftermath both of the Holocaust and the coming of atomic war had created a time of artistic uncertainty, a dislocation of artistic continuity. Writers who had paid pre-war homage to Communism in an age when massive solutions to economic and human problems seemed necessary, now surveyed the new order in Europe and spoke of the God That Failed. The tentative new liberalism born out of the aftermath of war looked over a world that seemed no more stable than what had gone before, and the great new ideological division of the age depressed the imagination and encouraged a naive provincialism.

It was in these circumstances that a few American writers suddenly emerged to provide the literary energy, the moral vitality, the new tone of voice that was needed. The United States was now a Superpower, its economic affluence restored, its political power and world influence made massive. It had also entered on an era of social and moral conformity and of high materialism, the fruition of one aspect of the American Dream. Its image was ambiguous, a lure and a nightmare to others. The writers who mattered are those who tested the ambiguities both of the age and the new cultures that were born out of the age. It was not surprising that Jewish writers spoke with a special authority, and Jewish-American writers above all. They spoke for the moral novel, for the liberal theatre, for the burden of human responsibility that fell on all writers in difficult and ambiguous times, when the paradoxes of morality, politics and human freedom called for reassessment. For me as a writer there were two in particular who spoke and wrote with the moral force and complexity that the times made necessary. One of them, in the novel, was Saul Bellow. The other, in drama, was Arthur Miller.

Miller's idea of the purpose of theatre and the role of the playwright was firm at that time, and has varied very little since. Theatre was and is a public art, a popular art that solicitied its audiences with vivid human recognition, or rather a vivid recognition of being human. Being human meant recognising the complex nature of our responsibilities, testing the nature of our limits, our courage, and our endurance. Drama was therefore an art which explored the difficult bridge we always cross between individualism and social existence, and it meant looking with due scepticism at the American Dream, a Dream of intense value that had grown ever more materialistic in the new world of affluence and urbanism. It was, of course, no accident that Bellow and Miller were both Jewish-American, conscious of immigrant origins, and that they had developed many of their preoccupations as well as their techniques in the left-leaning liberal climate of the 1930s. Both had clearly transferred that vision into an age of new powers that posed new questions and new quandaries, not the least of them the discrepancy between material emancipation and moral and psychic deprivation.

And it was very appropriate that the burden of exploring the relation between human responsibility and the new social and economic order should fall on American writers. America was not only an economic and military Superpower; it spread its radiation, extended its influence, fielded its metaphors and dreams across much of the globe. Miller was soon a world playwright in much the way that Bellow was soon a world novelist; both had a strong sense of history, and both tested the images and expectations of the time against a global meaning. Bellow's cramped victims in their urban alienation, dreaming their large dreams, and Miller's wartime entrepreneurs and small salesmen, those who were 'never anything but a hard-working drummer who ended in the ashcan like all the rest of them', evidently merited a world stage for their dramas, and their authors provided it. As Miller phrased it himself, in the most famous passage of *Death of a Salesman*, 'He's a human being, and a terrible thing is happening to him. So attention must be paid.'

For, I suspect, many young writers like myself, Bellow and Miller came along at quite the right time, and we were able to find in their spirit of moral enquiry and liberal decency a seriousness now needed if we were to find a significant postwar role for the writer. Amongst other things, this amounted to a high valuing of personal lives, a solemnity before experience that did not inhibit the playful discoveries of art, and a high estimation of authorial responsibility and conscience. Miller's writing has the grainy realism that evokes life, but this is never innocent; he also tests and challenges it. It tells us that all deeds are decisive, and that for each of them there is a price which we diminish if we set it too low. The price can be reasonably charged of both parties in the social bargain; if we as writers have a debt to pay to social reality, social realities in turn have a debt to pay to the conscience of the writer. Miller always knew about the price, and he paid a considerable one himself, for the nature of his own liberal and moral allegiance. Even self-avowedly democratic societies have an aversion to seeing their dreams and high expectations, their conformities and limitations, put through the rigorous test that great drama can bring to them. Miller's Ibsenite inheritance (how appropriate that he should adapt and amend *An Enemy of the People*) proved indurant in the grim age of American McCarthyism, when many American minds refused to accept the value of the challenge of conscience. It gave a bitter justification for the need for Miller's kind of theatre, the theatre of self-questioning democratic dissent.

Miller still remains, I suppose, an exemplary playwright of that time, but over the four and plus decades of his writing life he has weathered several kinds of social and ideological vicissitude, and several changes of critical and dramaturgical taste. The task of the Western writer has been assessed and reassessed very variously; social and political theatre have been in and out of favour, challenged by the age of performance, of randomness, of linguistic play and linguistic slippage, of the Death of the Author. Miller's is an authorial theatre, a theatre in which the playwright summons by stagecraft and force a moral as well as imaginative authority. That, I take it, is part of his claim that 'attention should be paid'; it is at once a moral and a dramatic principle. So it is that great writing transcends all talk of form and mannerism, of technique and vogue, and is able to pass beyond art's necessary play and randomness. To me that sense of art as humanistic enquiry – the 'paying of attention' – seems to lie at the heart of it all, and demands of each writer the moral strenuousness and strength to pursue it. Miller's work, through all its changes of rhythm and theme, through all its multiplicity of performances on stages all over the world, has sustained that. In Eastern Europe we have recently seen many expressions of the moral force of literature, its power to activate the decent human imagination. For four decades Miller has given the West the same sense of art's moral vigour, and that is one reason why there is not a Western writer who can fail to feel in his debt.

Peter Nichols

There was a marvellous point where we were discussing subsidy and Arthur Miller suddenly started speaking. And he spoke for about ten minutes. He said there's nothing else that's worth talking about in this country. It was as though he'd come down from the mountain, and he'd brought the tablets, and was just reading them out. And there is something very Mount Rushmore about him, very Moses bringing the tablets down. And it was very eerie.

Everything went very still, and I suddenly thought, he's the last generation who could say this kind of thing and say it in just this way. Since him there's been scepticism, there's been doubt, and that's been our style. Before him, and with him there was certainty, an absolute certitude that you couldn't argue with and it gave him a great eloquence.

Michael Billington

The Guardian

It is difficult to write objectively about Arthur Miller. It was from him that I learned that modern drama has the same capacity to handle pain and suffering as classical tragedy. I first came across his plays in the late 1950s when the amateur Talisman Theatre (a jerry-built tin-hut with epic pretensions) in Kenilworth staged two remarkable productions of *Death of a Salesman* and *A View from the Bridge*. At the time I was overdosing on Stratford Shakespeare and associated high drama with costumes, verse and the spectacle of great actors suffering emotional torments in sepulchral lighting. Modern drama, in contrast, seemed to me a flimsy, lightweight affair. But those two Miller productions enabled me to grasp personally something that is now a schoolbook commonplace: that tragedy is not defined by language or setting so much as by intensity of feeling and that an American salesman is as valid a candidate for heroic status as a Scottish thane.

But early exposure to those two Miller productions also subconsciously taught me something else: that a bedrock test of good drama is that private desperation is related to social conditions. I forget now who first pointed it out but the pivotal scene in *Death of a Salesman* is really the one where Willy Loman goes to talk to his 36-year-old boss, Howard, who is busy fiddling with his new toy, a wire-recording machine. On a human level, the scene is obviously deeply affecting: an old man is forced to crawl and beg before a boss he knew as a kid. But, on a social and political level, the scene is about the redundancy of the Loman style of salesmanship (based on the creation of a false 'personality') in a world where the technology and the values are changing fast. I doubt that at seventeen or eighteen I articulated the point. But coming to Miller's plays long before I discovered his American contemporaries or the European Absurdists, I naturally assumed that the job of the dramatist was to sew together, preferably with invisible thread, an exploration of the individual and a critique of society.

Over two years constant viewings of Miller's plays and random meetings with the man himself have also taught me another lesson: that the best dramatists are very like their work. As a man, Miller strikes one as liberal, ironic, open, humane: very much what you would expect from a close study of the plays. Two incidents stick in my mind. One is of Miller, at a weekend conference at the University of East Anglia, patiently listening to all the set-speeches and then gently but firmly pointing out to a left-wing English dramatist the danger of approaching play-writing with a set of cast-iron certainties. My other memory concerns a key Miller notion: responsibility. We had done a longish, exhausting interview at the National Film Theatre to celebrate the publication of *Timebends* ('Most of the time,' Miller revealingly remarked of the whole publicity-circuit, 'you end up interviewing yourself'). Over dinner afterwards, he was quietly ruminative. But he suddenly turned and asked me if I thought it was true that British critics were more prepared to reveal their political attitudes and private beliefs than their American counterparts. It struck me as a very Millerish question since it was based on the assumption that aesthetic judgements are related to social factors and that it was dishonest for critics to hide behind some mask of Olympian objectivity.

What is striking today, of course, is the vast discrepancy between

Miller's critical and popular reputation in Britain and the States. For a long time I put this down to external factors. On the one hand, the fact that the British subsidised theatre is largely run by a generation who grew up in the Miller era and who imbibed American culture from birth: on the other hand, the native American urge to abolish the past. But I am now convinced it goes much deeper than that.

Earlier this year I sent a group of American students I was teaching to see David Thacker's Young Vic production of *The Price*. These were bright students: the movers and shakers of tomorrow. Obviously one of the points of Miller's play is to achieve a fluctuating sympathy between the fraternal protagonists and to suggest that Victor's muted idealism needs to be harnessed to Walter's go-getting energy. What interested me was that, in my very English way, I leaned towards the wasted, defeated Victor whereas the bulk of the students sided with the worldly, pragmatic Walter. But even more revealing was the objection from some quarters in my class that the play was, apparently like a lot of Miller's work, too cynically realistic and offered little prospect of happiness, growth or change. It was, said someone, a 'downer'.

I argued that, in drama, there is always something bracing and tonic about the confrontation with reality: that *King Lear*, *Waiting For Godot*, *Death of a Salesman* send one out spiritually refreshed because the dramatist has, in each case, faced up to cruelty or despair or a life founded on lies with great honesty. But I could see that many of the students demanded more from a play than that: in the case of *The Price* they wanted specific assurances that Victor and Walter would be better men tomorrow. My hunch is that it is Miller's refusal to provide just such assurances or to yield to the built-in optimism of the American psyche that prevents him being as widely honoured in the States as he is in Britain. He retains to this day, as far as I can see, the liberal's faith in human perfectibility. But, for all the quintessential American-ness of his themes, he has the European dramatist's belief in the need to ask daunting questions rather than provide comforting answers. In the end, that to me is what makes him such a fascinating writer: he remains totally anchored in American life while challenging almost all of the values and beliefs that make the society tick. He is the late twentieth century's most eloquent critic of the devalued American dream.

Irving Wardle

The Sunday Independent

In his last book, *Recollections and Reflections*, Bruno Bettelheim refers to the Jewish myth of the thirty-six just persons. 'Only the existence of these righteous ones justifies humanity's continuation . . . otherwise God would turn his face from the earth and we would all perish. As long as these righteous ones walk on earth, nobody must know who they are.'

Leaving God out of the equation, a large part of the human race would unhesitatingly nominate Arthur Miller as one of the current thirty-six; a major artist who has consistently used his creative energy for the good of his fellow man, and set his art aside when the battle needed to be carried out in newspapers, international conferences, or in the witness box. His life is a famous model of constructive purpose and moral courage. The snag is that word 'famous'. Miller does not walk the earth unknown. Like Solzhenitsyn and Havel, he occupies a brilliantly lit platform where he is required to be good for the rest of us. Solzhenitsyn came in for belittling comment as soon as he lost status as an oppressed person; and the same thing is now happening to Havel, judging from accounts of snide attacks on American television. Miller has not been an oppressed person since the time of McCarthy; and there exists, particularly among the American Jewish community, a suspicious eagerness to find fault with him – on grounds of pharisaical self-righteousness, or artistic decline. So much acclaim, it is felt, is bound to have had a corrosive effect.

So far as I know, nobody has ever succeeded in nailing him on the first count. Watch Miller speaking in public and you are in the presence of a man who certainly knows his own worth; and, by that very fact, never overestimates it; and whose attention is wholly fixed on the world outside himself. Asked by Clive James (BBC Television, February 1990) about the long-term social influence of *Death of a Salesman* and *The Crucible*, he replied – after thinking over the question as if for the first time – that he doubted whether they had had any effect whatever. He then went on to describe a Kremlin conversation in which Gorbachev had told him that all the Marxist fundamentals were open to debate, because 'most of the things we're looking at now didn't exist in the nineteenth century.' Miller transcribed the conversation and offered it to the *Washington Post* which declined to publish it. After which, Miller said, 'Now I know where the party line is.' This was a story about the changing world of East Europe, and the static world of the Western media: it was not a famous author complaining about disrespectful treatment.

As for the plays, there is indeed a difference between those that made his name, and those he has written since *After the Fall*. It is summed up in two statements: from Dustin Hoffman, who calls Miller a great story teller; and John Lahr, who says his later work is plotless. The connecting element in this seeming contradiction is Miller's consistent endeavour to dramatise the workings of memory – which runs right through his output from *A Memory of Two Mondays* to *Danger: Memory!*. Memory plays are a prevailing species, one might almost say a disease, of the American stage. Sample, for instance, a season or two of the Louisville new drama festival, and time and again you find a character suddenly stopping the action to recall (at length) something that happened to him at the age of six, which is supposed to explain why he has been behaving so badly up to now and why (now he has got it off his chest) he will henceforth lead a blameless life.

Miller, for all his allegiance to Ibsen, has never written that kind of piece. But in *Salesman*, and *All My Sons* he did present an action governed by past events. Which obviously implies knowing precisely what those past events were; a bold claim for anybody to make. Whatever happened to Miller around the time of *After the Fall* seems to have involved an abdication from control of the past. It is still his obsessive concern; but one which he now approaches with modesty and doubt, knowing himself to be a prisoner of his own perceptions. This is not the basis for the vigorous linear narrative proceeding to a conclusion where the writer strikes the patiently waiting nail on the head. It is, however, concerned with truth, and with creating dramatic patterns that fit the facts rather than the writer's convenience. The detective piece in *Two-Way Mirror*, for instance, is a play about finding out whether there is a play there or not. And for sheer narrative excitement it is up to anything he produced in his story-telling phase. As one of our theatre magazines reported a couple of years ago, he is a promising writer.

Dan Sullivan

Los Angeles Times

The custom in Japan is to name respected artists of a certain age Living National Treasures. That would be a nice thing to do for Arthur Miller at seventy-five, except for the implication that the artist receiving the honour is being placed, ever so gently, on the shelf. Better just to say: Happy birthday.

But it would be foolish to pretend that Miller hasn't become a father figure for American and British theatre artists – and one that they need. They need to know that it is still just possible to have an honourable career in the theater, if you are good enough and if you are tough enough, in the right direction.

We are not discussing career moves here. I refer to integrity. It has something to do with not being too impressed with birthday honours or, conversely, with bad reviews. *Death of a Salesman* was not especially admired by the London critics in the 1940s and was very much admired by the London critics in the 1980s. What changed? Not the play.

Miller probably wouldn't be surprised to see himself go out of fashion again either. What counts, for him, is the quality of the workmanship, and he will be the judge of that. An easy enough attitude for Arthur Miller to maintain, the young playwight will say: he's an eminence. Right. But he wasn't always one.

As for his plays, what's interesting is how much less old-fashioned they look today than they did thirty years ago. If it needed to be said at that time that the world was absurd, it is now possible to notice that its absurdity often makes use of logic. What's really strange about the universe is how often things absolutely *do* add up.

That's what the old furniture dealer is chortling about at the end of *The Price*. But it has been Miller's theme since *All My Sons*: the sense that, whatever your choice, the bill will shortly be in the mail with the final payment being the killer (*Death of a Salesman*).

Anxious as he is to get the point across, Miller doesn't direct his characters' testimony. He gives them as much freedom as the fable will allow. That's true even of *All My Sons*, his most hammered-together play. What an interestingly mixed man Joe Keller is, a man with blood on his hands and also a man who can say, and almost believe, that he did it all for his family. What an elaborate rationale his wife Kate has worked out to prove that their son didn't really die in the Pacific. And what a suggestive picture the play offers of uneasy postwar America, trying to get back to tending its garden, as if it hadn't seen the snake.

Miller also keeps his most famous hero in double view. On the one hand Willy Loman is a dupe, sandbagged by the system. That's Charley's view from next door. On the other hand Willy is a genuine hero, laying down his life for his son. That's Willy's view. He dies exalted, and Miller admires him as much as he pities the poor sap.

The Crucible can seem a bit schematic, but not with the right actors. I saw it with my daughter at South Coast Repertory in California last season – her first experience of the play, my seventh or eighth. But there was a moment in the trial scene where we both thought that John Proctor had beaten the rap.

Why? Not just the acting. Not just the direction. The man writes in the present tense. Let's not put him on Mt Rushmore just yet.

Bigsby: Your next play, in 1980, was *The American Clock*, which was, on the face of it, rather strange because it was a 1930s play. Certainly it was a play about the 30s. What brought you to write it at this time?

Miller: I thought it would be interesting and useful and fun to recall what was probably one of the two greatest blows to the American psyche, the Great Depression (the other being the Civil War), and to see how it affected us. I have to say that my experience with this play tells you something about the Broadway theatre. It was brought in by a producer who did not have sufficient capital to advertise it. So it closed with full houses. And this is the insanity department. He simply didn't have the money for next week's advertising. So that was the end of that. You did it here at the National in a beautiful production, where, incidentally, you could use a live orchestra on stage where we would have used tape recorders. It made all the difference. It was to be a vaudeville, and in vaudeville, as you know, there was a live orchestra. You could also have more people in the play than we had. It's a kind of mural. It's supposed to pick up images of Depression America like a mural does, a large painting, and for that you need people. Well, we couldn't afford people. Not many. So that impoverished little play simply sank in the world of musicals. It's a system hostile to the drama.

Bigsby: The first play that you wrote, at the age of nineteen, in 1935 when you were at the University of Michigan, was a play about the Depression. Forty-five years on you wrote another play about the Depression. How differently do you see that period now?

Miller: Well, there are a lot of differences, I guess. One of them is that in 1935 there were two tremendous factors which either don't exist now or are less important. In 1935 there was the threat of Fascism. You woke to it every morning, and not only in Europe. We had counterpart organisations in this country and one of the fears one had then was that these guys could conceivably assume power. The anti-Semitism was very thick. Racism against the blacks was, of course, unrelenting and there was certainly anti-foreignism in the air. You see, when you get that kind of unemployment and the unemployed see some guy getting a job who doesn't speak English properly, inevitably there's resentment. So you had anti-foreign, anti-Jewish, anti-Catholic, anti-everything, feeling and it was pretty heavy for a while. Presumably we still have it and it's probably never going to go away but one sort of assumes that we can keep it under some kind of control and the majority of the people don't go with it. One wasn't so sure, in those days, if the majority wouldn't go with it. You see my people originally came from Austro-Hungary. They knew Germans a lot. The only language that was spoken in our house, aside from English, was a Germanised Yiddish, but it was like an Austrian dialect and they had tremendous respect for the Germans. We have all forgotten that Germany was the least anti-Semitic country in nineteenth-century Europe. The French and the British were not so hot but the Germans were civilised. After all, Heinrich Heine was a German and he wrote the national songs of Germany and he was a Jew. So when Hitler came in everybody thought, certainly those in our house thought, well, this is not going to last. The Germans are too intelligent for this. He's vulgar, doesn't speak German very well, speaks with a dumb accent like somebody yodelling in the mountains. You see, they understood that accent. They would go to the movies and hear him on the films and newsreels and come home laughing at him. Well, it turned out it was nothing to laugh about. That scared them. That this kind of irrationality could take hold of what they really thought was a far more intelligent country than the United States, better educated, more cultured, was frightening. So it wasn't simply a question of losing your job. Then, of course, there was the question of what the great mass was going to do, because no fix was working, even after Roosevelt got in. The stuff was brilliant. It was improvised, but somehow or another the great beast couldn't get up and breathe again. It was still floundering. Indeed, we didn't get out of the Depression until World War II. It was the war that cured the Depression. So now I can look back at it and see that it was a tremendously important incident in a long history. But we didn't know then whether history was going to end right there. And there were times when it seemed to me to be touch and go. The Government was obviously at a loss and one feared for the future that way, for the civilisation; you were scared that this damn thing was just going to go into the sewer. Of course an older generation might have had more perspective than I did. There had been depressions before in American history, one of them as recently as 1920. There had been a severe set-back on the Stock Market, a lot of unemployment, for about six or eight months or a year. They might have thought, well this is another one of them. When it got lengthened out, though, one sensed that this was the fate of America. There would be an indefinite period when people were simply not going to be able to work and a college graduate might assume that he would have to take any job, manual or labour, be a salesman, an usher in the theatre, selling something in a department store. Most of my classmates really never thought that they would work in the fields that they were trained for. It was a very rare thing. I had a good friend who was, of all things, a propeller engineer and propeller engineering is pretty complicated. There weren't many of them. I used to ask him, 'Who the hell is going to make an aeroplane any more?' The very idea was absurd. I remember him saying, 'Well, there's a place in Wako, Texas, where they still make planes for the army – small scouting planes.' But I doubt whether the army added more than six planes a year to the fleet. From where I stood the thing had simply come to a stop and what we were doing was living off of each other. If some guy needed a salesman for two weeks, you'd do that. I know a man up here in Connecticut whose father was a lawyer and at about the time we are speaking of he went to work for the State of Connecticut digging a viaduct with a pike and shovel. And he worked on that for about three years.

Bigsby: On the other hand, it was one of those periods in American history when people shared experiences across classes.

Miller: There was some of that. I wouldn't over-emphasise it though. Some people have pointed out that it was easier to make money in the Depression than at any other time. The reason for that is if you came out of that crash with capital, the value of that capital was *vastly* increased. You could buy a Cadillac car for eight hundred and fifty dollars. You could buy a pretty damn nice house for five thousand dollars. Imagine if you had a hundred thousand dollars cleverly spread around, you could own half the state. Many people did. Of course, the banks were in great shape, then, the ones that survived. They could buy cheap and wait. They could afford to do that. It was a great time to be alive but ninety-nine per cent of the people couldn't do that. As to sharing, well I remember one incident. I bought a car for twenty dollars, at Ann Arbor, a model T Ford, which at that time was ten years old. And I drove back in 1936 carrying a friend of mine, who was going to the Spanish Civil War where he would get killed, and the car began to sound funny. So I pulled over to a country garage in Ohio and I said to the man there, 'Look, don't do anything because I've only got two dollars and my friend here has three dollars.' That's what we had needed for gas and that's all we had. 'If it's going to cost anything much more than that, let's stop right here because I'll have to hitch-hike home and do something about the car.' He said, 'Well, let me look at it.' He looked at it and the next thing I knew, he took the head of the engine off and he found a valve in a garbage pail that would fit the car. He got very interested in that engine. He hadn't seen one of them in ten years. He repaired the thing, put it all back, started it up and was obviously happy to hear it running well. So I said to him, 'OK, what do I owe you now?' He said, 'Well, I think twenty five cents would be alright.' Now you see he was sure we didn't have anything. If he'd had the least suspicion that I was having him on, it wouldn't have worked that way. But he knew we were in the same bucket as he was and these guys were living on the edge of the world, nobody paid them. They were getting stuck all the time for unpaid bills. You find some of that in Steinbeck's work, perhaps a little bit sentimentalised but not much. Certainly by about 1936 one was pretty sure that this was endless. The New Deal had been in for four years, or something like that. And they'd tried a lot of stuff, the WPA, all those programmes which were supposed to have raised purchasing power, get the pump primed, as they said. They tried all kinds of programmes to generate business; they worked for about three months and then collapsed. And we generally assume that this was the final crisis of capitalism. It was going to give up the ghost. Maybe there was a sense of sharing; we were sharing our misery. Everybody was hitch-hiking everywhere; hundreds of people were on the road. One assumed that they were honest people. Nobody was ever afraid to pick me up. I did nothing but travel that way, so did my friends. It was assumed that it was simply somebody who didn't have any money, who was a basically honest person. You see, the perverse hadn't yet taken hold as normal. The perverse was still perverse, lousy behaviour, ungrateful behaviour, people being dishonourable, all that. Of course it happened all the time but you kept thinking it was an exception, that really the way man was, was a hard-working guy who was simply out of luck. We had people sleeping in our basement all the time, some old, some not. Some guy would show up at the back door and ask for a hand-out and then my mother would swear she would never do it again and she'd say, 'Where are you living?' Well, he was living in his shoes; he wasn't living anywhere. And they'd wash the windows for twenty-five cents or something and sleep down the basement. One of them didn't leave for six years.

Bigsby: And this surfaces in *The American Clock*?

Miller: That's the thing in *The American Clock*, yes. The difficulty in writing a play like that is the background is difficult to establish. You see, it's not just deprivation. It's a whole atmosphere.

Bigsby: You always said that the Depression was to the twentieth century what the Civil War was to the nineteenth century. Why is that?

Miller: I think that Americans, and possibly it's true of other people in Western Europe, live with the unspoken fear of falling, the sense that the whole system would simply stop working. I had a friend who used to be one of the editors of *Reader's Digest*, and he spent a week with various officials of the Eisenhower administration, one of whom was a banker named Humphrey, who was the Secretary of the Treasury. And he asked him whether we could have another Depression. This was 1953 when Eisenhower was President. It was a prosperous time, the boom was on again, and Humphrey, who was a very conservative man, said, 'Why not? We never understood why the first one happened.' And that's the real truth. There are so many theories about it that there is no theory. Some people think it started in Europe. Some people think it happened because of the Stock Market. But I think its's important in American history because it was the moment we realised that the whole thing is fragile. It can stop and hence it's vulnerable to any alternative system. Perhaps that explains the ferocity of the anti-Communism in this country. The Depression was a mystical event like the Civil War, and any great event of this size finally outranges the human intelligence. You know, odd things happened in the Depression when it struck. We suddenly had a drought in the west, unheard of since time began, unbroken; the sun seemed never to set. That's when the so-called Okies, farmers in Oklahoma and other states, were simply blown out of their farms by dust storms which had never occurred in known history. It was like nature had decided that we were finished. And there were enormous numbers of people wandering the face of the United States. People from Chicago decided it must be better in New York. People in New York figured it must be better in St Louis. People would get into a little car – gasoline then cost eight gallons for a dollar – and just drive. You could go a long way on a dollar and they'd scrounge around on the way. There was a kind of disassociation of cause and effect, because nobody had an answer to the damn thing that rocked the soul of this country. It's been covered up as pain always is. Nobody wants to remember painful things and so we have tended to deny that on the one hand we are afraid of it and on the other hand that it might happen again.

Bigsby: That being so, why did you not write *The American Clock* until the end of the 70s?

Miller: One obvious reason was that by the end of the 70s I was in a country that had seemingly no relationship to any country I knew. The 60s were over. That rebellion, which I never believed in, incidentally, since I always felt it was cosmetic and totally middle-class and had no reality, was finally ground down to nothing. So we were living in what to me was a kind of an oblong blur. There was simply no definition to the society and I had an urge to tell people, 'this is when there was such a thing as necessity, when you didn't have to invent your necessity.' By the 70s the sons and daughters of the middle class were trying to figure out something that made life necessary. Earlier, Kennedy created a necessity in the Peace Corps. That excited a lot of people. They would go into poverty. They wouldn't have to go wash their blue jeans and make them look old. They would really have old blue jeans and they'd be in a place where they couldn't wash their hair all the time, a place beyond the reach of under-arm deodorants, and this was very attractive because this was a disoriented society. But by the 70s this had gone. People didn't know what was necessary any more and I was tempted by the idea of telling them that underneath all this prosperity there is a skeletal structure of human relations which is still there but is covered up by this prosperity. And I wanted to show them how when it collapses you can find it. I wanted to tell them that this thing that seems to go on forever, doesn't, that when you think it's OK you take the next step and start falling 3,000 feet over the abyss. That's why it started then and not earlier, I suspect.

Bigsby: Was there any sense that the conditions of the 30s were beginning to recreate themselves?

Miller: I have always been waiting for that to happen. I am still waiting for that to happen and am convinced its going to happen. One way or another. You see, we've got it now in certain parts of this country. The farm population, in some cases, are in a worse situation than they were in the 30s. There are more farmers being put out of business now than there were in the 30s. It's incredible, but it's true.

What we've got now is a different psychology because the rest of the country is operating. These people now figure, well there's something wrong with me. Again, you see, it's the great American self-blame thing. And we have the steel industry, which effectively is in the position it was in before the unions were organised in 1935. The steel towns of Pennsylvania are in a permanent state of Depression. The oil industry has gone to pot and they're walking around wondering what tomorrow morning is like. The difference is that in the 30s *everything* stopped together, almost. The manufacturing stopped. The farming stopped. The price structure simply collapsed. Nothing was worth anything so you had people starving in New York City and in Pennsylvania, New Jersey, Ohio and so on. They were dumping milk on the road while people were dying for it.

Bigsby: In *The American Clock* you draw an implicit portrait of the 1920s as a period of unreality, a period that fed on its own myths. On the other hand, didn't the 30s also feed on its own myths.

Miller: Every age does. From about 1937 or 1938 the country seemed radicalised. Everybody I knew was a radical. Even middle-class people. The vote for Roosevelt, who by conservative standards was an anarchist, was overwhelming. The Republicans could barely carry one state. The welfare state was accepted by everybody, which was a more or less radical position, *vis-à-vis* the hands off *laissez-faire* idea that the Government is some sort of referee and keeps its hands off business which runs the society. Most people didn't trust business to run anything. So I would have thought it was a radicalised country in those days. I remember thinking, 'Who is ever going to go to church again or a synagogue?' Well, within fifteen or twenty years friends of mine who agreed with me were officials in their synagogues and I used to look at them and say, 'Are you out of your mind? What has happened?' Well, they couldn't even remember. There hadn't been any other way. Its as though this episode simply passed into the realm of denial. I think the job of the artist, incidentally, is to remind people of what they have chosen to forget because it's too hard to remember. That's what *Salesman* does and that is why people who go to see it hate it at the same time. It's because it reminds them of this kind of treatment of human beings.

Bigsby: Why *The American Clock*? Presumably not simply because you are turning the clock back in time?

Miller: The idea is that there is a clock running on every civilisation. It has a beginning and presumably it has an end. What is the hour at the moment? That's the idea. And that would have been a very accurate way of characterising many people's idea of the 30s. They felt that they were on their way to something else. A lot of us thought that it would be some kind of socialism. Other people, whether openly or not, wanted it to be some kind of Fascism. The idea of a *laissez-faire* country, such as we'd had until Roosevelt came in, where the market and the needs of the market were supreme, was gone. That could never be again.

Bigsby: On the other hand, when you write about the past you are presumably partly inventing the past, not just recalling it.

Miller: Sure. That's true. I've gotten obsessed with the idea that we are literally creating our history. If you can't find three people out of a hundred who could tell you what Watergate was about, how the hell are we going to talk about history of a hundred years ago, or fifty years ago or thirty years. The fact is we can't remember the day before yesterday. The mind of an individual, like the mind of a group, selects certain mythic, convenient, easy to memorise characteristics, whether they be real or invented, of an era, and that's history. I have to go back into my notebooks to remember the 70s. They are far dimmer to me than the 30s or even the 50s and this is a fraud we commit on ourselves. I've come out of that playwrighting tradition which is Greek and Ibsen where the past is the burden of man and it's got to be placed on the stage so that he can grapple with it. That's the way those plays are built. It's *now* grappling with *then*, it's the story of how the birds come home to roost. Every play.

Bigsby: Yes. There's always seemed to be a Calvinist streak in you. In *The American Clock* the 30s were the price that had to be paid for the 20s.

Miller: That's true.

Bigsby: But that's true of most of your plays, the notion of the chickens coming home to roost.

Miller: I believe in it. Absolutely. You spend and then you want. Then you've got to retrieve what you've spent and you've got to account for it somehow. I don't mean to God, I mean to yourself, or else you are totally incomplete always. You never complete yourself.

Bigsby: But that suggests that you believe in the concept of justice.

Miller: I believe in it as an aim, sure. I realise that there are situations in which it's impossible. You get existential justice, where you do your best, but that's about it. History is so contradictory that the claims of contending parties have equal weight and then you're with Solomon; you have to cut the baby in half.

Bigsby: But surely the most terrible thought is that people do not actually have to play for their sins?

Miller: But we do. Somebody has to. We do with our forgetfulness. The Germans are paying by an amnesia, many of them, which is necessary, I think, for their mental health. It's not possible to confront this thing. We do it *vis-à-vis* American Indians. The British do it with God knows what, whatever your burden of guilt is. That's the way we carry on. You rationalise in a way. You deny it and it keeps coming back in one form or another. That is, it might be your claim to some kind of a life because you are a more moral people than other people. And somebody comes along and says, 'Well, what about (whatever) . . .' And there you are.

Bigsby: The Depression suddenly seems to be in vogue, especially in Hollywood, though usually with this sort of patina of sentimentality, doesn't it?'

Miller: I am afraid that unless you are, first of all, a witness, the air of futility that was over everything is almost impossible to recreate. I knew medical students at the university: I would say that out of the six that I knew fairly well, only one had any assurance he'd ever practice medicine. Why were the others studying medicine? They had managed to cadge enough money out of their parents and grandparents and loans to go to university. They loved the art of medicine. They wanted, like an artist wants to be an artist, to be doctors. But nobody really thought he was ever going to do anything that he was trained to do. You went to school to stay out of the work market, more than anything else. I remember, when I was at school I wanted to quit after my sophomore year because I realised all I needed was a library. I didn't have to go to the university and I thought, 'What the hell am I going to do with myself, though?' It's cheaper to live as a student, you see. You get away with murder because you had free medical care, free eye glasses, at the University of Michigan, and you had an excuse for living. People would say, 'Well, what are you doing?' and you'd reply, 'Well, I'm a student', even though you knew in your heart you didn't have to be a student. You know, I knew how to learn by this time. I knew how to study and I knew what I wanted to learn. I could have done it all in a room in New York. I knew guys who stayed at the University of Michigan for *ten* years; they were perpetual students, like in

Chekhov. They just were in dread of ever leaving that place and being asked, 'Well, what are you doing?' That kind of futility is very difficult to convey hard, although in certian parts of the United States, it's easy. I am reminded of it very often when I go through Harlem. There's about sixty per cent unemployed there. If you want to see what it was like through the whole country, go up there, because they're standing on the corner looking at each other, grown guys, tossing a coin, listening to the radio, watching the sun go down. Nothing tomorrow but more of this. That's really the Depression. What they do in Hollywood is find some of the styles of the Depression, the dances and so on.

Bigsby: On the other hand, *The American Clock* itself ends on an optimistic note, rather like an Odets play. Is that because you were trying to recreate that necessary optimism of the 30s or is it an optimism you actually felt in the present?

Miller: Well, its part both. I felt that I should end the play in the way that it would have ended then. You see, the crazy thing of it all was, we were so desperate that the popular songs of the time were all optimistic: 'Life is Just a Bowl of Cherries', 'The Sunny Side of the Street'. They were all upbeat titles. The best comedies that Hollywood ever made were made in the 30s.

Bigsby: Films like *Gold-Diggers of 1933*.

Miller: The musicals, yes. People say, 'Well, they were trying to keep the people's mind off their trouble.' That's only half of it. The people's mind was already half off their troubles. They were really thinking, 'Well, tomorrow, something good could happen.' Or else they'd commit suicide. They might do both; feel everything is coming on great and then commit suicide. Incidentally, speaking of suicide, there were a lot of them when the first shock occurred, especially among upper-class people, stockbrokers who couldn't face what they had done. But I would suggest that probably overall there were fewer suicides than normally. I don't know that for a fact, but I would be willing to bet that that was so, because underneath it all, you see, you were stripped of all your illusions and there's a certain perverse healthiness in all that. I wrote a line in a televison adaptation of *The American Clock*. The Government passes a law suddenly guaranteeing deposits and savings banks – this is after this family has lost all its money and has no more – and Rose, the mother, says, 'Well, thank God, now all our money is safe in the bank.' Well, that's Depression humour. That's really the way it was, sharp, but somehow smiling irony. That went on a lot. You see, some of the best comics came out of the Depression. Sid Caesar, Zero Mostel, all those guys. As Pearl Bailey used to say, 'cheer up – it can only get worse.' And I suppose that way in the back of the back of the brain, you knew you were in America and that somehow it was going to work out. God knows how. But alongside that, running along parallel to that idea, you felt it was never going to work out. On the other hand, if you stuck around long enough people would say, 'I'd kill myself but I want to find out what happens.'

Bigsby: And are you still waiting?

Miller: Always. Sure. You can't be an American without a future. A future is part of the present always. The past isn't. We never remember anything. When I wrote *The Creation of the World and Other Business*, I had the Devil say to God, 'Never remember anything.' It's Lucifer who remembers everything. See, he's the intellectual, he's trying to make it all logical, consistent. God's an improvisor. He's an American.

Bigsby: I wonder, though, if there isn't a rather more benign tone in your work now. I was thinking the other day of the self-destructiveness of your characters, the number who actually die or kill themselves: Joe Keller kills himself in *All My Sons*, Willy Loman does; John Proctor dies in *The Crucible*, Eddie Carbone destroys himself in *A View from the Bridge*. Maggie does in *After the Fall*. A character in *Incident at Vichy*. It goes on and on and on. But for the last twenty years there seems to be a more benign spirit.

Miller: Yes, I've noticed that myself. I suppose I'm closer to the end so it's not so easy to knock people off. Maybe that's part of it. But I think I'm more interested in continuity than I used to be and in time. You see most conflicts are settled, in this country anyway, in two ways. People become indifferent to them, get used to the contradiction, simply live it out. They form a kind of membrane and carry it into their graves with them; it doesn't kill them. The other way is when they can't do that and they go crazy. We have a lot of crazy people in this country. More hospital beds in the United States are occupied by depressives than any other disease, by far. More than cancer, more than tuberculosis, more than anything. People are simply unable any longer to get up in the morning and do the thing that they did yesterday. That's another way you see, but explosive endings are less characteristic of us. Maybe we got Swedish or something in our old age. It always seemed to me in Sweden that that's the way they did it. They simply stay out of the war longer until the light comes up in June. Then they go out and do a few push-ups.

Bigsby: Your plays have always been very precisely located in time and in space, *The American Clock* perhaps more so than most. Are you surprised at the extent to which those plays find an international audience?

Miller: You know, I don't understand any of that or I understand only a little bit of it. Take a play like *Death of a Salesman*. It's about a family and the family situation is fundamentally unchanged wherever the human society is. I did it in China and I discovered that this was a Chinese family. It really and truly was and that play will be running in China a hundred years from now. They adore that play and they all kept saying, 'It's so Chinese.' Well, what's Chinese about it? What's Chinese is that the parent wants his children to do better than he did. They find an ego satisfaction and gratification in saying, 'My son is a dentist, whereas I was a ditch-digger.' That apparently goes on all around the world, regardless of what the system is. In the Soviet Union there's a whole class of people who fixes up their children's future by making contacts for them, sending them to the right school, corrupting everything around them so that they don't ever have to compete for real against the great unwashed out there. It reassures me somehow (it probably shouldn't, but it does), that Willy Loman, for example, is a universal human being, more or less, because, if we're not profoundly different, then there's hope for us, maybe, if we last another thousand years. That there is such a thing as a human culture rather than a tribal one means we have some means to create a permanent peace of some kind, that we've a common interest, common characteristics, anway. Because I can tell you that when I went to China the experts all told me that they are never going to understand *Salesman*. Now the mistake they made is the one we generally make; there hasn't been a salesman in China since, the latest, 1949, and even then they were gone. Of course, it doesn't depend on the salesman; it depends on the father and the mother and the children. That's what it's about. The salesman part is what he does to stay alive. But he could be a peasant, he could be, whatever.

Bigsby: Do you think the same thing would apply to such a play as *The American Clock* which grows out of a specifically American experience?

Miller: Well, if you think about it for a moment, any catastrophe that a country's gone through, whether it be a war or a depression, that shakes it up so that the structure of the society is questionable, would probably result in something similar. Now I should think that because *The American Clock* is preoccupied, a lot more than my other plays, with the social side of man, how he relates as a citizen, it might prove difficult. It might possibly seem exotic, but, of course, especially in England now, the American experience is so familiar to a lot of people that probably even that won't be the case. In other words, if it's humanly valid it will probably have an audience.

Bigsby: Of course all of your plays make that connection between the public world and the private world. But here, it's actually a part of the structure of the play, isn't it?

Miller: Yes. Also *The American Clock* is validly about people in social trouble. That's not an incidental part of their lives; it's the centre of their lives, because the one thing about the Depression was that society was in the bedroom, it was in the living room, it was in the kitchen. You could no longer talk about a private life in the normal sense of the word. You know, when seventy per cent of the people on the block had lost their jobs, what the hell else are you going to talk about? Then the petty mother-in-law jokes and problems with sex become, relatively speaking, boring. The interesting thing is what's going to happen tomorrow; what's Roosevelt going to say tomorrow? You know, people woke up in the morning and got the newspaper to see whether he'd invented something. Maybe he'd got a new idea, you see, because it was all being improvised. We weren't Russians with a Five Year Plan, with some heavy thinkers that worked it out. We were Americans, and every week he'd start up anew. Sometimes a programme would go on for six months, and he'd say, 'Well, that didn't work. I don't know what got into me to start that! Let's scrap it, and start something else in its place.' So *The American Clock* is preoccupied with the common fate, put it that way, of people caught in a national dilemma. It's really about the survival of a country. Well, I suppose, after all, the British were in the Depression just as much, if not worse, than we were.

Bigsby: It's not hard to see certain elements of your own personal history appearing in that play. Are you, in a way, not merely tackling a public and a social issue, but laying to rest the ghosts from your own past?

Miller: Oh, definitely, sure. I made no real attempt to disguise that at all. I'm looking at a very young man, and maybe a little more warmly than I ought to, but this way I felt better when I was writing it. I suppose I'm looking at a survivor; it didn't kill me. I managed to get myself through it. But it did injure a lot of people; it injured them permanently. It dented their sense of security about the world. But their children put it out of mind completely. They don't remember any part of it. They now criticise the New Deal. Their children say that it's too socialistic. Of course, they all survived because of the New Deal. Today, when the Stock Market drops in one day sixty points – that's more than the drop in any one day in 1929 – nobody goes screaming around, because there are certain regulations put in by the New Deal which prevents it from unravelling. There are certain guarantees that automatically come into play when this structure begins to shake. We've had bank failures on a scale in some cases greater than in 1929/30. The Continental/Illinois Bank failed. I think it was the third largest bank in the United States. Well, within about three days it was taken over by a couple of other banks. The depositors hardly knew there was a ripple. This thing had been bankrupted! It's because the new legislation had guaranteed the depositors, so that everybody didn't show up Monday morning demanding his money. They went right on about their business and they said, well, we'll get paid one way or another.

Michael Bryant

The American Clock, *National Theatre, August,*
1986

I discovered Arthur Miller at Oxford Rep. in 1955. We thought we were very advanced when we put on *All My Sons*. I was deeply influenced by Marlon Brando and James Dean and mumbled and grunted my way through the text.

My next Miller was *An American Clock* at the National Theatre. By this time I had realised that he was a great writer, and like all great writers, the words are more important than the actor speaking them.

I played Mo, a man with whom I had very little in common. Or so I thought. Though the part never fitted me like a glove, I let the words dictate the mood and pace of each scene and discovered that if you do this it's hard to make a complete hash of a part in an Arthur Miller play.

Neil Daglish

From the first readthrough of *The American Clock* we all knew we were on to a winner. The characters just jumped off the page and the narrative was so strong we sailed away. The play was a huge success at the National Theatre. On meeting Arthur Miller after a performance of the play we all behaved like 'groupies', rushing around trying to find 'prop' dollar notes, anything we could lay our hands on, for him to sign.

A totally rewarding and happy experience never to be forgotten by those involved with that production.

Sarah Kestelman

I can't recall what age I was when I first saw the film of *Death of a Salesman* but I do recall that its emotional impact made a profound impression. So when I eventually decided to become an actor it was with Arthur Miller that I applied for a grant to Drama School, with Arthur Miller that I tentatively presented myself to stern faced boards set to deter me from acting by refusing a grant unless I chose a teaching course. I wasn't sure I could act but I sure knew I couldn't teach so it was with Arthur Miller that I returned three times until sick of the sight of me they gave in! At the Central School of Speech and Drama I played Beatrice in *A View from the Bridge* and shortly after leaving Central I played Abigail in *The Crucible* at the Manchester Library Theatre, where I also played the mother in a workshop production of *Death of a Salesman*. Many years later I was to play Esther in *The Price* at the Palace Theatre Watford.

In 1986 I was asked by director Peter Wood to be in *The American Clock* at the National Theatre. The author describes his play as a vaudeville – the epic nature of its subject, the devastation wreaked upon men and women by the Depression, stripped bare of dignity by poverty and degradation, is told in a series of fast moving tableaux, the action interspersed with songs, as it travels across the vast span of America pitching us into a world of high finance back to back with the starving farmers in Iowa; from the lush, plush apartments of the rich to the slums of the tenements; from the powerful offices of General Electric to the push and shove of meal lines and relief offices; people on the street, people cramped and claustrophobic, people on the run – begging, penniless, hopeless – people simply struggling to stay alive. It is a huge play moving with immense speed like a movie, driving the audience right into the very heart and organs of a society ripped apart by the terrible tide of events. These are ordinary people, some good, some bad, some smart, some not, who deftly draw with the minimum of strokes a sketch of their lives, their pain, their humour, frailty, tenderness, fear, corruption, persecution, bigotted ignorance, brutality, death and with these fifty or so characters and their show of courage and strength, however pitiful, we feel the overwhelming pressure of the millions in the collapse of a nation.

At the centre of the play is a family, the Baums: Moe a rich and successful businessman, his wife Rose, his son Lee. Their story weaves through the action as their dramatically changing circumstances unfold. It was Rose that I was to play. Rose Baum's philosophy of life is an adorable and crazy mix of intuition and superstition; she's a good wife and mother, loyal, strong, generous, fiercely maternal, passionately romantic. In adversity her wit and her optimistic refusal to be defeated by injustice, along with her driving ambition for her son, give her her strength while for shelter her comfort is in her books and music, her memories and dreams. But as the pressures mount and those things that have helped keep her dreams intact are stripped away, fear begins to erode her sense of self and gradually breaks her spirit. Re-reading the end of the card scene, as I did recently, I was again helplessly moved by the intensity of heat in that tiny house in Brooklyn, the four women sharing a waiting game, each blocking out her pain and loss in her own way; the sickening despair in Rose erupting into hysteria; the surprise of where her mind takes her so unexpectedly affecting; her final plea to her God so unbearably naive. I knew the emotional demands of the scene, let alone playing a card game at the same time, never mind doing a fortune as well (I'm hopeless with cards!), would make it a fiend to rehearse. The only way I know of stripping a scene bare so that I can begin to inhabit the skin of it is by learning it, so I began from day one with Rose's 'memory' speech. My method is a laborious one, writing out the entire part over and over to test the accuracy of my memory, Miller is not difficult to learn, though, because there is a natural flow and music to his words, and the thought processes of his characters focus the scene and give it its rhythm. On the other hand, the idiom he has adopted in this play, with its short dense scenes as in a vaudeville sketch, demands that the performer be absolutely precise about the centre of the scene so that the leap into it is clean, and the emotional demands, mood, nuance, all perfectly balanced as on a circus spinning plate. Vaudeville requires immense energy and attack, a delicate touch, a lightness of foot – it's tightrope stuff – one slip and the whole damn thing crashes into the net. *The American Clock* was to open in the Cottesloe Theatre, the smallest of the NT's three auditoria and the most beloved, especially by actors, because of its flexibility and intimacy of space. Later the production transferred surprisingly happily to the huge Olivier stage, but these early days in the Cottesloe were the best. Rehearsals began on Monday June 16th at 12 pm. There were nineteen in the cast, most of us performing every night in repertoire: I was playing Mrs Frail in Congreve's *Love For Love* and Katarina

Binder in Arthur Schnitzler's *Dalliance*, adapted by Tom Stoppard, both in the Lyttleton Theatre, and Mrs Peachum in Brecht/Weill's *The Threepenny Opera* in the Olivier. We had six weeks rehearsal, not long at all, but we were a strong team and having worked so closely together for so long we had established a shorthand that gave us great freedom. I don't play the piano so Robert Lockhart, our musical director, and I had to find a technique for Rose. On cue we'd both raise our hands at our respective pianos and on a second cue we'd lower them onto the keyboards (mine was mute) and he would play. Rather than attempting to mime the fingering I simply placed my hands on the keys, resting them there until the music ended. The effect was completely successful and the audience happily accepted the convention. Each actor, with the exception of the Baum family, played three or four parts. As the characters became more sharply defined and we got a clearer picture of the whole sweep of the play, all the music and songs seemed to fall into their natural place. The show began with an empty stage. From the back of the auditorium a lone whistler, unaccompanied and very slightly amplified, began the first few bars of 'I found a million dollar baby'. One by one we joined in, some humming, some whistling, some singing the words, moving through the theatre till we filled the stage. As the band took up the melody we began speaking, as a chorus, the opening speech of the play which linked straight into the shoe-shine scene and a reprise of 'million dollar baby' hummed barely audibly to clear the stage. This segued into the first Baum scene and 'I can't give you anything but love, baby'; a night-club smooch, 'Ten cents a dance,' linked the Baum chauffeur on his car-repair trolley into Rose's Schumann; 'The Joint's a jumping' set up a marathon dance competition, a repeating theme – each scene hooked by music, a one-liner, a song: 'We're in the money'; 'On the Sunny side of the street'; 'Life is just a bowl of cherries'; ''Swonderful!' 'Love and a dime' . . . We had no set, only props; huge prop tables at either side and costume rails. The entire cast became the subway blocked together strap-hanging; the packing cases from the farm in Iowa transformed into a box car on a freight train. Add to that a bicycle, a baby's pram, a table, a chair, a bed, a flag, a piano and finally we evolved a style that invoked a real spirit of vaudeville. The first preview, on July 31st, received a tremendous ovation and the press night on August 6th was a triumph. We continued in the Cottesloe until November 27th and moved into the Olivier from December 17th till February 10th, 1987. It was a wonderfully happy experience for us all and for me it was a perfect marriage. I loved Rose: she liberated me and I hope I liberated her. When the author came to see us on October 21st, 1986 he paid me a great compliment by saying: 'You were my mother – thank you!' Toasting us afterwards he looked a proud and happy man.

In all his plays Arthur Miller unexpectedly touches on emotions universal to man; suddenly he'll strike a chord so deeply personal, stir memories so sharp and vivid, re-visiting, maybe, some part of ourselves long held concealed for better or worse. Mysteriously bonded in a darkened auditorium, laughing together, crying together, there is comfort in the sharing because great theatre is catharsis, it purifies and when we come through to the end there is real fulfillment and elation in the survival. Relief too!

David Schofield

In the Autumn of 1986 I worked on *The American Clock* at the National Theatre.

In this production many of the roles were 'doubled up'. In fact I was lucky and got to play four parts: an auctioneer, a deep South redneck sheriff, a dispossessed Slavic misfit and Theodore K. Quinn, the all-singing, all-dancing head of America's General Electric Corporation.

Although Quinn was the largest of these roles, my favourite was the Sheriff, a part, I may add, rejected by some other actors as being too small. And yet in this short scene we saw the predicament of so many people during the Depression – a love of life, however, painful, coupled with a hidden unspoken despair. Huge issues dealt with on an intensely personal level.

At the time of writing I am playing John Proctor in *The Crucible*, a large part in anyone's book, yet I would happily play any part for the gift of thinking, feeling and speaking the words of this storyteller of the brightest magnitude.

Bigsby: You were saying that *The American Clock* has elements of your own life that you were re-encountering. In writing your autobiography you also revisited that former self. Was the young Arthur Miller that you met a stranger or somebody that you still recognised?

Miller: I had to continually keep correcting what I put down. I'm not the doctor who doesn't contract the disease. I only know about the disease because I have it. I'm one of the patients, and he is a stranger until I pierce certain levels of denial, and then it starts getting painful, and I realise what a fragile thing I was. You see, the process of time is like geology; the living organism gets encrusted by salts and various kinds of deposits, and all you get back is the impression it makes in previously soft material that is hardened. But the palpitating organism that made that is gone. It's only in your memory, and to provide that requires a kind of act of grace. And sometimes, with the greatest will in the world, you can't get it back. And I tried not to write about it unless it started to pulsate. I didn't want to write about fossils. I wanted to write about the actual organism, and a lot of the time there's no way to get it back and I knew it. That recollection in tranquillity that art is supposed to be – I've never found that. There's no tranquillity about it. It's very agitated. It's in many ways excruciatingly painful.

Bigsby: Writing an autobiography surely isn't that distinct from writing a work of fiction. Indeed, it is in some senses, surely, a work of fiction. You're creating a character, the character which is Arthur Miller. What sort of a character does this person turn out to be?

Miller: I don't know, it's hard for me to tell. I'm trying to be the witness, that's all. I'm not the judge, hopefully. If I've succeeded in doing what I wanted to do, I won't be the judge, I'll be the witness. I'll be the accused, if you want to put it that way. I've attempted to justify myself from time to time – just as in the courtroom, you know, unless you want to get killed by the judge. So the equanimity, which is generally associated with memoirs, is missing here. I hope, anyway. That's not what I was aiming at. I think that we've lost our history. I think we always do, especially at this time. Too much happened too soon, too quickly. I'll give you a quick example. There's a playwright who lives around here. We play tennis sometimes. He's a very nice man, a good playwright, and I mentioned in passing (now he's about fifteen years younger than I am) that I had had some difficulties with the American passport bureau, and he was astonished. He said, 'Why?' I said that I was denied a passport for five years. They wouldn't let me travel. We were talking about American PEN protesting that some guy in Russia was not permitted to leave to attend some congress or something. I said that I know how he feels because I was prevented from leaving the United States to see a production of *The Crucible* in Belgium, and they wouldn't give me a passport for about four and a half years. He'd never heard of all this. He was brought up in Boston; he had taught at Harvard. He was an extremely knowing guy, and I thought, OK, if it had happened with some incident in the life of some writer in the 1890s maybe I could understand but he'd lived right through this. So I thought, it's a good idea I'm writing my memoirs just to tell him, 'Look this was what was going on, fellows.' Because, as God said, 'They'll never remember anything', and, what you don't remember, catches up with you.

Bigsby: Presumably, in the process of writing it, there were aspects of your life which you were now able to detail but which were closed to you before. I'm thinking of the material you could get through the Freedom of Information Act from the FBI. Did anything interesting emerge out of those documents?

Miller: I tell you, the truth is that, as with everybody who gets the freedom of information material, they go through it first – the FBI does – and they ink out anything that they choose to, and they don't have to explain anything. So you have a sentence composed of the words 'the' 'he' 'it' and 'Frank', or something like that. There's a lot of that. What you're given is what you already knew, though there was one event which I'd never known, and that was, when I was living in Brooklyn, it was my first marriage, they had apparently been trailing guests at our dinner party, from our dinner party to where they went home. I can't imagine who the heck had been trailing, but they actually had been tracking people from our house to wherever they were going. Maybe they forgot to ink that out. They don't give anybody the name. They don't say who that was. They have somebody reporting that so-and-so (un-named, that is, it's inked out) left at eleven o'clock and went directly home. What the hell they thought they were going to find from one of our dinner parties, I can't imagine. But there it was. This was referring to the years around 1950, and I don't know what else was in there that would have been interesting because it's gone. You see, they give you a certain amount of information, but the principle is that they're never going to reveal their sources, so if you have some bosom buddy who's actually an agent, they're not going to tell you about it. So I didn't find out a hell of a lot from it that I didn't know before, quite frankly.

Bigsby: There is a certain polarity in your concern with fathers and sons, that's to say, the father tends to represent authority and power, the son some kind of moral integrity, some sense of a spiritual dimension. Can you conceive of those two things being united; can power be united with moral integrity?

Miller: Up to a point. But I think that power is, by its nature amoral; it's got to do with continuing power, which may, at any one point, coincide with moral demands, but not necessarily. If it does, it's incidental. And that's true in every society; I think it's true in the American, English, Russian, anything. I don't see any hope of bringing those two together. I say that, curiously enough, as an American, because in this country you can't rule excepting by consensus. That's why we have no real political parties; political parties are meaningless, really, because the President has to represent unemployed people, millionaires in Chicago, artists in New York, and so on. It's an immense society, and there is no way of logically dividing it up and saying, 'Well, I represent the poor, and I hope to be President', or, 'I represent the well-to-do, and hope to be President'. No. You've got to represent the poor and the well-to-do to be President. So, automatically, you're starting with lying. Your impulses may be the best – you want to make the poor happier – but you can't get to that without telling a lot of lies. And as soon as you start that, you know what happens. It starts to rot you out, and pretty soon all you've got left is, 'Love me. What I do is good, because I'm doing it.' And that's Lyndon Johnson, it's Mr Nixon, it's even to a degree Mr Roosevelt. They all finally end up saying, 'I don't remember where I came in here, but I'm here and I mean well. And if you don't believe it, watch out, because I'll get you before you get me.' It all comes down to that. The rules are a little bit better here than they are in some places.

Bigsby: But you live away from the centre of power; you live really in a small village. Is there some significance in that, in terms of your life and beliefs?

Miller: I tell you, living in a city, in New York City, which is the only city I recognise as a city – the rest of them are all large neighbour-hoods – there's a certain kind of repetition that wears you down. It wears me down. You see, I was born there; I spent most of my life there. The repetition of celebrating the demise of the city and the end of the world while at the same time saying, 'Isn't this the most exciting place you've ever been in your life . . .' becomes tedious. The point comes when you don't want to hear any more of that. I would suspect, too, that most of the writers who are writing are not living in the big cities, anyhow, now. It's just a fact. Why, I don't know. I have a clear route from my bedroom into the studio. I don't have to park my car; I don't have to argue with anybody before I get in here in the morning. And I've got more than enough subject matter to keep me going for the rest of my life. Of course, I'm in touch with more than it seems that I am. I don't have any problem in understanding what's going on in the city, because, as I say, it is vastly repetitive. As a kid in Harlem, I used to have to defend my property every day against thieves. Our apartment was robbed regularly once a year. It just came with the seasons. About August it got robbed. It's fundamentally the same thing, except now the weapons are better; they're more like the army, you know. They're better armed and possibly a little less inured to human suffering. But we were in a bad way in the thirties, as far as that was concerned. The one big difference now in the city is drugs, and that is a difference. That's a big one, because, those people are simply pathological. They're sociopathic people; they're against any society but the one-member church that they belong to. And you're fair game to them.

Bigsby: But is there a sense that you're closer in some respects to democracy here. I mean a town meeting makes no sense in Manhattan.

Miller: Very definitely. Oh yes.

Bigsby: So the public and private are much closer here.

Miller: Oh, absolutely. You can't have a conversation out there without bringing in the society. And that's the impulse behind a play like *The American Clock*, which is devised as a mural, which means that it is a large picture of a society, with the details being individual portraits that are seen up close. But from a distance, it should show a vast movement of a whole society. Part of my impulse was not only to deal with the Depression itself, but with the idea of survival, because the fact of the matter is that these were the same people who fought World War II and who went on to create a new age with all its faults and its hopes. They were not defeated by it.

Bigsby: What was it that suddenly, at the age of seventy, made you decide to write your autobiography? Why had you waited that long and why did you decide to do it then?

Miller: It was a pre-emptive strike. I had been approached over the years by three or four threatening scholars who were going to write my biography and from time to time I got tempted in order to give them my version of events, but the prospect was awful because I saw myself sitting there talking to someone when I could have been writing it myself and probably taking more time talking to them than I would writing it. The other thing was that for ten or fifteen years now I had been making stabs, not at an autobiography but at more or less giving my feelings about various events that I lived through, for historical purposes, because I found that even people in my own generation had very dim memories of what, to me, had been vivid and very important. So I accumulated probably a hundred and fifty pages like that over the years but I realised I had no form for them and that they would probably remain fragments. But my friend and former editor, Aaron Asher of Grove Press, kept leaning on me to do this, so I thought that, if I could find a form for it, it might be worth doing, if I could find some pleasure in doing it, because the idea of writing an account that was at all day by day or year by year was boring. So I started to fool around with it and arrived at this form which has the virtue of expanding to wherever I wanted it to expand and contracting when it needed to contract, meaning that I could follow themes and people instead of following chronology in any way.

Bigsby: Yes, that's the fascination of it. It isn't just the recording of events or experiences. It is shaped, maybe partly like a history book or even like a novel.

Miller: Well I don't wish it to be mistaken for a novel but I found in reading back over it that what you are getting, a lot of the time, is several views of people. On page ten you get one slant on somebody, then he returns on page twenty-nine with a difficult slant. On page one hundred he is back, different again. So it gives you the feeling, I think, as it did me when I was writing it, of going down deeper and deeper into the event.

Bigsby: One result is that it brings together moments and experiences which are separated by time. But isn't that, in a way, what you did also in *Death of a Salesman* or *After the Fall?*

Miller: It only occurred to me when I was practically finished that I had done more or less what I had done in *Salesman*, that is to seize some major motion of the mind when it occurs instead of holding off until its proper time is ripe. So that if something occurs to me on page ten, instead of waiting because it does not yet happen chronologically for fifty pages, I go right to it and the result I think is to reproduce the way the mind works, because we don't really remember chronologically. When you remember something, you remember clusters, clusters of images, clusters of feelings; one feeling invokes another and the calendar has absolutely nothing to do with it. When you think back, a scent, or a vision of some kind, just speeds through the calendar with the speed of light. That is the way this book was composed.

Bigsby: And is it memory that we are getting here or did you rely on diaries, letters and so on?

Miller: I relied very little on diaries because I found that once I had committed something to a diary it was usually, for some reason I am not sure I understand, the least interesting part of that period. What got engraved on my mind was the nub of it all, really the part of an experience that helped to form me. What I put into a diary was its shell and so very early on I found that useless. I have never kept diaries systematically, anyway, more so in recent years but even there I suspect if I went back to them I would find that the stuff that I remembered was more vivid.

Bigsby: How difficult is it to recapture innocence, the sharpness of the original experience?

Miller: I believe I can do that. I am able, when I am sufficiently moved by something, to put myself back in time quite quickly and without too much trouble. In other words I can dispel the succeeding years so that I am as naive when I am writing it as I was when I experienced it.

Bigsby: How difficult is it to tell the truth in an autobiography?

Miller: Well, there are truths that no one can tell because they don't know them. Nobody's view of themselves is the same as the view of others of them. But I think that if you can withstand a certain amount of anguish you can approach it and imply it even if you can't really come out and say it in so many words. I think there is a lot of anguish involved but there is a lot of anguish in writing anything that matters in terms of art. I used to say that unless a work somehow made me blush, it probably wasn't any good. And I think that there is something of that in everybody who is really writing out of his blood.

Bigsby: But isn't there a temptation both to protect the people you care about and to become your own defence attorney?

Miller: Yes, well there is, sure, you have to negotiate all that with yourself and finally I think there are compromises made that you are not even aware of, because we heal, so to speak; great anguish and pain create a healing process and you are looking at pain after you have recovered from it, so that you can never really quite re-establish it, but I think on the whole it is reasonably possible.

Bigsby: *Timebends* is a book that brings together not only different moments but also the public world and the private world.

Miller: I had hoped, through this way of writing and through the whole project, that, at least in principle, I could make people, the reader, see my experience as part of an age, because I do. It's quite obvious to me that we can't begin to get the impact of a person without setting him in his time, in the context of the main drift of events that he has lived through. We lose track very quickly of what the temper of the time was, what everybody was absolutely fascinated by at only one moment. For example, what did the Russians mean in 1943 to any democratically inclined person? General Douglas MacArthur said that civilisation depended upon the bayonets of the Red Army at Stalingrad. I am sure a lot of people can't visualise it today but they were really being crucified by the German Army and refusing to lie down. This example of human endurance, courage and intrepid values was burned into the mind at the time. I do believe that without them the world would have been Nazi, regardless of the Americans.

Bigsby: That interests me because running through this book there seems to be an argument that you are having with America, and the nub of that seems to be your feeling that America wants to deny history.

Miller: We are always denying the past, it's not just now. Americans are only very slightly interested in what's happened. They want to know what is going on now and tomorrow. The future, youth, the way things are going to change, that's what's interesting. We romanticise the past a lot. The greatest example is *Gone with the Wind* which, after all, is about the bloodiest civil war in the history of the world and yet the image that the novel and picture give is one of nostalgia. It's a fairly painless picture, I think; you are not really involved in the agonies of the people involved in this catastrophe, not to speak of the viciousness of the politics of the time. It was really a brutal, brutal thing. We will go back that way in the popular arts but hardly with any real analytical sense. So there is a constant war on forgetfulness, if you want to get any truth going in the world, and I think a lot of our novelists are involved in trying to set the record straight. Styron does and Updike does, a number of writers are trying to recover what they think are the realities of the past, primarily because they have been skipped over. We don't want to hear about them much.

Bigsby: And what about your own history? This is a book that takes the reader back to Arthur Miller as a child, as a teenager, as a young writer. Looking back now do you feel a sense of continuity with that young person, the writer beginning a career, or is it the differences, the discrepancies that most strike you?

Miller: Both. I feel, especially after having written this book, incidentally, that I am the older fellow who I am describing here as a young chap, and I hadn't been aware, really, until I wrote the book how continuous I am, in my own psyche. However, that does not take away from the absurdity of some of the things that I believed. I was sure they were true and I got very angry when they were contradicted. But I accept the contradictions, somehow, I don't know why: I don't feel bitter about them, in other words. I don't feel bitter that I was so wrong about so many things. I just stand in awe, sometimes, of my own denseness, given the obviousness of my mistakes. I can't imagine how I could have been so dumb but then that makes me investigate further: why did I persist in thinking certain things about people, about politics, about myself, in face of the evidence? And that makes an interesting kind of investigation. It's not enough to sit back and say I was fooled, tricked or whatever.

Bigsby: You are prone in your own interviews, I have noticed, to confess to a sense of doom, a sense, not absolute, but of an inevitable catastrophe. I have to tell you, however, that I have never seen any evidence of that either in you as an individual or in the work. Your tragic sense of life is surely a long way removed from doom.

Miller: You have to be optimistic to approach tragedy. It's a form of optimism, actually. The unspoken question is why bother with this story at all, why do we have to go through all this? The only answer is that the author, the audience, the society, the work is optimistically struggling to discover a relationship with ultimate forces. Pessimism is comedy because it is saying in effect there are no ultimate forces, it's all accidental; we are a joke and anyone who tries to press on further than that is another kind of idiot. The optimist is required to ask ultimate questions. That is what tragedy is about. Therefore I think that somebody who rather enjoys existence can approach tragedy better than someone who is bitterly disappointed.

Bigsby: And your own work is laced with a resilient irrepressible humour, not often commented on by critics.

Miller: You know people go to see my plays, and I stand in the back watching. They laugh a lot and then, at the end, they come out and I say, 'Well you had a lot of good laughs,' but they don't remember. They forget completely the way Loman was so funny.

Bigsby: *Timebends* is obviously only an interim report. Do you think that in the process of writing the book you learned something, not so much about your own work as about yourself?

Miller: Oh yes, we mentioned it earlier, the subtlety of the continuities is more apparent to me now. I have had, like everyone else, difficulty from time to time imagining how I could have done some things that I have done in my life. I can't relate myself to that fellow of twenty, thirty, forty years ago who was doing all that. We are more various than we like to think. You tend, in your estimates of yourself, to sort of shave off what does not logically seem to cohere and you come up with a kind of neat puppet that you can appreciate with one glance and estimate with one glance. But we are far more various and more foolish. And those foolish things come back and you can relate to yourself better through them. I found that was far more possible now I have written a book and I feel better about it.

Bigsby: When you were relatively young you very briefly underwent Freudian analysis. Then you abandoned it, partly because you said you were afraid that it might destroy something in you that was the root of your creativity. But in a way writing an autobiography seems a little like a Freudian analysis.

Miller: Well, I probably am a Freudian by birth. I say that because what I learned in psychoanalysis was far less surprising than I would have liked, given the cost of it all. There was a struggle on my part with my brother, whom I love, for the affections of my mother. I was doing that all the time. I was always putting my foot out to get him to fall on his face and I would triumph in her eyes. There was always a conflict between imitating my father, modelling myself after him, and wanting to destroy him. But I was perfectly conscious of all that; that was no great surprise, and that is why I say I was probably Freudian to start with.

Bigsby: So writing the autobiography didn't pose that threat to creativity that you were afraid it might.

Miller: No, as a matter of fact I feel now that if there is time left me I will have far more to write than if I had not written the autobiography.

Bigsby: Why is that?

Miller: All sorts of subjects have shot up in my head as a result of confronting this, including the possibility of doing them as novels.

Bigsby: I was going to ask about that, because this is the most extended prose piece that you have written. Might you return to the novel?

Miller: Well, I am tempted. As a matter of fact I began working on one just to see whether it was something I wanted to do. And of course the expansiveness and the freedom involved in novel writing is very tempting to a playwright who has got to use every syllable so that it works on stage. It is very tempting. But I get more excited about the theatre and I don't know why, since there isn't any. I may write another book, but I'm writing a play now. I don't know, we'll see what happens.

John Guare

A couple of years ago I went into Lincoln Center Theater looking for my friend and associate, Gregory Mosher, its Artistic Director. Mosher wasn't around so I sat down at his desk thinking what it would be like to run Lincoln Center and suddenly, as my first visitor, I heard a voice around the corner. 'Mosher, we're going to lunch.' In came Arthur Miller.

'Mosher's not here any more,' I said, feet on the desk, 'I now run the store.'

'Then you're coming to lunch with me. I just handed the publishers 1038 pages of my life and I'm not celebrating alone.' We went over to the local for what turned into three hours. 'By the way, what have you done with Mosher?'

I have only read about Buddhist satori, that crystal clear moment of epiphany. That day, at that bar, Arthur was as weightless as shining and free as a human being can be who's just handed over his life to an outside force.

The impromptu celebration had a free fall lunacy to it. We roared with laughter at flights and insights that can never survive the moment but transcend time forever.

Towards the end of the lunch, I told Arthur how my feelings about him as a writer had changed. I had at one time thought him the enemy, consigned to the poetry-free pits of naturalism Hell. Not until I saw *The American Clock* did I realize how shot through to its very bones the play was with surrealistic imagery and that this surrealism was indeed responsible for that which was most powerful about the play. I subsequently saw a conventional revival of *All My Sons*. I closed my eyes and simply listened to the play's madness and realised one day some visionary director will find a way to liberate Arthur's plays from their cage of traditional psychological realism (much as Bergman had done in his Munch-inspired *Hedda Gabler*).

Lunch was over. A man who that morning had typed The End to his autobiography had to get back to the business of living.

We went back to the Lincoln Center. Mosher sat behind his desk, 'Hi, guys. What's up?'

Jacques Huisman

Théâtre National de Belgique, *in conversation with*
Gilbert Debusscher

Towards the end of *Timebends*, Arthur Miller casts a backward glance
at his 1978 encounter in grey-weathered Brussels with the American
consul-general who obligingly got him a new passport to replace the
original forgotten in Paris. The diplomat then swapped stories with the
playwright about his own former problems with the State Department
in the McCarthy era. The anecdote smacks of the author's justified
glee in view of another 'bending of time' that makes him 'feel good to
have lived this long'. The occasion of the visit was the twenty-fifth
anniversary production of *The Crucible* in Brussels, a commemoration
that triggered recollections of more somber days but also provided the
opportunity of the first meeting of Miller with Jacques Huisman who
had been at the head of the *Théâtre National de Belgique* for thirty years
by then. During that period he had championed Miller's work so that
only Molière's had been seen more often on the National's stage. He
could claim credit for the French speaking world premières of *Death of
a Salesman* in 1952, *The Crucible* in 1954, *The Price* in 1968 and *The
Creation of the World and Other Business* in 1974. Jacques Huisman
answered my questions in his home on the outskirts of the Forêt de
Soignes in Brussels. On the table I had put my copy of *Timebends*.

HUISMAN: I like the book for its balance and serenity. It is not a
settling of accounts except perhaps with Elia Kazan who deserved
what he gets and, then, most of all with Lee Strasberg. I saw him in
New York at work on Marilyn Monroe. He was directing her in a
scene from Anouilh's *Colombe*. His sole aim was to reduce her to
tears in front of forty or fifty voyeurs who attended the course. It was
scandalous and totally useless: he was not a teacher but a guru and
the attendants were disciples not pupils. I have known many of these
acting instructors who entertain very intimate relationships with their
pupils; they are part priest and part doctor, dominating and doping
those who come to them for advice or instruction.

DEBUSSCHER: From Arthur Miller's description of her, Marilyn
Monroe emerges as a considerable actress. Did you have that
impression?

HUISMAN: There are no miracles in this field. Marilyn Monroe had a stunning figure but also an enormous sensitivity which probably destroyed her in the end. Careers like hers are never to be ascribed to chance alone; an international reputation, and a lasting one at that, is never achieved without tremendous talent and she had it.

DEBUSSCHER: It is symptomatic that starting with *Timebends* we should immediately focus on Marilyn Monroe. You expressly forbade any question about his private life at the press conference in 1974 when *The Creation of the World and Other Business* premièred in Brussels.

HUISMAN: Yes, out of respect for the artist and the man I wanted the newspaper people to stick to enquiries about the play at hand or his work and artistic views in general. But they got around to it obliquely. I was struck then by the equanimity with which Miller answered the questions. The initial embarrassment was mine rather than his and it evaporated altogether in view of the simplicity with which he faced the press. His wife Inge Morath confirmed that the subject was strictly unavoidable. It still is, obviously.

DEBUSSCHER: Your acquaintance with Miller's work starts much earlier, in 1952.

HUISMAN: I had secured the rights from his agent in Paris, a Mr Rothschild I believe, to produce *Death of a Salesman* which I had read and for which I shared Raymond Gerôme's enthusiasm. Gerôme was perfectly bilingual and familiar with the English-speaking theatre. He was in part responsible for the National's long tradition of English and American plays. The production of *Salesman* was a passionately interesting piece of work and went very well until, one day, the agent called with the shattering news that Mr Miller did not want us to do the play. At least, not unless Peter Brook agreed to supervise it. I had every reason to welcome this suggestion having had an opportunity to see his work on *Romeo and Juliet* the year before at the Old Vic. I had met him after the performance to express my admiration and ask what is probably the most stupid question on earth 'How do you manage? What is your method?' to which he replied 'Trial and error', a lesson I have always cherished for its pragmatism. Peter Brook came to Brussels in the final stages, for the last four or five rehearsals, and made useful and important suggestions. We have remained very good friends ever since that time.

DEBUSSCHER: Do you remember what his suggestions were about?

225

HUISMAN: Not with any degree of precision but I know that they all went in the direction of greater naturalness. He had not directed *Death of a Salesman* before but offered advice that the actors could immediately integrate and feel comfortable with because it tended to do away with mannerisms or artifice.

DEBUSSCHER: Did *Death of a Salesman* appear to you as difficult to describe in terms of genre?

HUISMAN: No. As far as I was concerned it was one of the first in a long series that I did at the National of contemporary works that reflect the problems of the public for which they are produced. In 1952 the problems of Willy Loman, who loses his grip on reality and is subsequently thrown out of his job, were real enough for any member of our audience.

DEBUSSCHER: Were you aware then, as we are now, that the play was not strictly naturalistic, that it had overtones that took it well beyond the anecdotal?

HUISMAN: I produced it as a strictly contemporary play. But I became aware gradually that it was a poetic play, a work for all times. It is indeed a classic drama. And our almost two-month long run in Paris, which was greeted enthusiastically by the French critics, helped to convince me of this. Had it been experienced by the French as a strictly American tale they would have reacted negatively, as they always do; worse still, had it struck them as a specifically Belgian production, they would have rejected it with hostility, as is often the case. Our success in Paris indicated that the play transcended its geographical location to become an exemplary story. The relationships between husband and wife, or father and sons, and between Willy and his brother were immediately perceived as those within a very ordinary family and therefore to be found in all societies under all latitudes.

DEBUSSCHER: This appears clearly from the reviews both in Brussels and Paris. The critics indulged in considerations about 'modern tragedy' or 'the tragedy of the ordinary man' wondering if the genre could exist without a hero of traditional 'tragic stature'. But all seem to have discerned immediately that beyond his American-ness, this 'commis-voyageur' was rather the archetypal Voyageur, the existential traveller, a modern version of Everyman.

HUISMAN: It is often the case with major works that they grow out of apparently limited, anecdotal material to reach a wider, even universal applicability. Most classics are that way. The play is neither place- nor time-bound. It exemplifies, among other things, the moment in life, which comes sooner or later for everybody, when existential strength is flagging, when readjustment to changing realities, inside and outside thc self, becomes imperative. That it should take place in the United States, at a time when the American Dream is devitalised to the point of being reduced to a frantic search for success or material possessions, is unimportant. One could easily find equivalent pressures bearing on the protagonists in different cultural or geographical contexts. The atmosphere in 1952 in Brussels as well as Paris was basically anti-American yet the reviewers of the conservative *Le Figaro* as well as the communist *L'Humanité* found reason to praise the play which further suggests that it also transcends ideologies of right and left.

DEBUSSCHER: The critics unanimously praised your work on *Death of a Salesman* but all seem to have been surprised, not necessarily pleasantly, by what they call the cinematographic structure of the play by which they mean the oscillation in time, the flexibility of space and the simultaneousness of several locations, the apparent close-ups on characters or groups, the movement from one plane of reality to another. Was all this so innovative?

HUISMAN: The reviewers may have found this revolutionary. It was not. And the audience had no difficulty adjusting to the shifts. We had an outsize calendar in Loman's living room that allowed for swift changes in time and as to the scenes with Ben, changes in light – we had an intense white-blue light instead of the then customary orange-yellow for those scenes – sufficiently indicated that the action was midway between dream or reminiscence and reality. In those matters the audience can be trusted to adapt more readily than reviewers.

DEBUSSCHER: In January 1954 you followed suit with *La chasse aux sorcières* this time adapted by Herman Closson. At the very end of that year it opened in Paris under the title of *Les sorcières de Salem*. Neither of these titles were faithful to the original: *The Crucible*.

HUISMAN: To this day I am puzzled by the title Miller chose for this play and I have never had an opportunity to ask him what he really meant with that crucible. But I myself gave it its Brussels title: it seemed quite obvious to me that a witchhunt was its central theme. In a country like ours which had to suffer from the Spanish Inquisition the parallels were immediately apparent; the contemporary relevance was as blinding as was Tyl Uilenspiegels's under the Nazi occupation. Here was a play recognisably about the freedom of conscience and the dark forces that attempt to repress that fundamental right. But nobody could suspect that by making explicit the originally mysterious title I was about to create trouble for Miller. He had been invited to attend the opening in Brussels and was refused a passport to leave the United States. Miller himself did not expect this and the incident created quite a stir in Brussels. Two years later, as I was preparing for my first trip to the States, I was made to wait until the very last minute to get a visa: the witches were still haunting us. And yet it had been an evening full of irony: the première was a gala organised by the Belgo-American Association to which the Ambassador came with a number of officials. Ours was after all a 'National' theatre and accredited diplomats usually attended our gala evenings. In fact the Ambassador's absence would have created an even greater scandal to which must be added that not all Americans present in Brussels were in favour of McCarthy, whose days were numbered by then anyway. The success of the play in Brussels confirmed a number of them in their feeling that the nightmare was almost over.

DEBUSSCHER: The newspapers devoted a good deal of space in their political columns to the 'passport affair', which was good publicity for the play, and the drama critics unanimously praised your production. Once again, the Parisian reviewers came to Brussels.

HUISMAN: Yes, and they were followed quickly by Yves Montand, Simone Signoret and Raymond Rouleau who liked the play well enough to decide to do it in Paris. They opened in December that same year.

DEBUSSCHER: A number of critics also went to Berlin to see Karl Heinz Stroux's version which seems, more than yours, to have laid the stress on historical, almost documentary accuracy.

HUISMAN: I was never interested by the folkloric, the local colour aspect of a play. I have always considered that a director's task was to make evident, even in plays of or about the past, the contemporary relevance of a drama for the audience. That is what I would call its 'classical resonance'. That was not very hard in this case; the antiquarian's preoccupation with surface accuracy would here only obscure the central concern of the play by diverting attention to the unimportant historical details to the detriment of the fundamental truths.

DEBUSSCHER: Some of the reviewers suggested that by comparison with Tennessee Williams's plays, which Brussels had been discovering alongside those of Miller, this work lacked 'poetry'.

HUISMAN: It is difficult to say exactly what they meant. To me its poetry resides in the unspoken as much as in what is expressed, in the depth of its human sympathy, in its rejection of realism and its universal applicability.

DEBUSSCHER: You were so attached to the play that you decided to do it again almost twenty-five years later in 1978. Was your conception of the play fundamentally different in the altered circumstances of the seventies?

HUISMAN: Unfortunately it was not and I blamed myself for it. Another director could have done a better job of recreating the play. I was merely copying myself at so many years' distance. I have often regretted that Miller should finally have seen this version rather than the first. I had a similar experience only one other time, with *Romeo and Juliet:* theatre is an art of the moment, eminently non-repeatable and you should never look back.

DEBUSSCHER: Did the play at first appear to you as illustrative of a specific ideology?

HUISMAN: Neither of the left nor of the right. It is not an anti-American play, any more than *Death of a Salesman* can be reduced to an anti-capitalist tract. It is, as I said, a plea for freedom of conscience and maybe that is more highly respected on the left than on the right. But then, dictatorships can be found at both ends of the political spectrum.

DEBUSSCHER: With *The Price*, which you directed in 1968, one gets the feeling that it is a less socially – or politically – oriented play.

HUISMAN: I have never considered Miller's plays as belonging to one ideology or another. What attracted me to them first was their profound humanity. They may *afterwards* appear as revealing Miller's special social consciousness. In *The Price* existential pain, the sheer emotional misery of the two brothers and the wife of one of them – an important character by the way – implies a harsh assessment of the society in which they live. By the end of the sixties it had become abundantly clear that the left had no model to offer, no doctrine that would reduce social inequalities. That is why Solomon, the used furniture dealer who is also the philosopher of the play, casts a derisive eye on the brothers' aborted reconciliation. As he listens to the laughing record, which he has purchased with the rest of the family possessions, he breaks into uncontrollable laughter himself, a 'pure' laughter, prompted not by immediate circumstances, but by a deeper sense of tragic ridicule, of the senselessness of our petty quarrels and their unending repetition. *Timebends* reveals that the play is rooted in autobiography, Walter and Victor hardly disguised versions of the Miller brothers, but all plays spring from the personal experience of their author and, by that token, albeit for different reasons and to different degrees, *Death of a Salesman* and *The Crucible* would qualify equally well as autobiographical documents.

DEBUSSCHER: The play attracted the Paris reviewers to Brussels again. J. J. Gautier in *Le Figaro* praised your work and that of the actors but found the stage too large for the play.

HUISMAN: That was probably a well founded criticism. Although the set by Denis Martin representing the attic was full of superb details, it was entirely too big for a drama as intimate as this; also when you have that much space at your disposal, you tend to have your actors fill it and their movements contribute to dissipating the tension which is integral to this family confrontation.

DEBUSSCHER: Claude Olivier in *Les Lettres Francaises* talks of a 'flattened out' direction by which he means a deliberate refusal on your part to break away from the 'psychological rut'.

HUISMAN: Yes, he is absolutely right. My first concern has always been with the psychological truth of the characters. And I still believe that this approach works best with Miller's plays and should precede any other consideration.

DEBUSSCHER: Did this psychological preconception influence your decision not to direct *The Creation of the World and Other Business* yourself and entrust it to Walter Tillemans in 1974.

HUISMAN: Yes, this new play was written in an apparently mythical or mythological vein and such a referential work required a man of greater fantasy and inventiveness. A 'flattened out' production would have been detrimental to a play of this kind. Not that it is a purely comic play: it starts on a funny note but as it progresses the tone changes and the colours darken. The final scene with Adam asking for pity – that is for man in general, for mankind – reveals the seriousness of Miller's message. *Creation* is as dark in its existential intent as any of its predecessors. It bears re-reading and has not yet found, I am afraid, a production that does it justice. He did it as a medieval play: the set designer John Bogaerts had imagined a series of mansions simultaneously present on the stage. We were all

anxiously waiting for Miller's reaction since this was his first visit
ever to the Théâtre National. This is one of my fondest memories:
he seemed genuinely pleased with our work and said so during the
press conference at which he appeared perfectly happy and relaxed
in spite of the embarrassingly personal questions of the newspaper
people.

DEBUSSCHER: He also expressed his gratitude on that occasion to you
personally for having championed his work all those years. Was that
an oblique comment on the way he had fared in Paris?

HUISMAN: Maybe. You see, Paris tends to Parisianise whatever they lay
hands on. Some plays, particularly English and American, are too
idiosyncratic for such a treatment and as a result look strangely
hybrid when submitted to it. That explains, to a large extent, their
lack of success in Paris.

DEBUSSCHER: Miller says somewhere that in the theatre the devil
always plays an important role. On the stage, he always gets the best
lines. And God, the last word . . .

HUISMAN: Who could add anything to that?

DEBUSSCHER: Over the years, Miller's physique has changed, not only
with age.

HUISMAN: Yes, with time his face has mellowed and his voice
deepened. They are now the face and voice, someone said, of a
modern Abraham Lincoln, a revered kind of a sage, a recorder of
the tribulations of his period and his nation. In times of trouble,
personal I mean, intimate even, I have turned to him for counsel or
services and I have never been disappointed. Over the years our
professional relationship has evolved into a personal friendship.

Carlos Fuentes

There is a photo of a crowd of several thousand Parisians walking
down the Rue Soufflot on the day of François Mitterrand's
inauguration in May, 1981. One man stands head and shoulders above
the multitude. His friends can easily identify Arthur Miller, head bare
in the stormy afternoon, raincoat slung over one shoulder, eyeglasses
firmly set on the Mount Rushmore profile. 'He looks like a Jewish
Abraham Lincoln', said Bill Styron that day.

But this physical height, I then thought, is nothing compared to the moral, political and literary stature of my friend Arthur. Nothing has cut him down: personal tragedy, political opportunities, intellectual fads. I grew up in the USA in the 1930s, when America counted on its human capital to face its problems and believed that greatness meant joining ideals with practice. When North America became fat and complacent and thought that it had interests, but not friends, and belied its paranoid search for security through the insecurity of intimidating dissident individuals and picking on small nations, I knew that I could always look towards Arthur Miller and renew my faith in that great country, my neighbour, to which I am inexorably linked as a Mexican.

He stood up to the McCarthys and the McCarran-Walters. They are forgotten, and rightly so. Their menace is not and should not be forgotten. Miller wrote it down forever in *The Crucible*. And the human aching America, that must not be forgotten under the trappings of Trump Towers and Star Wars, goes on living, reminding us of all that we have forgotten, in *Death of a Salesman*. And bigotry, xenophobia, fear of the Other, the coming sin of the 21st Century, is already staring at us in *A View from the Bridge*.

In 1965, he received me and several other excludable or undesirable aliens under the shelter of PEN International in New York. Pablo Neruda and I then wrote hoping that this meant the end of the Cold War, at least in the realm of culture. The Cuban literary bureaucracy did not like that; the Cold War should go on, they said, because the two ideologies were irreducible: Capitalism or Communism. Again, Miller saw beyond the Manichean mentality, towards a world in movement, a world of encounters, where men and women and their ideas and longings meet and sometimes hurt, but finally create one another.

Arthur Miller has always found that grain of truth in every idea and in every individual that, ever since Aeschylus, has been the kernel of theater and tragedy. Tragedy is the recognition of the truth of the other, not of his or her evil. Theater is the time required for experience – pain or joy – to become knowledge.

Bigsby: Any chance of you slowing down?

Miller: Well, I slow down every day. But I pick up toward evening.

Bigsby: Looking back over a career that has already lasted over fifty-five years are you able to say what has given you the greatest satisfaction as a writer?

Miller: All these years later when I see a play of mine that I wrote thirty-five years ago, and I see that the audience is screwed into it in the way that they were in the first place, I like to believe that the feeling that they have is that man is worth something. That you care about him that much is a miracle, I mean considering the numbers of ourselves that we have destroyed in the last century. I think art imputes value to human beings and if I did that it would be the most pleasant thought I could depart with, apart from the fact that it entertains people, keeps them amused for a while. If it left behind that much value, it would be great. I also have a weakness for actors and when they are transformed, or seem to be, by something I wrote, it's a miracle to me. When they become somebody I imagined it moves me very much. I guess the other thing is the wonder of it all, that I'm still here, that so much of it did work, that the people are so open to it, and that we sort of clasped hands somehow, in many places and many languages. It gives me a glimpse of the idea that there is one humanity, there's just one homo sapiens. Underneath all the different etiquette and the incomprehensible languages we are one. And I think it's a sort of miracle. What does a writer want? He wants to have left his thumbprint on the world.

Bigsby: That sounds like Willy Loman.

Miller: That's right. Who does not want that?

Index

Page numbers in italics refer to the pieces by the book's contributors.

237

Wall Street Crash (1929), 15–16, 17–19, 21, 49, 207
Walter, Congressman, 108–9
Wanamaker, Zoë, *96*
Ward, Robert, 99, 101, 102
Warden, Jack, 179–80
Wardle, Irving, *190–1*
Washington, Joan, 116
Washington Post, 191
Watergate, 163, 201
Weill, Kurt, *The Threepenny Opera*, 211
Welles, Orson, 71
Wesker, Arnold, *65–6*; *Chicken Soup and Barley*, 65
West, Timothy, *152*
West Australian Theatre Company, 72–3
Whitehead, Bob, 138
Whitman, Walt, xiv
Wiest, Diane, 145

Wilkinson, Tom, 86, *95–6*
Williams, Tennessee, 26, 29, 115, 123, 150, 179, 229
Witness (film), 94
Wood, Peter, 209
Wooster Group, New York, 136
WPA (Works Progress Administration), 197; theatre, 26
Wyndham's Theatre, 50-1

Yarrow, Arnold, *153–5*
Yates, Marjorie, *157*
Young Vic Theatre Company, 137; *The Crucible*, 88; *An Enemy of the People*, 85–8; *The Price*, 156–61, 189; *Two Way Mirror*, 172
Yulin, Harry, 152

Zeffirelli, Franco, 143
Zinman, Toby, 144